中文详注剑桥莎士比亚精选

柔密欧与茱丽叶

原版创始主编：[英] 瑞克斯·吉布森（Rex Gibson）
原版主编：[英] 瑞查德·安褚斯（Richard Andrews）
　　　　　[英] 维姬·维南德（Vicki Wienand）
原版编注：[英] 罗布·史密斯（Rob Smith）
总主编：陈国华
分册主编：李亮

社图号 20164

Cambridge School Shakespeare: Romeo and Juliet [Fourth edition] [978-1-107-61540-3] was first published by Cambridge University Press in 2014. All rights reserved.

This Simplified Chinese edition for the People's Republic of China is published by arrangement with the Press Syndicate of the University of Cambridge, Cambridge, United Kingdom.

© Cambridge University Press & Beijing Language and Culture University Press 2020.

This book is in copyright. No reproduction of any part may take place without the written permission of Cambridge University Press or Beijing Language and Culture University Press.

本书版权由剑桥大学出版社和北京语言大学出版社共同所有。本书任何部分之文字及图片，如未获得出版者书面同意，不得用任何方式抄袭、节录或翻印。

This edition is for sale in the People's Republic of China (excluding Hong Kong SAR, Macao SAR and Taiwan Province) only. 此版本仅限在中华人民共和国境内销售。

北京市版权局著作权合同登记图字：01-2020-4098 号

图书在版编目（CIP）数据

中文详注剑桥莎士比亚精选. 柔密欧与茱丽叶 / 陈国华总主编；李亮分册主编. -- 北京：北京语言大学出版社，2020.11

书名原文：Cambridge School Shakespeare：Romeo and Juliet

ISBN 978-7-5619-5770-7

Ⅰ. ①中⋯ Ⅱ. ①陈⋯ ②李⋯ Ⅲ. ①悲剧－剧本－英国－中世纪 Ⅳ. ① I561.33

中国版本图书馆 CIP 数据核字（2020）第 188975 号

中文详注剑桥莎士比亚精选：柔密欧与茱丽叶
ZHONGWEN XIANG ZHU JIANQIAO SHASHIBIYA JINGXUAN: ROUMI'OU YU ZHULIYE

项目策划：李 亮	**责任编辑**：孙冠群
封面设计：乔 剑	**排版制作**：北京创艺涵文化发展有限公司
责任印制：武晓东	

出版发行：北京语言大学出版社

社　　址：北京市海淀区学院路 15 号，100083
网　　址：www.blcup.com
电子信箱：service@blcup.com
电　　话：编辑部　8610-82301019/0178
　　　　　　发行部　8610-82303650/3591/3648
　　　　　　北语书店　8610-82303653
　　　　　　网购咨询　8610-82303908
印　　刷：北京博海升彩色印刷有限公司

版　次：2020 年 11 月第 1 版　　**印　次**：2020 年 11 月第 1 次印刷
开　本：787 毫米 × 1092 毫米 1/16　　**印　张**：15.75
字　数：472 千字
定　价：79.00 元

PRINTED IN CHINA

序

由于观察角度不同，评判标准不同，关于哪个国家哪位诗人或小说家的成就最大，世人可能难以达成一致；可是说到剧作家，大家的共识是，莎士比亚不仅是英语国家有史以来最伟大的剧作家，也是全世界最伟大的剧作家，在知名度、影响力和传世作品的数量上，没有任何一位剧作家可以与之比肩。正是由于其公认的文学成就和人文精神，在过去400多年里，莎士比亚戏剧的演出在英语国家和许多非英语国家经久不衰，莎剧的阅读和鉴赏已成为这些国家英文教学的必选内容。

莎剧进入中国，已经有100多年历史，莎士比亚全集已经有了四个中文译本。不懂英文的人可以通过译本来欣赏莎士比亚剧作。然而文学作品的语言，尤其是诗歌的语言，具有相当程度的不可译性，而几乎所有莎剧的大部分台词都是素体诗（blank verse）。例如《哈慕雷》（*Hamlet*）里主人翁的名言"To be, or not to be, that is the question"，不论怎样译，都难以完全再现原文的深刻内涵和形式特点。要想真正欣赏莎士比亚的语言和戏剧艺术，还得阅读其英文原作。最早由剑桥大学出版社出版的这套莎剧精选，收录了最受读者和观众喜爱的14部剧目，涵盖莎剧的各个类别，以其独具匠心的设计和编排，成为所有英文原版莎剧中最适合英语学习者阅读、最适合戏剧爱好者排演的莎剧选集。

本选集的创始主编瑞克斯·吉布森（Rex Gibson）在本书引言（Introduction）里指出："不论做什么，都要记住，莎士比亚写下他的剧本是为了演出、观看和享受的。"秉承这一宗旨，这一新版莎剧选集有四个鲜明的区别性特点：

一、书的开本和页面的宽高比例特别适合学校的老师和学生以及剧团的导演和演员在排练莎剧时把书打开，拿在手里，随时参阅，而且左边页面上有许多有关排演活动的建议。

二、书中配有大量世界各国莎剧演出的彩色剧照，为莎剧爱好者和剧团排演莎剧提供了灵感。

三、书的正文部分打开后，右页是未经删减、原汁原味的剧本原文，左页是多种不同栏目，包括导演技巧（Stagecraft）、剧中语言（Language in the play）、人物分析（Characters）、主题分析（Themes）、写作练习（Write about it）及词语注释等。每幕之间（本幕回顾）和最后一幕后（本剧回顾）有与剧情相关的各种思考题。

四、在剧本之后有各种针对全剧的专题论述，以《哈慕雷》为例，包括视角与主题（Perspectives and themes）、人物分析（Characters）、《哈慕雷》的语言（The language of *Hamlet*）、《哈慕雷》的演出（*Hamlet* in performance）、笔论莎士比亚（Writing about Shakespeare）、笔论《哈慕雷》（Writing about *Hamlet*），还有一份莎翁年表（William Shakespeare 1564–1616）。

左页上的栏目对于解读和排演莎剧特别有帮助，剧本后面的专题论述对于撰写有关莎士比亚的文章特别有帮助，而参加莎剧排演，背诵台词，撰写论文，又是提高英语水平的极好途径。

为了方便更多的中国读者阅读、欣赏、排演莎士比亚原作，北京语言大学出版社携手剑桥大学出版社，将这套莎剧精选引入中国。我有幸应邀担任这套书的中文版总主编，组织起一个团队，对原版进行一定程度的改编和汉化，以适应中国读者的需求。我们不仅将原版提供的关键注释基本译成了中文，而且针对中国英语学习者和莎剧爱好者阅读理解上的难点，主要做了以下四件事：

一、参考 The Oxford Dictionary of Original Shakespearean Pronunciation (David Crystal 2016)、Oxford Dictionary of Pronunciation for Current English (Clive Upton 2003) 和 Shakespeare's Names: A Pronouncing Dictionary (Helge Kökeritz 1950)，给每个剧本前面人物表里的人名加上了国际音标。为了便于读者识别，我们将第一本发音词典里一般中国读者不认识的个别音标替换成了大家熟悉的近似音标。

二、为左页顶端的剧情简介添加中文译文。

三、左页中以及剧本后面论文部分里有一些具有挑战性的词和术语（如tableau），我们为其中的大部分添加了相应的中文释义。

四、适当增加了原版里没有的词语注释。

给剧中人物的名字加了国际音标之后，我们发现，现有莎剧中文译本里一些人名的中文译名与原文的读音差别较大且互不相同。根据定名不苟、译音循本、音义兼顾、音系对应的原则，我们给出了新译名。根据前两个原则，我们将剧本 Julius Caesar /ˈdʒuːlɪəs ˈsiːzə(r)/ 译成《儒略·恺撒》，而没有采用《尤利/力乌斯·恺撒》《裘利/力斯·凯撒》《居里厄斯·恺撒》等现成译名中的任何一个，因为从公元前1世纪到公元16世纪西方使用的儒略历（Julian calendar）就是以这位 Julius Caesar（拉丁文读音是 /ˈjuːlɪʊs ˈkaesar/）命名的。根据音义兼顾的原则，我们将剧本 Hamlet /ˈ(h)amlət/ 译成《哈慕雷》而不是《哈姆莱特》或《哈姆雷特》，因为"慕雷"比"姆莱"或"姆雷"更适合用来给男子起名，结尾的辅音 /t/ 在实际说话中往往不发音。根据音系对应的原则，我们借鉴了曹禺的译法，将剧本 Romeo and Juliet 译成《柔密欧与茱丽叶》，没有将 Romeo 译成更常见的"罗密欧"，因为"柔 /rou/"比"罗 /luo/"更接近原名 Romeo /ˈroːmɪoː/ 的读音；同时我们将 Juliet /ˈdʒuːlɪət/ 译成"茱丽叶"而不是"朱丽叶"，因为这样做不容易让人误以为这个女孩姓"朱"。

这套经过改编并且带中文注释的《中文详注剑桥莎士比亚精选》不仅可以用作中国高中和大学的英文教材，而且适合中国所有具有较高英语能力的莎剧爱好者阅读和欣赏，将戏剧从书中提升到自己心中，将剧本从课堂搬演到戏台。

相信《中文详注剑桥莎士比亚精选》会带给中国广大英语爱好者一个惊喜。

陈国华

北京外国语大学

2020年5月于英国剑桥家中

Contents 目录

Introduction 引言 iv
Photo gallery 剧照精选 v

Romeo and Juliet 《柔密欧与茱丽叶》

List of characters 人物表 1
The Prologue 序幕 3
Act 1 第1幕 5
Act 2 第2幕 49
Act 3 第3幕 91
Act 4 第4幕 141
Act 5 第5幕 171

The story of Romeo and Juliet 《柔密欧与茱丽叶》故事介绍   202
Characters 人物分析 204
Perspectives and themes 视角与主题 209
Why did Romeo and Juliet die? 柔密欧和茱丽叶为什么会死?   212
The language of Romeo and Juliet 《柔密欧与茱丽叶》的语言   214
Romeo and Juliet in performance 《柔密欧与茱丽叶》的演出   220
Writing about Shakespeare 笔论莎士比亚   230
Writing about Romeo and Juliet 笔论《柔密欧与茱丽叶》   232
William Shakespeare 1564–1616 莎翁年表   234
Acknowledgements 鸣谢   235

Cambridge School Shakespeare

Introduction 引言

This *Romeo and Juliet* is part of the **Cambridge School Shakespeare** series. Like every other play in the series, it has been specially prepared to help all students in schools and colleges.

The **Cambridge School Shakespeare** *Romeo and Juliet* aims to be different. It invites you to lift the words from the page and to bring the play to life in your classroom, hall or drama studio. Through enjoyable and focused activities, you will increase your understanding of the play. Actors have created their different interpretations of the play over the centuries. Similarly, you are invited to make up your own mind about *Romeo and Juliet*, rather than having someone else's interpretation handed down to you.

Cambridge School Shakespeare does not offer you a cut-down or simplified version of the play. This is Shakespeare's language, filled with imaginative possibilities. You will find on every left-hand page: a summary of the action, an explanation of unfamiliar words, and a choice of activities on Shakespeare's stagecraft, characters, themes and language.

Between each act, and in the pages at the end of the play, you will find notes, illustrations and activities. These will help to encourage reflection after every act and give you insights into the background and context of the play as a whole.

This edition will be of value to you whether you are studying for an examination, reading for pleasure or thinking of putting on the play to entertain others. You can work on the activities on your own or in groups. Many of the activities suggest a particular group size, but don't be afraid to make up larger or smaller groups to suit your own purposes. Please don't think you have to do every activity: choose those that will help you most.

Although you are invited to treat *Romeo and Juliet* as a play, you don't need special dramatic or theatrical skills to do the activities. By choosing your activities, and by exploring and experimenting, you can make your own interpretations of Shakespeare's language, characters and stories.

Whatever you do, remember that Shakespeare wrote his plays to be acted, watched and enjoyed.

Rex Gibson
Founding editor

This new edition contains more photographs, more diversity and more supporting material than previous editions, whilst remaining true to Rex's original vision. Specifically, it contains more activities and commentary on stagecraft and writing about Shakespeare, to reflect contemporary interest. The glossary has been enlarged, too. Finally, this edition aims to reflect the best teaching and learning possible, and to represent not only Shakespeare through the ages, but also the relevance and excitement of Shakespeare today.

Richard Andrews and Vicki Wienand
Series editors

This edition of *Romeo and Juliet* uses the text of the play established by G. Blakemore Evans in **The New Cambridge Shakespeare**.

'Star-crossed (时运不济) lovers'. *Romeo and Juliet* dramatises the story of two young people who fall deeply in love. But their families are locked in an age-old bitter feud (世仇). As Romeo (a Montague) and Juliet (a Capulet) seek happiness, the hatred between their families, together with misfortune and accident, makes everything go wrong. They kill themselves rather than be separated from each other.

The play opens as the feud between the Montague and Capulet families erupts afresh. The servants of the two households clash violently in public.

Later, after order has been restored, Lord Capulet arranges a lavish party. His guests dance in celebration.

A forlorn (孤苦伶仃) Romeo has riskily gatecrashed Capulet's party. Disguised behind a mask, and at first unrecognised, he falls in love with Juliet, not yet knowing that she is the daughter of Lord Capulet. They kiss for the first time.

'What light through yonder window breaks?' After the party, Romeo catches sight of Juliet while she thinks of him. Shakespeare never mentions a balcony, but all productions strive to find an inventive way of staging Act 2 Scene 2 – the 'balcony' scene.

◀ 'Parting is such sweet sorrow'. Juliet agrees to marry Romeo the following day and bids him a reluctant farewell.

▼ 'Tybalt, you rat-catcher, will you walk?' Mercutio (right), Romeo's close friend, is disgusted by Romeo's refusal to fight Tybalt (a Capulet). Mercutio challenges Tybalt to a duel (决斗).

▲ Romeo tries to stop the duel, but Tybalt fatally wounds Mercutio (centre). Romeo, furious about Mercutio's death, kills Tybalt in revenge and is banished (流放) from Verona.

▼ Friar (修士) Lawrence has secretly married Romeo and Juliet. Juliet refuses to marry Paris, her father's choice. She seeks advice from the troubled Friar about what she can do. Paris continues to promote his own qualities as Juliet's husband-to-be. Friar Lawrence proposes a hazardous (危险) plan, in which Juliet will drink a potion (药水) that will send her into a death-like sleep.

'What if this mixture do not work at all?' Juliet fears that the Friar's 'poison' may not act, and she will have to obey her father's commands and marry Paris. But in spite of her misgivings, and her dread of the horrors that may await her in the Capulets' tomb, she finally drinks the potion.

Juliet's parents (and Paris, right) think their daughter is dead, and grieve at their loss. But the Friar and the audience know that she is merely drugged. She will be placed inside the Capulets' tomb and Romeo will return from his banishment to rescue her when she wakes.

'Here's to my love!' Romeo arrives at the tomb and, thinking that his beloved Juliet is really dead, he resolves to kill himself. Tragically, as Juliet awakes she finds her dead husband beside her. She, too, takes her own life.

▶ Lords Montague and Capulet are reconciled (和解) in their grief as they mourn Romeo and Juliet.

▼ 'For never was a story of more woe / Than this of Juliet and her Romeo'. Franco Zeffirelli's 1968 movie set the play in Renaissance Italy and used outdoor locations in Tuscany and Umbria (but not in Verona). The film ended with the funeral procession (送葬，出殯) of Romeo and Juliet.

List of characters 人物表

CHORUS (叙事人)

The house of Capulet 卡普莱家族

JULIET /ˈdʒuːlɪət/ (茱丽叶)
CAPULET /ˈkapjəˌlet/ (卡普莱) Juliet's father
LADY CAPULET (卡普莱夫人) Juliet's mother
TYBALT /ˈtɪbɒlt/ (提巴尔) Juliet's cousin
NURSE (奶妈) to Juliet
PETER /ˈpiːtə(r)/ (皮特) the Nurse's servant
COUSIN CAPULET (卡普莱堂亲) Juliet's kinsman
SAMPSON /ˈsamsən/ (萨慕森) servant to Capulet
GREGORY /ˈgreg(ə)rəɪ/ (格莱戈瑞) servant to Capulet
CLOWN (小丑) servant to Capulet
PETRUCHIO /pəˈtruːkɪoː/ (珀楚丘) Tybalt's friend

The house of Montague 芒特鸠家族

ROMEO /ˈroːmɪoː/ (柔密欧)
MONTAGUE /ˈmɒntəˌgjuː/ (芒特鸠) Romeo's father
LADY MONTAGUE (芒特鸠夫人) Romeo's mother
BENVOLIO /benˈvoːlɪoː/ (本沃琉) Romeo's friend
BALTHASAR /ˈbaltəˌzɑː(r)/ (巴尔特扎) Romeo's servant
ABRAM /ˈeɪbrəm/ (艾伯润) Montague's servant

The Court 宫廷

ESCALES /ˈeskələs/ (艾斯克勒) Prince of Verona /vəˈroːnə/ (维罗纳亲王)
MERCUTIO /mə(r)ˈkjuːsɪoː/ (莫丘休) Escales's kinsman, Romeo's friend
PARIS /ˈparɪs/ (帕瑞) Escales's kinsman, suitor to Juliet
PAGE (小厮) to Paris

The Church 教会

FRIAR LAWRENCE /ˈlɒrəns/ (劳润修士) Franciscan priest (方济各会祭司)
FRIAR JOHN /dʒɒn/ (约翰修士) Franciscan priest

The City 市民

Musicians, Gentlemen and Gentlewomen, Maskers, Torch-bearers, Citizens and Officers of the Watch, Captain of the Watch (乐师、男女宾客、戴面具者、持火把者、市民及巡夜、巡夜队长)

Mantua /ˈmantjʊə/ 曼托瓦

An apothecary (药剂师)

The Play is set in Verona and Mantua.

Chorus (a narrator) gives a preview of the play: the bitter quarrels of the Montagues and Capulets are ended only by the death of their children, Romeo and Juliet.

剧情简介：叙事人预告本剧因果：芒特鸠与卡普莱两个家族的世代深仇直到两家的孩子柔密欧和茱丽叶死后才得以化解。

1 Chorus speaks the Prologue (in threes)

The role of the Chorus originated in classical Greek drama over two thousand years ago. Back then, the Chorus was a group of characters who took no actual part in the play, but who introduced it and commentated on the action as it developed. Deciding how to play the Chorus can be a challenge for directors of *Romeo and Juliet*, as the main elements and outcomes of the plot are clearly explained before the play even begins.

In the production pictured here, the actor playing Prince Escales delivered the Chorus's lines, giving him the first and last words in the play. In another production, the Prologue was delivered collaboratively by the whole cast (全体演员).

- In groups of three, talk about how well you think these ideas would work and then come up with some other ideas for staging the Prologue. After the discussion, offer your most unusual suggestion to the class.

1 **alike in dignity** 拥有同样高的地位
2 **ancient grudge** 宿怨
3 **mutiny** 内乱
4 **civil … unclean** 市民的鲜血脏污了同伴的手
5 **From … foes** 这两家死敌不吉祥的娘胎里孕育出的
6 **star-crossed** 煞星笼罩，厄运注定
7 **take their life** 降生
8 **misadventured piteous overthrows** 悲惨的意外发生
9 **strife** 冲突，不和
10 **fearful passage** 恐怖展开
11 **nought** = nothing
12 **traffic** 往来；表演
13 **What … mend** 如果（我的讲述）有什么遗漏，我们努力（通过表演）加以弥补

Language in the play 剧中语言

Antithesis (对偶) (in pairs)

The Prologue is written in the form of a fourteen-line **sonnet** (十四行小歌) (see p. 216). A key feature of such poems – and of this play – is the use of **antithesis** (see p. 215), or oppositions, especially in the type of language Shakespeare uses. Here, Montagues are set against Capulets ('Two households'), and in line 3 'ancient' is set against 'new'. The remaining eleven lines contain several other antitheses.

a Take turns reading aloud lines 1–14. As one person reads, the other listens out for examples of antithesis and writes them down. Swap roles and compare notes.

b Start a Language file and give one of the sections the heading 'Antithesis'. Collect examples and add to this list as you read on.

The Tragedy of Romeo and Juliet

The Prologue

Enter CHORUS.

Two households, both alike in dignity[1],
In fair Verona (where we lay our scene),
From ancient grudge[2] break to new mutiny[3],
Where civil blood makes civil hands unclean[4].
From forth the fatal loins of these two foes[5]   5
A pair of star-crossed[6] lovers take their life[7];
Whose misadventured piteous overthrows[8]
Doth with their death bury their parents' strife[9].
The fearful passage[10] of their death-marked love,
And the continuance of their parents' rage,   10
Which but their children's end nought[11] could remove,
Is now the two hours' traffic[12] of our stage;
The which if you with patient ears attend,
What here shall miss, our toil shall strive to mend[13].   [*Exit*]

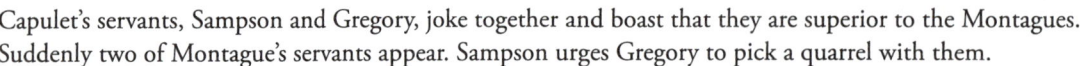

Capulet's servants, Sampson and Gregory, joke together and boast that they are superior to the Montagues. Suddenly two of Montague's servants appear. Sampson urges Gregory to pick a quarrel with them.

剧情简介：卡普莱家的用人萨慕森和格莱戈瑞一起开玩笑，吹嘘卡普莱家族比芒特鸠家族厉害。芒特鸠家的两个仆人突然出现，萨慕森怂恿格莱戈瑞找他们的碴儿。

1 Servants' banter (玩笑) (in pairs)

The play begins with Capulet's servants, Gregory and Sampson, joking about sex and women.

a Read lines 1–36 aloud together several times, changing roles. Try to emphasise all Sampson's and Gregory's wordplay – their **puns** (words that sound the same but have different meanings, see p. 218) and double meanings. For example, in lines 3–4 Sampson's 'we be in choler, we'll draw' means 'being angry, we'll draw our swords'. But Gregory's reply, 'draw your neck out of collar', turns the meaning into 'pull your head out of the hangman's noose' ('choler' = anger, 'collar' = noose [套索]). In addition, 'stand', 'thrust', 'maidenheads', 'tool' and 'weapon' all have crude double meanings.

b Talk together about why you think Shakespeare chose to begin the play with this kind of dramatic episode. Write a paragraph each, summarising your thoughts. Afterwards, swap your writing with another pair to read and comment on.

Stagecraft 导演技巧

Set the scene

At the beginning of each scene, a location is given (here it is 'Verona A public place'). But in Shakespeare's theatre the action took place on a bare stage, with little or no scenery.

a Look at the illustration in the '*Romeo and Juliet* in performance' section on page 220, showing the interior of Shakespeare's Globe. Suggest two or three simple ways in which you could convey to the audience that the scene in the script opposite takes place in the open air in Verona. Then think about where you might set this scene in a modern production. For example, Baz Luhrmann's movie version places the action in Verona Beach, a mythical modern Hispanic-American (西语美洲) city. One modern theatre production was set on a volcanic fault line (断层线) that constantly generated fire and steam 'to represent the ever-present threat of violence'.

b As you read on, look out for and make notes on the way in which Shakespeare alternates scenes that are played out in public arenas and those that have intimate domestic settings.

1	*bucklers*	小圆盾
2	*carry coals*	背煤；受侮辱，干脏活儿
3	*colliers*	背煤的，煤黑子
4	*and* = if	
5	*in choler*	动肝火
6	*draw*	拔剑，拔刀
7	*draw … collar*	把你的脖子从套索中抽出来（collar是双关语，也表示"绞刑的套索"）
8	*moved*	惹恼，挑逗
9	*valiant*	勇敢
10	*stand*	挺住（接下来的stand暗指挺起或勃起）
11	*take the wall*	靠墙走（伊丽莎白时代的街道中间是排污沟，因此靠墙的路边更干净；这里表示"占上风、占女性便宜"）
12	*weaker vessels*	较弱的器皿（出自《圣经》；以前的人们认为女性比男性弱，因此男性需要让着女性一些）
13	*thrust to the wall*	抵到墙根（进行猥亵）
14	*The quarrel … men*	纠纷只是两家男主人和我们男仆之间的事儿
15	*'Tis all one*	都是一回事儿，都一样
16	*civil*	文雅（这里是反话，实际上表示"残忍"；有的版本这里用cruel）
17	*maidenheads*	处女膜；童贞
18	*flesh*	鲜肉（与后面的tool、naked weapon均暗指男性的性器官）
19	*fish*	鱼肉
20	*poor-John*	咸鱼（伊丽莎白时代的便宜食物，暗指性无能）
21	*two other* SERVINGMEN	（一个是艾伯润[Abram]，另一个可能是巴尔特扎[Balthasar]）
22	*naked weapon*	裸剑（参见注解18）

Act 1 Scene 1
Verona A public place

Enter SAMPSON *and* GREGORY, *with swords and bucklers*[1].

SAMPSON   Gregory, on my word, we'll not carry coals[2].
GREGORY   No, for then we should be colliers[3].
SAMPSON   I mean, and[4] we be in choler[5], we'll draw[6].
GREGORY   Ay, while you live, draw your neck out of collar[7].
SAMPSON   I strike quickly, being moved[8].
GREGORY   But thou art not quickly moved to strike.
SAMPSON   A dog of the house of Montague moves me.
GREGORY   To move is to stir, and to be valiant[9] is to stand[10]: therefore if thou art moved thou runn'st away.
SAMPSON   A dog of that house shall move me to stand: I will take the wall[11] of any man or maid of Montague's.
GREGORY   That shows thee a weak slave, for the weakest goes to the wall.
SAMPSON   'Tis true, and therefore women being the weaker vessels[12] are ever thrust to the wall[13]: therefore I will push Montague's men from the wall, and thrust his maids to the wall.
GREGORY   The quarrel is between our masters, and us their men[14].
SAMPSON   'Tis all one[15], I will show myself a tyrant: when I have fought with the men, I will be civil[16] with the maids; I will cut off their heads.
GREGORY   The heads of the maids?
SAMPSON   Ay, the heads of the maids, or their maidenheads[17], take it in what sense thou wilt.
GREGORY   They must take it in sense that feel it.
SAMPSON   Me they shall feel while I am able to stand, and 'tis known I am a pretty piece of flesh[18].
GREGORY   'Tis well thou art not fish[19]; if thou hadst, thou hadst been poor-John[20]. Draw thy tool, here comes of the house of Montagues.

Enter two other SERVINGMEN[21], [*one being* ABRAM].

SAMPSON   My naked weapon[22] is out. Quarrel, I will back thee.
GREGORY   How, turn thy back and run?

Sampson and Gregory begin a quarrel with the Montagues. Benvolio (a Montague) tries to make peace, but Tybalt (a Capulet) adds flames to the fire, seizing the opportunity to fight.

剧情简介：萨慕森和格莱戈瑞与芒特鸠的家丁吵了起来。芒特鸠家的本沃琉试图劝架，卡普莱家的提巴尔却火上浇油，借机打斗起来。

Stagecraft 导演技巧

Stage fight (in pairs)

Would you make the street fight ritualised (仪式化) and symbolic (as above) or brutally realistic (for example, one production had a servant's bloodied head smashed against a wall of the set; it remained evident throughout the performance)? Weigh up the merits of both approaches. Which do you think would have the greater impact in the theatre? Why? In your pairs, come up with some alternative ways of staging this fight.

Themes 主题分析

Love versus hate (in small groups)

Shakespeare's plays contain many themes (key ideas or concepts that run throughout the script). Often these are presented in the form of tensions or oppositions, one set against another. *Romeo and Juliet* is famous for being a great love story, but in this first scene the Montague and Capulet servants engage in a violent fight.

- Suggest two or three reasons why Shakespeare might have decided to begin the play with a scene of hatred and anger rather than love.

1 Benvolio versus Tybalt (in pairs)

Benvolio's first words in the play ('Part, fools!') are an attempt to halt the riot that has developed between the Montagues and the Capulets. Tybalt seeks only to inflame it (his second line threatens death to Benvolio).

- Take parts as the two men and read aloud lines 55–63, emphasising their contrasting attitudes. Then perform the parts, adding actions that fit the language. Afterwards, in role as Benvolio and Tybalt, write down your thoughts about each other's behaviour.

1. Fear me not 不用担心，我会支持你
2. marry 马利亚啊（圣母马利亚 [Virgin Mary] 的简称，功能与今天的 Jesus 相似，表示对事实的感叹或惊奇、义愤等情感）
3. take … sides 让法理站在我们这边
4. as they list 如他们所愿
5. bite my thumb 咬我的大拇指（伊丽莎白时代一种挑衅、猥亵的手势）
6. sir 老兄，老弟（反复轻蔑地说）
7. quarrel 打架
8. kinsmen 亲戚
9. washing blow 力劈猛砍
10. Part 分开（让他们住手）
11. heartless hinds 没有胆的下人（这一说法意带双关，heart 与 hart [公鹿] 音同，hind 有"雌鹿"的意思）
12. manage 处理，应付
13. Have at thee 看剑

SAMPSON	Fear me not[1].	
GREGORY	No, marry[2], I fear thee!	
SAMPSON	Let us take the law of our sides[3], let them begin.	
GREGORY	I will frown as I pass by, and let them take it as they list[4].	
SAMPSON	Nay, as they dare. I will bite my thumb[5] at them, which is disgrace to them if they bear it.	35
ABRAM	Do you bite your thumb at us, sir[6]?	
SAMPSON	I do bite my thumb, sir.	
ABRAM	Do you bite your thumb at us, sir?	
SAMPSON	[*Aside to Gregory*] Is the law of our side if I say ay?	40
GREGORY	[*Aside to Sampson*] No.	
SAMPSON	No, sir, I do not bite my thumb at you, sir, but I bite my thumb, sir.	
GREGORY	Do you quarrel[7], sir?	
ABRAM	Quarrel, sir? No, sir.	45
SAMPSON	But if you do, sir, I am for you. I serve as good a man as you.	
ABRAM	No better.	
SAMPSON	Well, sir.	

Enter BENVOLIO.

GREGORY	[*Aside to Sampson*] Say 'better', here comes one of my master's kinsmen[8].	50
SAMPSON	Yes, better, sir.	
ABRAM	You lie.	
SAMPSON	Draw, if you be men. Gregory, remember thy washing blow[9].	

They fight.

BENVOLIO	Part[10], fools! Put up your swords, you know not what you do.	55

[*Beats down their swords.*]

Enter TYBALT.

TYBALT	What, art thou drawn among these heartless hinds[11]? Turn thee, Benvolio, look upon thy death.	
BENVOLIO	I do but keep the peace. Put up thy sword, Or manage[12] it to part these men with me.	60
TYBALT	What, drawn and talk of peace? I hate the word, As I hate hell, all Montagues, and thee. Have at thee[13], coward.	

[*They fight.*]

A furious riot develops. Capulet and Montague join in. Prince Escales, angry and exasperated, stops the fight. He rebukes Montague and Capulet, and threatens death if they fight in public again.

剧情简介：一场激烈的骚乱开始上演，卡普莱和芒特鸠都加入其中。艾斯克勒亲王十分生气，制止了这场打斗。他斥责芒特鸠和卡普莱，威胁说下次他们再公开打斗就处死他们。

1 A snapshot (快照) at the height of the riot (in large groups)

Each group member takes a part. There are at least eleven speaking characters so far. You can add as many other servants and officers as you wish. Use the hall or drama studio if you can, but this activity will work just as well in the classroom if you clear some space.

- Each group prepares and presents a **tableau** (定格；活画) (a 'human sculpture', like a still photograph) showing the height of the riot at line 72, 'Rebellious subjects (臣民，子民), enemies to peace'. Your tableau should show precisely what each character is doing at that moment. This means thinking carefully about what your character has said so far, then 'freezing' as that person at this moment in the riot. Remember, each character is doing something in relation to other characters, so try to show those relationships. For example, both Lady Capulet and Lady Montague seem to rebuke and mock their husbands. It will take time to think out, experiment with and then present the most dramatic picture.
- Hold your tableau for at least sixty seconds – with no movement at all. The other groups spend that time working out exactly who is who.

Language in the play 剧中语言

The all-powerful Prince (in fours)

The Prince is a figure of absolute power and authority. His language is suitably elaborate and impressive (e.g. bloodstained swords are 'neighbour-stainèd steel').

a Identify other examples of the Prince's striking way of speaking, then compare his language style with the way the servants speak at the start of the scene. What differences do you notice?

b Write notes advising an actor playing the Prince how to speak the different sections of his speech opposite.

1 *fray* 骚乱
2 **Clubs, bills and partisans** （这些都是长柄武器；clubs：棍棒，bills：长矛，partisans：宽头长戟；这里用来招呼市民抄家伙）
3 *in his gown* 身着睡袍（他刚被吵醒）
4 **crutch** 拐杖
5 **flourishes his blade** 挥舞兵刃
6 **in spite of me** 存心让我恼怒
7 **foe** 对头，仇敌
8 **train** （亲王的）随从
9 **Profaners** 亵渎者（因为他们的剑上沾了邻居的血）
10 **quench** 熄灭
11 **pernicious** 邪恶，险恶
12 **On pain of torture** 如果不想遭受刑罚的痛苦
13 **mistempered** 锻造粗糙；脾气暴躁（拟人）
14 **movèd** 生气，愤怒
15 **airy word** 毫无意义的斗嘴
16 **thrice** 三次
17 **ancient** 年迈
18 **Cast by** 抛却，脱掉
19 **grave beseeming ornaments** 符合其年长尊贵的饰物（指拐杖，是一种挖苦）
20 **Cankered / cankered** （前者表示"生锈"，后者表示"生病"）
21 **forfeit** 丧失
22 **old Free-town** （根据原故事记载，这是卡普莱家的一座宅邸，位于维罗纳城外）
23 *Exeunt* （剧本中的说明，两个以上演员）退场，下场

Enter [several of both houses, who join the fray¹, and] three or four Citizens [as OFFICERS *of the Watch,] with clubs or partisans.*

OFFICERS Clubs, bills, and partisans²! Strike! Beat them down!
Down with the Capulets! Down with the Montagues! 65

Enter old CAPULET *in his gown³, and his wife [*LADY CAPULET*].*

CAPULET What noise is this? Give me my long sword, ho!
LADY CAPULET A crutch⁴, a crutch! why call you for a sword?
CAPULET My sword, I say! old Montague is come,
And flourishes his blade⁵ in spite of me⁶.

Enter old MONTAGUE *and his wife [*LADY MONTAGUE*].*

MONTAGUE Thou villain Capulet! – Hold me not, let me go. 70
LADY MONTAGUE Thou shalt not stir one foot to seek a foe⁷.

Enter PRINCE ESCALES *with his train⁸.*

PRINCE Rebellious subjects, enemies to peace,
Profaners⁹ of this neighbour-stainèd steel –
Will they not hear? – What ho, you men, you beasts!
That quench¹⁰ the fire of your pernicious¹¹ rage 75
With purple fountains issuing from your veins:
On pain of torture¹², from those bloody hands
Throw your mistempered¹³ weapons to the ground,
And hear the sentence of your movèd¹⁴ prince.
Three civil brawls, bred of an airy word¹⁵, 80
By thee, old Capulet, and Montague,
Have thrice¹⁶ disturbed the quiet of our streets,
And made Verona's ancient¹⁷ citizens
Cast by¹⁸ their grave beseeming ornaments¹⁹
To wield old partisans, in hands as old, 85
Cankered²⁰ with peace, to part your cankered²⁰ hate;
If ever you disturb our streets again,
Your lives shall pay the forfeit²¹ of the peace.
For this time all the rest depart away:
You, Capulet, shall go along with me, 90
And, Montague, come you this afternoon,
To know our farther pleasure in this case,
To old Free-town²², our common judgement-place.
Once more, on pain of death, all men depart.
Exeunt²³ [all but Montague, Lady Montague, and Benvolio]

Benvolio recounts the story of the riot. He tells Lady Montague how Romeo has avoided meeting him. Lord Montague confirms that Romeo has been keeping to himself, preferring night to day.

剧情简介：本沃琉讲述骚乱的来龙去脉。他告诉芒特鸠夫人柔密欧如何一直躲着不见他。芒特鸠老爷证实柔密欧一直不与人来往，喜欢夜晚胜过白天。

Characters 人物分析
Focus on Benvolio (in pairs)

Benvolio's name means 'well-wishing' (the opposite of Malvolio in *Twelfth Night*, whose name means 'ill-wishing'). Benvolio seems to be a peacekeeper. He has already tried to stop the street brawling. Now he recounts to the parents of his good friend Romeo how the riot unfolded (lines 97–106) and describes Romeo's current dejectedness (lines 109–21).

- Take turns to read these two groups of lines, then discuss what characteristics you would look for in casting Benvolio in a production of your own. How closely does this Benvolio (on the right in the picture) match your own ideas for this character?

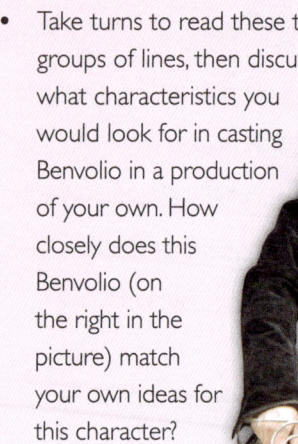

1. abroach （如同在酒桶上开个口子让酒流出来一样的）引流口
2. adversary 对手，对头
3. ere = before
4. drew 拔剑
5. breathed defiance 出言不逊
6. nothing hurt withal 无丝毫伤害
7. hissed him in scorn 发出嘲讽的嗞嗞声
8. on part and part 有的向着我们，有的向着他们
9. either part 双方
10. abroad 去外面
11. sycamore 西卡莫树（人们常将这种树与忧郁的恋人联系起来）
12. ware 警惕，谨防
13. covert 隐蔽处
14. my weary self 只有我这烦闷的一个人
15. humour 性情，心情
16. shunned 躲避
17. augmenting 增加
18. Aurora 奥婼菈（罗马神话中的曙光女神）
19. heavy 忧郁，悲伤
20. pens 封闭
21. portentous 不祥
22. good counsel 好言相劝

Write about it 写作练习
Lord and Lady Montague (in pairs)

In pairs, take one of the following activities each.

a Lady Montague speaks only two lines, then is silent. The fact that she never speaks again in the play suggests the powerlessness of women in Verona. Step into role as Lady Montague and break her silence by writing a **monologue** (独白), in which she expresses her previously unspoken thoughts about Romeo, her husband, the feud with the Capulets and the fight she has just witnessed.

b Lord Montague describes Romeo's current perplexing behaviour (lines 122–33 and 137–46). Write an additional monologue for Lord Montague, in which he voices his thoughts about his son and considers Romeo's reluctance to talk to him.

Read aloud your monologues to each other in ways that bring out Lord and Lady Montague's contrasting attitudes and perspectives.

MONTAGUE	Who set this ancient quarrel new abroach[1]?	95
	Speak, nephew, were you by when it began?	
BENVOLIO	Here were the servants of your adversary[2],	
	And yours, close fighting ere[3] I did approach:	
	I drew[4] to part them; in the instant came	
	The fiery Tybalt, with his sword prepared,	100
	Which, as he breathed defiance[5] to my ears,	
	He swung about his head and cut the winds,	
	Who, nothing hurt withal[6], hissed him in scorn[7];	
	While we were interchanging thrusts and blows,	
	Came more and more, and fought on part and part[8],	105
	Till the Prince came, who parted either part[9].	
LADY MONTAGUE	O where is Romeo? saw you him today?	
	Right glad I am he was not at this fray.	
BENVOLIO	Madam, an hour before the worshipped sun	
	Peered forth the golden window of the east,	110
	A troubled mind drive me to walk abroad[10],	
	Where underneath the grove of sycamore[11],	
	That westward rooteth from this city side,	
	So early walking did I see your son;	
	Towards him I made, but he was ware[12] of me,	115
	And stole into the covert[13] of the wood;	
	I, measuring his affections by my own,	
	Which then most sought where most might not be found,	
	Being one too many by my weary self[14],	
	Pursued my humour[15], not pursuing his,	120
	And gladly shunned[16] who gladly fled from me.	
MONTAGUE	Many a morning hath he there been seen,	
	With tears augmenting[17] the fresh morning's dew,	
	Adding to clouds more clouds with his deep sighs,	
	But all so soon as the all-cheering sun	125
	Should in the farthest east begin to draw	
	The shady curtains from Aurora's[18] bed,	
	Away from light steals home my heavy[19] son,	
	And private in his chamber pens[20] himself,	
	Shuts up his windows, locks fair daylight out,	130
	And makes himself an artificial night:	
	Black and portentous[21] must this humour prove,	
	Unless good counsel[22] may the cause remove.	

Benvolio promises to find out the cause of Romeo's sadness. Romeo says it is because his love for Rosaline (whom he doesn't name) is not returned. He suddenly notices the signs of the riot.

 剧情简介：本沃琉答应搞清楚柔密欧为什么伤心。柔密欧说是因为自己追求若泽兰（他没提名字）却没有回应。他忽然注意到发生了骚乱。

Characters 人物分析

Focus on Romeo (in small groups)

Shakespeare holds back Romeo's introduction to the play. After the seething violence of the opening, Romeo cuts a forlorn figure. His first words express weariness and melancholy (忧郁): his 'love' is unrequited (not returned). In some productions, Romeo is presented as a young man who is lonely and isolated (in one recent production, the director costumed him in modern dress as a contrast to the other male characters, who were all in traditional Elizabethan outfits).

- How would you stage Romeo's first appearance to highlight his state of mind at the start of the play? How might you mark him out as being at odds with the world around him? Produce an annotated drawing showing your ideas.

▶ What are your initial impressions of this Romeo?

1. importuned　询问
2. his own affections' counsellor　他自己情感的密友
3. sounding　试探，探究
4. whence = where
5. grievance　委屈，苦恼
6. shrift　（柔密欧的）告白
7. Good morrow = Good morning
8. hence = away
9. so … proof　看起来很亲切，实际却很残酷
10. muffled still　总是被蒙住眼睛
11. brawling　争吵的
12. of nothing first create　最初从虚无中创造

Language in the play 剧中语言

Imagery: 'bit with an envious worm'

In lines 142–4, Montague compares Romeo to a bud that is destroyed by a malicious (恶毒) ('envious') worm before it can fully flower. In lines 162–3, Romeo says that although Love is blind ('muffled') it can still impose its will on lovers. Both these examples are vivid and striking images typical of the **imagery** to be found throughout the play.

- Look ahead to the information on imagery in the 'Language' section on pages 214–15. Use the guidance there to help you explore these two images. Then write a couple of sentences about the effectiveness and impact of each one.

Romeo and Juliet Act 1 Scene 1
柔蜜欧与茱丽叶

BENVOLIO	My noble uncle, do you know the cause?	
MONTAGUE	I neither know it, nor can learn of him.	135
BENVOLIO	Have you importuned[1] him by any means?	
MONTAGUE	Both by myself and many other friends,	
	But he, his own affections' counsellor[2],	
	Is to himself (I will not say how true)	
	But to himself so secret and so close,	140
	So far from sounding[3] and discovery,	
	As is the bud bit with an envious worm	
	Ere he can spread his sweet leaves to the air,	
	Or dedicate his beauty to the sun.	
	Could we but learn from whence[4] his sorrows grow,	145
	We would as willingly give cure as know.	

Enter ROMEO.

BENVOLIO	See where he comes. So please you step aside,	
	I'll know his grievance[5] or be much denied.	
MONTAGUE	I would thou wert so happy by thy stay	
	To hear true shrift[6]. Come, madam, let's away.	150

Exeunt [Montague and Lady Montague]

BENVOLIO	Good morrow[7], cousin.	
ROMEO	Is the day so young?	
BENVOLIO	But new struck nine.	
ROMEO	Ay me, sad hours seem long.	
	Was that my father that went hence[8] so fast?	
BENVOLIO	It was. What sadness lengthens Romeo's hours?	
ROMEO	Not having that, which, having, makes them short.	155
BENVOLIO	In love?	
ROMEO	Out –	
BENVOLIO	Of love?	
ROMEO	Out of her favour where I am in love.	
BENVOLIO	Alas that Love, so gentle in his view,	160
	Should be so tyrannous and rough in proof[9]!	
ROMEO	Alas that Love, whose view is muffled still[10],	
	Should, without eyes, see pathways to his will!	
	Where shall we dine? O me! what fray was here?	
	Yet tell me not, for I have heard it all:	165
	Here's much to do with hate, but more with love:	
	Why then, O brawling[11] love, O loving hate,	
	O any thing of nothing first create[12]!

Romeo, melancholy because he loves a girl (Rosaline) who does not love him, plays with words to express how love confuses and mixes up all kinds of things, turning order into chaos.

 剧情简介：柔密欧爱上一个姑娘（若泽兰），但姑娘不爱他，所以郁郁寡欢，他玩弄词句，表示爱情如何使各种事物混在一起，将秩序变成了混乱。

Language in the play 剧中语言
The contradictions of love (in pairs)

Take a closer look at Romeo's language. Here is a different way of setting out parts of lines 167–72:

>'loving' v. 'hate'
>'heavy' v. 'lightness'
>'serious' v. 'vanity'
>'Misshapen chaos' v. 'well-seeming forms'
>'Feather' v. 'lead' (铅)
>'bright' v. 'smoke'
>'cold' v. 'fire'
>'sick' v. 'health'
>'Still-waking' v. 'sleep'

The love poetry of Shakespeare's time put together contradictory words in this way to express the turmoil (动荡) that love causes. Phrases like this, composed of 'opposite' words placed directly next to each other, are called **oxymorons** (矛盾修辞法) (see p. 215). You can think of them as very condensed antitheses (see p. 2).

a With your partner, choose one pair of words from the list above and prepare three tableaux. The first two tableaux should show the two separate words (e.g. 'loving' and 'hate'). The third should show the oxymoron ('loving hate'). The class guesses which oxymoron each pair has chosen.

b As you read through to the end of Scene 1, write a couple of paragraphs about how the oxymorons and antitheses have helped shape the characters and themes being explored at the start of the play.

1 Cupid and Diana (in pairs)

Take parts as Romeo and Benvolio and read aloud lines 195–202, which contain several references to two classical figures:

- Cupid, who was famed for his ability to inspire love and desire in anyone hit by an arrow fired from his bow
- Diana, the goddess of hunting and chastity.

As each person reads their lines, the other listens out for and echoes any words connected with either Cupid or Diana. Afterwards, research these classical figures further, then talk together about why Shakespeare might have included these particular references at this point in the play.

1	Misshapen	扭曲变形
2	Still-waking	永远清醒
3	coz = cousin	(本沃琉是柔密欧的亲戚，并不是真正的 cousin)
4	oppression	负担
5	transgression	过度，出格（引申为犯罪）
6	propagate	增加
7	fume	气息
8	purged	净化
9	vexed	沮丧，懊恼
10	gall	苦楚
11	Soft	等一下
12	Tut	（表示反对、厌烦或同情的啧啧声）
13	sadness	严肃，认真（本沃琉让柔密欧说老实话；注意柔密欧在第193—195行中说的双关语）
14	mark-man = marksman	（神射手）
15	fair mark	漂亮的靶子（暗指漂亮女人）
16	Dian = Diana	（狄阿娜，罗马神话中的狩猎和贞洁女神，她避开了爱神丘比特射出的箭）
17	proof	盔甲
18	chastity	贞洁，贞操
19	uncharmed	没被迷住

ROMEO AND JULIET ACT 1 SCENE 1
柔密欧与茱丽叶

	O heavy lightness, serious vanity,
	Misshapen¹ chaos of well-seeming forms,
	Feather of lead, bright smoke, cold fire, sick health,
	Still-waking² sleep, that is not what it is!
	This love feel I, that feel no love in this.
	Dost thou not laugh?
BENVOLIO	No, coz³, I rather weep.
ROMEO	Good heart, at what?
BENVOLIO	At thy good heart's oppression⁴.
ROMEO	Why, such is love's transgression⁵:
	Griefs of mine own lie heavy in my breast,
	Which thou wilt propagate⁶ to have it pressed
	With more of thine; this love that thou hast shown
	Doth add more grief to too much of mine own.
	Love is a smoke made with the fume⁷ of sighs,
	Being purged⁸, a fire sparkling in lovers' eyes,
	Being vexed⁹, a sea nourished with loving tears.
	What is it else? a madness most discreet,
	A choking gall¹⁰, and a preserving sweet.
	Farewell, my coz.
BENVOLIO	Soft¹¹, I will go along;
	And if you leave me so, you do me wrong.
ROMEO	Tut¹², I have lost myself, I am not here,
	This is not Romeo, he's some other where.
BENVOLIO	Tell me in sadness¹³, who is that you love?
ROMEO	What, shall I groan and tell thee?
BENVOLIO	Groan? why, no;
	But sadly tell me, who?
ROMEO	Bid a sick man in sadness make his will –
	A word ill urged to one that is so ill:
	In sadness, cousin, I do love a woman.
BENVOLIO	I aimed so near, when I supposed you loved.
ROMEO	A right good mark-man¹⁴! and she's fair I love.
BENVOLIO	A right fair mark¹⁵, fair coz, is soonest hit.
ROMEO	Well, in that hit you miss: she'll not be hit
	With Cupid's arrow, she hath Dian's¹⁶ wit;
	And in strong proof¹⁷ of chastity¹⁸ well armed,
	From Love's weak childish bow she lives uncharmed¹⁹.

Line numbers: 170, 175, 180, 185, 190, 195, 200

15

Romeo complains that because she refuses to marry, the woman he loves will leave no children. Her beauty will die with her. Benvolio advises him to look at other girls – that will cure him! Romeo isn't convinced.

剧情简介：柔密欧抱怨说，因为他爱的女人拒绝与他结婚，就不会（与他）有孩子，她的美貌会同她一起逝去。本沃琉建议他放眼其他姑娘，这样会治好他的相思病！柔密欧不以为然。

1 Is Romeo really in love? (in small groups)

Romeo uses the language of classical poetry, and many people today think that because he speaks in this elaborate way, his emotions are 'artificial', not genuine and sincere. But what do you think? Does this manner of speaking (for example, using extravagant imagery, wordplay, antitheses and rhyming couplets [押韵二行连句；对偶句]) show that he is really in love, as he claims to be, or just infatuated (痴情)?

a Focus on Romeo's language in the script opposite. With your group, identify which words and phrases sound heartfelt and which sound forced and contrived (做作). One person draws a pair of scales, with one side labelled 'genuine' and the other 'false'. Discuss which extracts of text should go on either side, and see what kind of balance results.

b Individually, rewrite Romeo's twenty-three lines opposite in simple modern English. In your groups, compare your versions, then look again at Shakespeare's original script. Discuss the different effects created by the two types of writing.

2 A link with Shakespeare's sonnets?

Romeo's lines 206–7 pick up an idea that frequently appears in Shakespeare's sonnets: to die childless is a waste of one's earthly beauty, as there will be no legacy for future generations.

- Why do you think Shakespeare included such an image at this point in the play? What does it add to your understanding of the theme of love?

Write about it 写作练习

The conflict of love, the conflict of hate

Act 1 Scene 1 includes several key episodes that dramatise the conflicting effects of love and hate. For example, it begins with crude jokes, simmers (酝酿) with tension, then explodes into violent action. Benvolio is immediately cast as a peacekeeper and Tybalt as an uncompromising aggressor. Romeo is clearly torn apart by feelings of love.

- Re-read the scene, then write a review exploring how it addresses the theme of conflict. Focus on the different characters' attitudes to one another, on the specific types of language they use and on how Shakespeare structures the scene to create a dramatic interplay (相互影响) of contrasting viewpoints and attitudes.

1 stay ... terms   屈服于甜言蜜语的围攻（柔密欧把求爱比作一场军事进攻）
2 bide ... eyes   经受炽辣目光的相遇
3 ope her lap to   为……张开她的大腿 (ope = open)
4 still = always
5 live chaste   守身如玉
6 sparing   吝惜，节俭
7 severity   严苛
8 posterity   子孙后代
9 merit bliss   有资格享受极乐
10 forsworn to love   发誓不恋爱
11 Be ruled by me   听我的话
12 strucken blind   突然失明
     (strucken = struck)
13 passing   非常，极其
14 pay that doctrine   给你上一课

	She will not stay the siege of loving terms[1],	
	Nor bide th'encounter of assailing eyes[2],	
	Nor ope her lap to[3] saint-seducing gold.	205
	O, she is rich in beauty, only poor	
	That when she dies, with beauty dies her store.	
BENVOLIO	Then she hath sworn that she will still[4] live chaste[5]?	
ROMEO	She hath, and in that sparing[6] makes huge waste;	
	For beauty starved with her severity[7]	210
	Cuts beauty off from all posterity[8].	
	She is too fair, too wise, wisely too fair,	
	To merit bliss[9] by making me despair.	
	She hath forsworn to love[10], and in that vow	
	Do I live dead, that live to tell it now.	215
BENVOLIO	Be ruled by me[11], forget to think of her.	
ROMEO	O teach me how I should forget to think.	
BENVOLIO	By giving liberty unto thine eyes,	
	Examine other beauties.	
ROMEO	'Tis the way	
	To call hers (exquisite) in question more:	220
	These happy masks that kiss fair ladies' brows,	
	Being black, puts us in mind they hide the fair;	
	He that is strucken blind[12] cannot forget	
	The precious treasure of his eyesight lost;	
	Show me a mistress that is passing[13] fair,	225
	What doth her beauty serve but as a note	
	Where I may read who passed that passing fair?	
	Farewell, thou canst not teach me to forget.	
BENVOLIO	I'll pay that doctrine[14], or else die in debt.	

Exeunt

Paris wishes to marry Juliet. Capulet says his daughter is still only thirteen, but he will agree if Juliet consents. He invites Paris to a party that night, where there will be many beautiful women.

剧情简介：帕瑞想娶茱丽叶。卡普莱说他女儿只有13岁，但如果茱丽叶愿意他就会同意。他邀请帕瑞当晚来参加宴会，到时候会有许多漂亮女士到场。

Stagecraft 导演技巧

Capulet's mansion

The action moves swiftly from an outdoor space to the interior of Lord Capulet's grand house. After a brief exchange between Capulet and Paris, the scene switches again to the street outside.

- Sketch a set design that you think could work well for this, and then compare your ideas with the images in the section on 'Romeo and Juliet in performance' on pages 220–7. Refine your original design in light of your reflections on other stagings.

1 | COUNTY = Count （伯爵）
2 | *Clown* 仆人（在大多数现代演出里这个角色通常是茱丽叶奶妈的仆人Peter）
3 | bound 被勒令
4 | In penalty alike 同罪论处
5 | reckoning 声望
6 | at odds 结怨
7 | suit 求婚
8 | saying o'er 重申 (o'er = over)
9 | She … years 她还不满14岁
10 | marred （身体）受损，损毁
11 | within her scope of choice 根据她的选择
12 | old accustomed 由来已久
13 | store 大批宾客
14 | Earth-treading stars 凡间的星星（比喻可爱的女士们）
15 | well-apparelled 花枝招展
16 | limping winter 步履蹒跚的冬天
17 | fennel buds 茴香芽（茴香被认为是一种春药；这里暗指年轻女子）
18 | Inherit 采到
19 | Which … none 您在宴会上看到其他女After后，小女或许就不是您最青睐的了

1 What were Capulet and Paris talking about?
(in pairs)

a Capulet and Paris enter in the middle of a conversation. In your pairs, make a list of some of the topics they might have been talking about before they entered. Remember, Capulet has already been involved in the action of Scene 1; Paris has not been involved.

b Improvise (即兴表演) their conversation so that it leads naturally to the opening line: 'But Montague is bound as well as I' (the Prince has ordered both me and Montague to keep the peace). First try it in modern English, then challenge yourselves by scripting it in Shakespearean language and fitting it to the rhythm of **iambic pentameter** (抑扬五音步) (see p. 216).

2 Marrying off Juliet (in pairs)

Shakespeare continues to hold back Juliet's first appearance in the play. But he uses part of the dialogue between Capulet and Paris to give some background information about Juliet and particularly about her father's attitude to her becoming a wife. Capulet explains that, amongst other things, Juliet is only thirteen and is therefore too young to be married. He also informs Paris that the 'Earth hath swallowed all my hopes but she' (all my other children have died).

- Focus on lines 6–19. Read them together and then jot down your own thoughts about Capulet's views. Do you think that he comes across as a reasonable and thoughtful father? Why, or why not? Identify quotations from the script opposite that back up your opinion of Capulet.

Act 1 Scene 2
Capulet's mansion

Enter CAPULET, COUNTY[1] PARIS, *and the Clown*[2] [SERVANT *to* CAPULET].

CAPULET But Montague is bound[3] as well as I,
In penalty alike[4], and 'tis not hard, I think,
For men so old as we to keep the peace.

PARIS Of honourable reckoning[5] are you both,
And pity 'tis, you lived at odds[6] so long.
But now, my lord, what say you to my suit[7]?

CAPULET But saying o'er[8] what I have said before:
My child is yet a stranger in the world,
She hath not seen the change of fourteen years[9];
Let two more summers wither in their pride,
Ere we may think her ripe to be a bride.

PARIS Younger than she are happy mothers made.

CAPULET And too soon marred[10] are those so early made.
Earth hath swallowed all my hopes but she;
She's the hopeful lady of my earth.
But woo her, gentle Paris, get her heart,
My will to her consent is but a part;
And she agreed, within her scope of choice[11]
Lies my consent and fair according voice.
This night I hold an old accustomed[12] feast,
Whereto I have invited many a guest,
Such as I love, and you among the store[13],
One more, most welcome, makes my number more.
At my poor house look to behold this night
Earth-treading stars[14] that make dark heaven light.
Such comfort as do lusty young men feel
When well-apparelled[15] April on the heel
Of limping winter[16] treads, even such delight
Among fresh fennel buds[17] shall you this night
Inherit[18] at my house; hear all, all see;
And like her most whose merit most shall be;
Which on more view of many, mine, being one,
May stand in number, though in reck'ning none[19].

Capulet orders his servant to deliver party invitations. But the servant can't read! Benvolio again urges Romeo to look at other women to cure his love-sickness. The servant asks Romeo to read the letter.

剧情简介：卡普莱命仆人送宴会请柬，但这个仆人不识字！本沃琉再次力劝柔密欧看看别的女子来治他的相思病。仆人请柔密欧帮他读请柬。

Benvolio (left) with Romeo. Which line of Benvolio's advice best matches this picture? Explain your choice.

1 Make Benvolio's advice active (in fours)

Benvolio's advice to Romeo (lines 44–9) is that the cure for love is to look at other girls, because then new love will replace old love. Here, he says the same thing in five different ways.

- Work out how you can show, without words, each part of the advice. It is probably easiest to begin with 'pain' (line 45 – new pain makes you forget earlier suffering), then 'giddy', then 'grief', then 'infection'. Finally, see if you can make up a mime (哑剧手势) for 'fire'. Show your actions to the class.

Themes 主题分析

Chance versus choice

Unwittingly, the Servant sets the plot moving towards its tragic conclusion. Unable to read the names of the guests invited to the Capulet party, he looks for someone to read the list to him and, by chance, comes across Romeo in the street. This is how Romeo discovers his 'beloved' Rosaline will be present at the ball which, in turn, encourages him to make the decision to gatecrash (强闯) the Capulet celebrations.

- Start to complete an Evidence Grid (证据网格). Head up a piece of paper with two columns: 'Chance' and 'Choice'. Review the action of the play so far and begin to fill up the columns as appropriate. How far do the characters seem in control of their own destinies? How far are they victims of the apparently random workings of fate? Add further details as the play unfolds.

1 sirrah 小子（旧时对下人的称呼语）
2 trudge about 走遍，跑遍
3 on their pleasure stay 等着他们做决定
4 meddle with 摆弄，捣鼓
5 the shoemaker … nets （仆人因为不识字而把鞋匠、裁缝、渔夫和画匠与他们使用的工具张冠李戴了）
6 writ = written
7 In good time! 得早早儿的！
8 anguish 痛苦
9 giddy 头晕
10 holp = helped
11 languish 憔悴
12 rank 臭烘烘
13 plantain leaf 车前草叶（可用来治疗刀伤和擦伤）
14 God-den = Good evening
15 gi' = give you
16 without book 牢记在心
17 Ye 你们；您；你
18 rest you merry 再见
19 beauteous = beautiful

ROMEO AND JULIET ACT 1 SCENE 2
柔密欧与茱丽叶

	Come go with me. [*To Servant*] Go, sirrah¹, trudge about²	
	Through fair Verona, find those persons out	35
	Whose names are written there [*Gives a paper.*], and to them say,	
	My house and welcome on their pleasure stay³.	
	Exit [*with Paris*]	
SERVANT	Find them out whose names are written here! It is written that the shoemaker should meddle with⁴ his yard and the tailor with his last, the fisher with his pencil and the painter with his nets⁵; but I am sent to find those persons whose names are here writ⁶, and can never find what names the writing person hath here writ. I must to the learnèd. In good time!⁷	40
	Enter BENVOLIO *and* ROMEO.	
BENVOLIO	Tut, man, one fire burns out another's burning,	
	One pain is lessened by another's anguish⁸;	45
	Turn giddy⁹, and be holp¹⁰ by backward turning;	
	One desperate grief cures with another's languish¹¹:	
	Take thou some new infection to thy eye,	
	And the rank¹² poison of the old will die.	
ROMEO	Your plantain leaf¹³ is excellent for that.	50
BENVOLIO	For what, I pray thee?	
ROMEO	For your broken shin.	
BENVOLIO	Why, Romeo, art thou mad?	
ROMEO	Not mad, but bound more than a madman is:	
	Shut up in prison, kept without my food,	
	Whipt and tormented, and – God-den¹⁴, good fellow.	55
SERVANT	God gi'¹⁵ god-den. I pray, sir, can you read?	
ROMEO	Ay, mine own fortune in my misery.	
SERVANT	Perhaps you have learned it without book¹⁶; but I pray, can you read any thing you see?	
ROMEO	Ay, if I know the letters and the language.	60
SERVANT	Ye¹⁷ say honestly, rest you merry¹⁸.	
ROMEO	Stay, fellow, I can read.	
	He reads the letter.	
	'Signior Martino and his wife and daughters,	
	County Anselme and his beauteous¹⁹ sisters,	
	The lady widow of Vitruvio,	65
	Signior Placentio and his lovely nieces,	
	Mercutio and his brother Valentine,	

Romeo discovers that Rosaline has been invited to Capulet's party. Benvolio urges Romeo to go. There he will see women more beautiful than Rosaline. Romeo refuses to believe Benvolio's claim.

 剧情简介：柔密欧发现若泽兰也在卡普莱夜宴受邀者之列。本沃琉撺掇柔密欧赴宴，因为他会在那里看到比若泽兰更漂亮的女子。柔密欧不相信本沃琉的话。

1 Make a grand entrance! (in large groups)

The names on the list of guests (lines 63–71) roll off the tongue.

- One person acts as Master of Ceremonies (司仪). He or she will announce the guests, line by line. Everyone else chooses a part and decides how their character will make their grand entrance to Capulet's party. At least twenty-three people are listed, so double up parts and make two entrances!

2 Advice to the Servant

The Servant only has a small part in this scene (some 16 lines), but he can still create a dramatic impact. Read through all the Servant's lines, from line 58 onwards. (Notice that in lines 39–40, he muddles up workers and their tools: a shoemaker uses a last, a tailor a yard, a fisherman a net and a painter a pencil.)

- Imagine you are directing a production of the play. The actor playing the Servant asks you how he should perform his part. Begin a Director's Journal, in which you will write notes to guide the actors playing various parts. To begin with, make notes for the Servant. For example, do you think he is dull-witted or clever? How comic would you make his interplay with Romeo? Add to your notes for various characters as opportunities arise throughout the rest of the play.

Characters 人物分析

What does Romeo think about love? (in pairs)

Romeo continues to protest that his love for Rosaline will never change. He even says that if he did see someone more beautiful than Rosaline, his eyes would burn out because they would be liars, unfaithful to the 'devout religion' they serve – his adoring belief in Rosaline's beauty (lines 88–91). Romeo's words seem to be inspired by the practice of burning heretics (people who did not believe in a Christian God) at the stake.

- Based on your reading of this scene and Scene 1, come up with five questions that you would like to ask Romeo about his attitude towards Rosaline, and what he thinks and feels about being in love.
- In pairs, take turns in the role of Romeo and answer your partner's questions. Compare your answers and then talk about your views of Romeo as a young man in love.

1 whither should they come? 他们要去哪里?
2 crush 喝
3 Go thither = Go there
4 unattainted 不带偏见
5 devout religion 虔诚的信仰
6 Transparent heretics 明显的异教徒
7 poised 衡量
8 crystal scales 水晶天平（指柔密欧的一双眼睛）
9 scant 不足，几乎没有
10 mine own （指若泽兰自己的美丽）

	Mine uncle Capulet, his wife and daughters,	
	My fair niece Rosaline, and Livia,	
	Signior Valentio and his cousin Tybalt,	70
	Lucio and the lively Helena.'	
	A fair assembly: whither should they come[1]?	
SERVANT	Up.	
ROMEO	Whither? to supper?	
SERVANT	To our house.	75
ROMEO	Whose house?	
SERVANT	My master's.	
ROMEO	Indeed I should have asked thee that before.	
SERVANT	Now I'll tell you without asking. My master is the great rich Capulet, and if you be not of the house of Montagues, I pray come and crush[2] a cup of wine. Rest you merry. [*Exit*]	80
BENVOLIO	At this same ancient feast of Capulet's	
	Sups the fair Rosaline whom thou so loves,	
	With all the admirèd beauties of Verona:	
	Go thither[3], and with unattainted[4] eye	85
	Compare her face with some that I shall show,	
	And I will make thee think thy swan a crow.	
ROMEO	When the devout religion[5] of mine eye	
	Maintains such falsehood, then turn tears to fires;	
	And these who, often drowned, could never die,	90
	Transparent heretics[6], be burnt for liars.	
	One fairer than my love! the all-seeing sun	
	Ne'er saw her match since first the world begun.	
BENVOLIO	Tut, you saw her fair, none else being by,	
	Herself poised[7] with herself in either eye;	95
	But in that crystal scales[8] let there be weighed	
	Your lady's love against some other maid	
	That I will show you shining at this feast,	
	And she shall scant[9] show well that now seems best.	
ROMEO	I'll go along no such sight to be shown,	100
	But to rejoice in splendour of mine own[10].	
	[*Exeunt*]	

Lady Capulet and the Nurse discuss Juliet's age. She is not yet fourteen. The Nurse remembers her own daughter, Susan, now dead. She recalls that Juliet was weaned eleven years ago.

 剧情简介：卡普莱夫人与奶妈谈论茱丽叶的年龄——她还不满14岁。奶妈回忆起自己过世的女儿苏珊，还想起11年前给茱丽叶断奶的情形。

1 The Nurse – first impressions (in small groups)

This is the first appearance of Juliet's Nurse (a 'wet nurse' [奶妈] who acted as a surrogate mother [替身母亲] to a young child, and a person to whom Juliet is naturally very close). Many productions exploit the Nurse's role for its comic potential. Her distinctive character dominates this scene, and her lines are often rude and very funny!

a Speak aloud all the Nurse says in lines 2–63. Each person reads a small **sense unit** (a portion of script that makes sense on its own – sometimes a sentence, sometimes a phrase), then hands the speech on to the next group member. Speak your own short extracts as you think the Nurse would say them. Refer to the glossary on the right if you are unsure about the meaning of any terms.

b In your groups, write down a list of words or phrases you think best describe the Nurse. Match them to quotations from the script where possible. Then compare your list with those of other groups. Add to your list as you learn more about the Nurse in later scenes.

1 **What** （感叹词，表示不耐烦）
2 **How now** = Why
3 **give leave** 让我们单独待着
4 **thou s' hear** = you shall hear （你应该听一听）
5 **counsel** 私下谈话
6 **lay** 下赌注
7 **teen** 悲哀，伤心
8 **Lammas-tide** 莱玛斯节（8月1日，英国的收获节；tide = time；茱丽叶将在7月31日 [后文的Lammas-eve] 满14周岁）
9 **odd days** 零几天（odd也指奇数）
10 **Even or odd** 不管（多出来的天数）是奇数还是偶数（这句话表明奶妈有些迂腐）
11 **marry** （见第6页注解2）
12 **the earthquake** （可能指1580年发生于伦敦的地震）
13 **aleven** = eleven
14 **laid wormwood to my dug** 在我的乳头上涂苦艾（为了给茱丽叶断奶）
15 **bear a brain** 有脑子；记性好

▲ What does this photograph suggest about the kind of relationship the three women share? What are your impressions of this Nurse (left)?

Stagecraft 导演技巧

Where are they? (in pairs)

Many productions set this scene in Juliet's bedroom. Talk together about why you think this is such a popular choice for directors. What alternatives can you suggest that might be similarly effective?

Act 1 Scene 3
A room in Capulet's mansion

Enter CAPULET'S WIFE *and* NURSE.

LADY CAPULET	Nurse, where's my daughter? call her forth to me.	
NURSE	Now by my maidenhead at twelve year old,	
	I bade her come. What[1], lamb! What, ladybird!	
	God forbid, where's this girl? What, Juliet!	

Enter JULIET.

JULIET	How now[2], who calls?	5
NURSE	Your mother.	
JULIET	Madam, I am here, what is your will?	
LADY CAPULET	This is the matter. Nurse, give leave[3] a while,	
	We must talk in secret. Nurse, come back again,	
	I have remembered me, thou s' hear[4] our counsel[5].	10
	Thou knowest my daughter's of a pretty age.	
NURSE	Faith, I can tell her age unto an hour.	
LADY CAPULET	She's not fourteen.	
NURSE	I'll lay[6] fourteen of my teeth –	
	And yet to my teen[7] be it spoken, I have but four –	
	She's not fourteen. How long is it now	15
	To Lammas-tide[8]?	
LADY CAPULET	A fortnight and odd days[9].	
NURSE	Even or odd[10], of all days in the year,	
	Come Lammas-eve at night shall she be fourteen.	
	Susan and she – God rest all Christian souls! –	
	Were of an age. Well, Susan is with God,	20
	She was too good for me. But as I said,	
	On Lammas-eve at night shall she be fourteen,	
	That shall she, marry[11], I remember it well.	
	'Tis since the earthquake[12] now aleven[13] years,	
	And she was weaned – I never shall forget it –	25
	Of all the days of the year, upon that day;	
	For I had then laid wormwood to my dug[14],	
	Sitting in the sun under the dove-house wall.	
	My lord and you were then at Mantua –	
	Nay, I do bear a brain[15] – but as I said,	30

The Nurse reminisces about Juliet's childhood and tells how her husband joked about Juliet's sexuality. Lady Capulet begins to talk to Juliet about marriage.

  剧情简介：奶妈追忆茱丽叶的童年，还提到她丈夫当时如何拿茱丽叶的性别开玩笑。卡普莱夫人开始跟茱丽叶谈她的婚事。

▶ This production was set in a care home for the elderly. By ageing the characters in this way, what might the director have been saying about the theme of love?

1 tetchy　易怒
2 Shake! = Shake a leg!（快跑！）
3 quoth　说
4 I trow　我确信
5 trudge　跑开
6 stand high-lone　自己站起来
7 th'rood　（基督受难的）十字架
8 broke her brow　磕破了额头
9 'A = He
10 fall backward　向后躺倒（暗指跟男人上床）
11 holidam = holy dame（圣母，指Virgin Mary）
12 warrant　保证
13 stinted　止住了（哭）
14 young cock'rel's stone　小公鸡的睾丸
15 perilous knock　危险的撞击
16 Peace = Silence
17 dispositions　意向，倾向
18 teat　奶头，乳头

Characters　人物分析

Focus on Juliet (in pairs)

The opening of Scene 3, our first glimpse of Juliet, creates the impression of just how young and vulnerable she is. Shakespeare gives her only seven lines to speak and, at first sight, most of them seem to suggest that she is submissive to the two older women. Even though Juliet is still only thirteen, Lady Capulet plans that she shall soon marry. One production made Juliet seem almost childlike. She entered eating chocolates, then sat cross-legged (盘着腿) on the floor ignoring all that the Nurse and her mother said. She continued to eat, and her face became more and more smeared with chocolate. In another production, Juliet played with a doll during this scene.

a Imagine that you are playing Juliet in a modern production. How would you enter this scene? What would you want the audience's first impression of her (and her age) to be? In rehearsal for this scene, test out your ideas with a partner.

b Take each of Juliet's lines in turn and decide whether she should speak them with respect and deference (敬重), or whether they should signal her independence and self-confidence. Write down your ideas in readiness for a discussion with your director.

	When it did taste the wormwood on the nipple	
	Of my dug, and felt it bitter, pretty fool,	
	To see it tetchy¹ and fall out wi'th'dug!	
	'Shake!²' quoth³ the dove-house; 'twas no need, I trow⁴,	
	To bid me trudge⁵.	35
	And since that time it is aleven years,	
	For then she could stand high-lone⁶; nay, by th'rood⁷,	
	She could have run and waddled all about;	
	For even the day before, she broke her brow⁸,	
	And then my husband – God be with his soul,	40
	'A⁹ was a merry man – took up the child.	
	'Yea', quoth he, 'dost thou fall upon thy face?	
	Thou wilt fall backward¹⁰ when thou hast more wit,	
	Wilt thou not, Jule?' And by my holidam¹¹,	
	The pretty wretch left crying, and said 'Ay'.	45
	To see now how a jest shall come about!	
	I warrant¹², and I should live a thousand years,	
	I never should forget it: 'Wilt thou not, Jule?' quoth he,	
	And, pretty fool, it stinted¹³, and said 'Ay'.	
LADY CAPULET	Enough of this, I pray thee hold thy peace.	50
NURSE	Yes, madam, yet I cannot choose but laugh,	
	To think it should leave crying, and say 'Ay':	
	And yet I warrant it had upon it brow	
	A bump as big as a young cock'rel's stone¹⁴,	
	A perilous knock¹⁵, and it cried bitterly.	55
	'Yea', quoth my husband, 'fall'st upon thy face?	
	Thou wilt fall backward when thou comest to age,	
	Wilt thou not, Jule?' It stinted, and said 'Ay'.	
JULIET	And stint thou too, I pray thee, Nurse, say I.	
NURSE	Peace¹⁶, I have done. God mark thee to his grace,	60
	Thou wast the prettiest babe that e'er I nursed.	
	And I might live to see thee married once,	
	I have my wish.	
LADY CAPULET	Marry, that 'marry' is the very theme	
	I came to talk of. Tell me, daughter Juliet,	65
	How stands your dispositions¹⁷ to be married?	
JULIET	It is an honour that I dream not of.	
NURSE	An honour! were not I thine only nurse,	
	I would say thou hadst sucked wisdom from thy teat¹⁸.	

Lady Capulet gives her reasons why Juliet should think of marriage. She tells her daughter of Paris's love, praising him in elaborate style. A servant tells them the party guests have arrived.

 剧情简介：卡普莱夫人给茱丽叶讲道理，解释为什么她要考虑结婚。她告诉女儿帕瑞向她提亲，把帕瑞仔仔细细地夸了一番。仆人进来禀报说宾客已经到了。

1 Juliet confides (by yourself)

Juliet says very little in this scene, but her young mind will certainly be working overtime. Just what are her thoughts after listening to her mother and the Nurse? What does she make of her father's plans for her and for the Capulet ball?

- Imagine you are Juliet. Write a diary entry explaining your thoughts and feelings at this point in the play.

2 Lady Capulet's admiration (in pairs)

Lady Capulet's lines 82–95 praising Paris are rather like a sonnet: there are fourteen lines, although the pattern of the rhymes is different from the usual sonnet form (see p.216). Lady Capulet elaborately compares Paris to an attractive book. To explore her language more closely, try the following activities.

a   Sit facing each other and read the lines aloud, each person taking just one line at a time. As you read your line, try to perform an action with the book you have in your hand. You'll find some lines quite easy to accompany with an action. Others are more difficult, especially lines 90–1, 'The fish lives in the sea … / … the fair within to hide'. This seems to mean that just as fish are at home in the sea, so good books deserve good covers, and handsome men deserve beautiful wives.

b   Make a list of the qualities that appear to make up Lady Capulet's perfect man. Find a suitable picture from a magazine and annotate it to show the qualities of the man in the picture. How closely do those characteristics match your idea of a *modern* 'ideal' man?

Write about it 写作练习

Three women

Scenes 1 and 2 focus strongly on male-dominated behaviour. In contrast, Scene 3 shows the play's three major female characters in an intimate domestic setting. The three women all have strikingly different personalities.

- Re-read the scene between the women and then write a paragraph about each character's specific personality.
- Then write a fourth paragraph exploring the relationships between them. Who do you think really controls what is happening in this scene? Why?

1 By my count   拿我来说
2 man of wax   十全十美的男人（就像雕塑家手中的蜡像一样）
3 married lineament   和谐的容貌
4 one another lends content   根根线条搭配匀称
5 margent = margin   （边缘）
6 unbound   未装订（这里指未婚）
7 cover   封面（这里指新娘）
8 fair without   美丽的外表（指书的封面，暗指妻子）
9 fair within   美丽的内心（指书的内文，暗指丈夫）
10 clasps   固定住精装书的锁钩
11 bigger women grow by men   女人借助男人变大（指怀孕）
12 endart   发射飞镖（丘比特之箭）
13 extremity   危机（指乱作一团）
14 wait   伺候
15 beseech   恳求，请求
16 straight   马上，立刻
17 the County stays   伯爵（帕瑞）在等着呢

LADY CAPULET	Well, think of marriage now; younger than you,	70
	Here in Verona, ladies of esteem,	
	Are made already mothers. By my count[1],	
	I was your mother much upon these years	
	That you are now a maid. Thus then in brief:	
	The valiant Paris seeks you for his love.	75
NURSE	A man, young lady! lady, such a man	
	As all the world – Why, he's a man of wax[2].	
LADY CAPULET	Verona's summer hath not such a flower.	
NURSE	Nay, he's a flower, in faith, a very flower.	
LADY CAPULET	What say you, can you love the gentleman?	80
	This night you shall behold him at our feast;	
	Read o'er the volume of young Paris' face,	
	And find delight writ there with beauty's pen;	
	Examine every married lineament[3],	
	And see how one another lends content[4];	85
	And what obscured in this fair volume lies	
	Find written in the margent[5] of his eyes.	
	This precious book of love, this unbound[6] lover,	
	To beautify him, only lacks a cover[7].	
	The fish lives in the sea, and 'tis much pride	90
	For fair without[8] the fair within[9] to hide;	
	That book in many's eyes doth share the glory	
	That in gold clasps[10] locks in the golden story:	
	So shall you share all that he doth possess,	
	By having him, making yourself no less.	95
NURSE	No less! nay, bigger women grow by men[11].	
LADY CAPULET	Speak briefly, can you like of Paris' love?	
JULIET	I'll look to like, if looking liking move;	
	But no more deep will I endart[12] mine eye	
	Than your consent gives strength to make it fly.	100

Enter SERVINGMAN.

SERVINGMAN	Madam, the guests are come, supper served up, you called, my young lady asked for, the Nurse cursed in the pantry, and every thing in extremity[13]. I must hence to wait[14], I beseech[15] you follow straight[16]. [*Exit*]	
LADY CAPULET	We follow thee. Juliet, the County stays[17].	105
NURSE	Go, girl, seek happy nights to happy days.	

Exeunt

Romeo and his friends, carrying masks and torches, prepare for their visit to Capulet's party. Romeo declares his unhappiness and says he will not dance. Mercutio tries to laugh Romeo out of his sadness.

剧情简介：柔密欧和朋友们带着面具和火把，准备去参加卡普莱家的夜宴。柔密欧说自己不开心，还表示不会在宴会上跳舞。莫丘休跟柔密欧开玩笑，想让他摆脱悲伤。

Characters 人物分析

Mercutio, the language trickster (魔术师)

In contrast to Benvolio, Mercutio is never bothered about getting into trouble. He seeks excitement and loves needling and verbally sparring with other characters. His language reflects his edginess (急躁，一触即跳) and, like Shakespeare's contemporaries, he relishes wordplay and puns. In fact, all three young men use puns in the script opposite: for example, 'soles'/'soul', 'soar'/'sore', 'pricks'/'prick', 'visor'/'visor'; and in Shakespeare's time 'heavy' (line 22) also meant 'sad'.

a Begin a Character file for Mercutio, in which you note down examples of his clever and inventive language. In each case, explain what makes it so effective.

b Add to these notes as you read through the rest of the play and look to see if any patterns emerge. For example, are there particular occasions or subjects that seem to inspire his wicked wordplay?

1 Lifting Romeo's spirits (in pairs)

Romeo continues to show his unhappiness, even as the young men approach the Capulet party. For example, in line 12 Romeo declares he is 'heavy' (sad) and only fit to carry one of their torches. Mercutio is intent on cheering him up, particularly by joking about sex.

- Take parts and read aloud lines 11–32. Mercutio should try hard to lift Romeo's spirits with every line. How does your Romeo respond? Afterwards, identify two or three ways in which Mercutio's attitude and choice of language remind you of the Nurse's language in the previous scene.

▶ Compare this image with the ones on pages 10 and 20. Can you find any similarities between the presentation of Romeo's relationship with each of his young male friends?

1 What … excuse? 怎么样，要说这段话作为借口吗？
2 The date … prolixity 这种啰唆客套已经过时了
3 hoodwinked 蒙住眼睛
4 Tartar's painted bow of lath 鞑靼人的彩绘木弓（形状像人的上嘴唇，与传说中丘比特手持的弓类似）
5 crow-keeper 稻草人
6 without-book 不用看书，会背
7 measure 评判
8 measure them a measure 跳一场舞（前一个measure指表演，后一个指舞蹈）
9 ambling 舞步
10 nimble soles 轻便的鞋底（sole与后文的soul是谐音双关）
11 stakes 固定住
12 bound 限制，束缚
13 bound 被束缚，被捆绑
14 bound 跳跃
15 pitch 高度
16 boist'rous = boisterous（狂暴）
17 case 面具
18 A visor for a visor! 一张丑脸再戴上个面具！
19 cote 注意，关注
20 beetle brows 浓密而突出的眉毛

Act 1 Scene 4
A street outside Capulet's mansion

Enter ROMEO, MERCUTIO, BENVOLIO, *with five or six other* MASKERS, TORCH-BEARERS.

ROMEO	What, shall this speech be spoke for our excuse[1]?	
	Or shall we on without apology?	
BENVOLIO	The date is out of such prolixity[2]:	
	We'll have no Cupid hoodwinked[3] with a scarf,	
	Bearing a Tartar's painted bow of lath[4],	5
	Scaring the ladies like a crow-keeper[5],	
	Nor no without-book[6] prologue, faintly spoke	
	After the prompter, for our entrance;	
	But let them measure[7] us by what they will,	
	We'll measure them a measure[8] and be gone.	10
ROMEO	Give me a torch, I am not for this ambling[9];	
	Being but heavy, I will bear the light.	
MERCUTIO	Nay, gentle Romeo, we must have you dance.	
ROMEO	Not I, believe me. You have dancing shoes	
	With nimble soles[10], I have a soul of lead	15
	So stakes[11] me to the ground I cannot move.	
MERCUTIO	You are a lover, borrow Cupid's wings,	
	And soar with them above a common bound[12].	
ROMEO	I am too sore enpiercèd with his shaft	
	To soar with his light feathers, and so bound[13]	20
	I cannot bound[14] a pitch[15] above dull woe:	
	Under love's heavy burden do I sink.	
MERCUTIO	And to sink in it should you burden love,	
	Too great oppression for a tender thing.	
ROMEO	Is love a tender thing? it is too rough,	25
	Too rude, too boist'rous[16], and it pricks like thorn.	
MERCUTIO	If love be rough with you, be rough with love:	
	Prick love for pricking, and you beat love down.	
	Give me a case[17] to put my visage in, [*Puts on a mask.*]	
	A visor for a visor![18] what care I	30
	What curious eye doth cote[19] deformities?	
	Here are the beetle brows[20] shall blush for me.	

Romeo refuses to be cheered up, in spite of Mercutio's joking. He has no wish to join in the dance. Mercutio begins to tell of Queen Mab, Queen of the Fairies. He describes the intricate detail of her coach.

剧情简介：即便莫丘休一直开玩笑，柔密欧仍然不愿振作起来，无心参加舞会。莫丘休的话题转到仙后麦布，描述她的座驾有多么精致。

1 Mercutio and 'Queen Mab' (in pairs)

Mercutio's tale of Queen Mab, Queen of the Fairies, is world-famous. However, it presents a challenge in production because it can delay the developing pace of the action. Is this long speech merely a self-indulgent (任性) flight of fancy by Mercutio, full of dazzling imagery and conceits (想法)? Or does it have a more serious purpose?

a   In pairs, one performs and the other directs an interpretation of the whole or part of Mercutio's speech (lines 53–94). Experiment with different ways of bringing it to life (for example, some actors have delivered the speech as if Mercutio is hallucinating [产生幻觉] or on the brink of madness).

b   Afterwards, talk together about your experiences of working with the speech from the perspectives of actor and director. What have you learnt about the way Mercutio's mind works and his use of language? Which version did you think was most effective and why?

c   Study the two photographs of Mercutio above. In the light of your own experiments and what you have seen of this character so far, which of these Mercutios comes closest to how you imagine him?

1 betake him to his legs 开始跳舞
2 wantons 寻欢作乐者们
3 senseless rushes 毫无知觉的灯芯草（伊丽莎白时代用灯芯草做地毯）
4 grandsire phrase 老祖宗的谚语
5 candle-holder 烛台
6 The game … done 只要戏好看，我就心满意足了（done = finished）
7 dun's the mouse 褐色的是耗子（与上文的done谐音）
8 the constable's own word 巡捕自己的说法（巡捕抓人时说Done [听起来和dun一样]，意思是"好了"，用来催促被抓捕者）
9 If … mire 你要是褐马，我们就把你拖出泥潭（褐色的马也叫dun；伊丽莎白时代有一种圣诞游戏叫drawing dun out of the mire，游戏中参赛者拖着一截沉重的树桩子赛跑，树桩子代表从泥潭里拖出来的褐马）
10 save your reverence = God save your reverence（恕我冒昧，用来为接下来说的冒昧的话做铺垫）
11 Or … ears = Or from love, in which you are stuck up to your ears
12 burn daylight 烧日光（浪费时间）
13 good meaning 善意
14 five wits 五种智慧（即人的五种感觉）
15 tonight 昨晚
16 agate-stone 玛瑙石
17 alderman 地方官
18 atomi 微生灵
19 spinners 蜘蛛
20 film 细丝线
21 gnat 蚊虫

BENVOLIO	Come knock and enter, and no sooner in,	
	But every man betake him to his legs[1].	
ROMEO	A torch for me: let wantons[2] light of heart	35
	Tickle the senseless rushes[3] with their heels;	
	For I am proverbed with a grandsire phrase[4],	
	I'll be a candle-holder[5] and look on:	
	The game was ne'er so fair, and I am done[6].	
MERCUTIO	Tut, dun's the mouse[7], the constable's own word[8].	40
	If thou art Dun, we'll draw thee from the mire[9],	
	Or (save your reverence[10]) love, wherein thou stickest	
	Up to the ears[11]. Come, we burn daylight[12], ho!	
ROMEO	Nay, that's not so.	
MERCUTIO	I mean, sir, in delay	
	We waste our lights in vain, like lights by day.	45
	Take our good meaning[13], for our judgement sits	
	Five times in that ere once in our five wits[14].	
ROMEO	And we mean well in going to this mask,	
	But 'tis no wit to go.	
MERCUTIO	Why, may one ask?	
ROMEO	I dreamt a dream tonight[15].	
MERCUTIO	And so did I.	50
ROMEO	Well, what was yours?	
MERCUTIO	That dreamers often lie.	
ROMEO	In bed asleep, while they do dream things true.	
MERCUTIO	O then I see Queen Mab hath been with you:	
	She is the fairies' midwife, and she comes	
	In shape no bigger than an agate-stone[16]	55
	On the forefinger of an alderman[17],	
	Drawn with a team of little atomi[18]	
	Over men's noses as they lie asleep.	
	Her chariot is an empty hazel-nut,	
	Made by the joiner squirrel or old grub,	60
	Time out a'mind the fairies' coachmakers:	
	Her waggon-spokes made of long spinners'[19] legs,	
	The cover of the wings of grasshoppers,	
	Her traces of the smallest spider web,	
	Her collars of the moonshine's wat'ry beams,	65
	Her whip of cricket's bone, the lash of film[20],	
	Her waggoner a small grey-coated gnat[21],	
	Not half so big as a round little worm	

Mercutio continues his description of Queen Mab, telling of the dreams she creates in the minds of all kinds of sleepers. He dismisses dreams as nothing but idle fantasies.

剧情简介：莫丘休继续描述仙后麦布，讲她在各类睡觉者头脑中创造的各种梦境，然后说梦境不过是空虚的幻想。

1 Act out Queen Mab's trickery (in pairs)

In lines 70–94, Mercutio describes what Queen Mab does to different people: lovers, courtiers (朝臣), lawyers, churchmen, soldiers and others.

- One person reads the speech a line at a time, the other mimes the actions described. Then change over reader and mimer. Afterwards, discuss which actions you think best fit each line. Show your final version to the class.

Write about it 写作练习

A modern version of Queen Mab (in pairs)

a Take lines 59–94 and write your own version of Queen Mab, turning the lines of poetry into modern prose and making it as simple and direct as possible. Notice that the speech is very structured. It has two main sections:

- the description of her carriage (lines 59–69)
- what she does to people (lines 70–94).

Passages within those sections begin with 'Her', 'O'er', 'Sometime', and 'This is'.

b When you have completed your own prose writing, place it alongside Mercutio's original verse speech and compare the two versions. What opportunities to heighten the impact of this speech on the audience's imagination are presented by Mercutio's poetry, language and imagery? Are these opportunities missing in your contemporary reworking?

2 Romeo listens … and interrupts (in threes)

Romeo listens silently for some time whilst Mercutio speaks. He finally interrupts at line 95. Why do you think he does so at this point?

- Individually, come up with two possible reasons and share them with the other group members. Which reason do you think is most plausible?

3 Benvolio listens … and thinks

Benvolio is largely an observer in this scene. But what does he make of the way his two friends, Romeo and Mercutio, behave?

- Imagine that he later shares his thoughts with a close friend in a letter. Write Benvolio's account of what he has observed.

---

1 gallops 飞奔，疾驰
2 cur'sies = curtsies (屈膝礼)
3 oft = often
4 blisters plagues 长水泡的疾病（暗指性病）
5 sweetmeats 果脯，蜜饯
6 smelling out a suit 闻出来有人要求他（为升官而贿赂他）
7 tithe-pig 用来抵什一捐（个人收入的十分之一）的猪（当时人们有时把猪交给教会充当会捐）
8 benefice 有俸圣职（油水更足）
9 ambuscadoes 伏击
10 Spanish blades 西班牙剑（一种产自西班牙托莱多的高品质佩剑，也指时髦小伙）
11 healths 酒水；干杯
12 fathom 英寻（测量水深的长度单位）
13 anon 不久，很快，立刻
14 plats = plaits (编织)
15 bakes 缠在一起
16 elf-locks 蓬乱的头发
17 sluttish 邋遢，肮脏
18 hag 妖婆
19 learns = teaches
20 bear 承受（男人压在身上的重量）；生儿育女
21 good carriage 能生会养
22 nothing = nothing (but …)
23 thence 那里
24 ourselves 咱们的目的

                Pricked from the lazy finger of a maid.
                And in this state she gallops[1] night by night   70
                Through lovers' brains, and then they dream of love,
                O'er courtiers' knees, that dream on cur'sies[2] straight,
                O'er lawyers' fingers, who straight dream on fees,
                O'er ladies' lips, who straight on kisses dream,
                Which oft[3] the angry Mab with blisters plagues[4],   75
                Because their breaths with sweetmeats[5] tainted are.
                Sometime she gallops o'er a courtier's nose,
                And then dreams he of smelling out a suit[6];
                And sometime comes she with a tithe-pig's[7] tail
                Tickling a parson's nose as 'a lies asleep,   80
                Then he dreams of another benefice[8].
                Sometime she driveth o'er a soldier's neck,
                And then dreams he of cutting foreign throats,
                Of breaches, ambuscadoes[9], Spanish blades[10],
                Of healths[11] five fathom[12] deep; and then anon[13]   85
                Drums in his ear, at which he starts and wakes,
                And being thus frighted, swears a prayer or two,
                And sleeps again. This is that very Mab
                That plats[14] the manes of horses in the night,
                And bakes[15] the elf-locks[16] in foul sluttish[17] hairs,   90
                Which, once untangled, much misfortune bodes.
                This is the hag[18], when maids lie on their backs,
                That presses them and learns[19] them first to bear[20],
                Making them women of good carriage[21].
                This is she –

ROMEO   Peace, peace, Mercutio, peace!   95
                Thou talk'st of nothing[22].

MERCUTIO   True, I talk of dreams,
                Which are the children of an idle brain,
                Begot of nothing but vain fantasy,
                Which is as thin of substance as the air,
                And more inconstant than the wind, who woos   100
                Even now the frozen bosom of the north,
                And being angered puffs away from thence[23],
                Turning his side to the dew-dropping south.

BENVOLIO   This wind you talk of blows us from ourselves[24]:
                Supper is done, and we shall come too late.   105

In spite of his fearful misgivings, Romeo decides to go along with the others to Capulet's party. The following scene begins with Capulet's servants joking together as they prepare for the dancing.

 剧情简介： 即便心中充满担忧和顾虑，柔密欧还是决定跟其他人一起去参加卡普莱家的夜宴。下一场开始，卡普莱家的仆人们一边准备舞会一边合伙开玩笑。

1 What did Romeo dream? (in pairs)

Romeo looks uneasily into the future and has a premonition (不祥预感) of death. His tone is ominous (不吉利), filled with foreboding. He uses legal language prophesying (预言) that his premature ('untimely') death will result from what he begins tonight ('date') by going to Capulet's feast. His life will be the penalty (处罚) ('forfeit') he must pay when the time is up ('expire the term'). Notice, too, that there are several words in lines 106–11 that describe fear or loss.

- Earlier (line 50), Romeo spoke of his dream. Explore lines 106–11 together and then imagine that Romeo goes to a fortune-teller or an expert on interpreting the significance of symbols in dreams. One of you gives an account of Romeo's dream (no one knows the details of this, so don't be afraid to use your imagination to fill them out). The other person takes the role of the expert and interprets the dream, explaining its significance.

1	*date*	时段
2	*expire the term*	度过这一时期
3	*He … course*	上帝，他引导我人生的旅程
4	*trencher*	木盘
5	*join-stools*	木凳
6	*court-cupboard*	餐具柜
7	*look to the plate*	收拾好餐具
8	*marchpane* = marzipan（杏仁饼）
9	*Susan Grindstone and Nell*（这二人是仆人们请来在夜宴后参加舞会的女友或妓女）
10	*longer liver*	长寿者
11	*retire*	退至（幕后）

Themes 主题分析

'Some consequence yet hanging in the stars'

Romeo's language, directly echoing the Prologue's 'pair of star-crossed lovers', adds to the darkly ominous sense of the random workings of fate and destiny generated by Romeo's dream.

- Add the relevant details to the Evidence Grid on 'Chance versus Choice' that you began on page 20. Continue to look out for other references to stars and the heavens as you read on.

2 Change the scene swiftly

The stage direction at the end of Scene 4 suggests that Romeo and his friends do not actually leave the stage. But how is the scene change made from outside Capulet's house to inside?

- Step into role as director and write your ideas about how you would make the change so Scene 4 flows swiftly into Scene 5, without a long pause. First, try to make the most of the limited opportunities provided by Shakespeare's original stage (see '*Romeo and Juliet* in performance', pp. 220–1). Then produce some further ideas showing what you could achieve in a modern theatre with no budgetary restrictions. Be as creative as you can with both scenarios (情形).

ROMEO | I fear too early, for my mind misgives
Some consequence yet hanging in the stars
Shall bitterly begin his fearful date¹
With this night's revels, and expire the term²
Of a despisèd life closed in my breast,   110
By some vile forfeit of untimely death.
But He that hath the steerage of my course³
Direct my sail! On, lusty gentlemen.
BENVOLIO | Strike, drum.

They march about the stage [and stand to one side].

Act 1 Scene 5
The Great Hall in Capulet's mansion

SERVINGMEN *come forth with napkins.*

FIRST SERVINGMAN Where's Potpan, that he helps not to take away? He shift a trencher⁴? he scrape a trencher?

SECOND SERVINGMAN When good manners shall lie all in one or two men's hands, and they unwashed too, 'tis a foul thing.

FIRST SERVINGMAN Away with the join-stools⁵, remove the court-cupboard⁶, look to the plate⁷. Good thou, save me a piece of marchpane⁸, and as thou loves me, let the porter let in Susan Grindstone and Nell⁹.   5

[*Exit Second Servingman*]

Anthony and Potpan!

[*Enter two more* SERVINGMEN.]

THIRD SERVINGMAN Ay, boy, ready.   10

FIRST SERVINGMAN You are looked for and called for, asked for and sought for, in the great chamber.

FOURTH SERVINGMAN We cannot be here and there too. Cheerly, boys, be brisk a while, and the longer liver¹⁰ take all.

[*They retire*¹¹ *behind*]

Capulet welcomes the dancers. He reminisces with his cousin about past times. Their conversation suggests that Capulet is well into middle age. Romeo catches sight of Juliet for the first time.

 剧情简介：卡普莱欢迎舞者们的到来。他跟堂亲追忆过去的时光，二人的对话暗示卡普莱已人过中年。柔密欧第一次目睹茱丽叶的芳容。

1 The dancing begins (in small groups)

Many productions take the opportunity to accompany the energetic dancing at the Capulet ball with atmospheric music (for example, with pulsating [有节奏感] beats and strong rhythms).

- Think about the mood you wish to create for this scene. Choose your style of music and then try making up a short dance routine that you feel would fit your Capulet party. You don't necessarily need instruments – you could use clapping and stamping sounds and movements. What other types of music and movement might be used instead of those you tried?

1 *Maskers* 戴面具的舞者
2 corns 鸡眼
3 walk a bout 跳上一阵
4 makes dainty 扭扭捏捏（不愿跳舞）
5 Am … now? 我是不是说到你们心眼里了？
6 visor 面具
7 knaves 奴才（称呼下人）
8 turn the tables up 把桌子垒起来
9 unlooked-for sport 意外的娱乐
10 Berlady = By her lady （以圣母起誓）
11 nuptial 婚礼
12 Pentecost 五旬节（复活节后50天，又称圣灵降临节；Come Pentecost = When Pentecost comes）
13 ward 受监护者（指未成年的娃娃）
14 yonder = at or in that place; over there; that

Stagecraft 导演技巧

Action within action (in pairs)

a Amidst the energy of the dance, Romeo becomes aware of Juliet (line 40). Talk together about how you would stage this critical moment in the play. Is Romeo's attention suddenly focused on Juliet or does he become aware of her more gradually? What about Juliet? When and how does she notice Romeo?

b Imagine that you are two actors rehearsing this scene. Based on your discussions, experiment with different ways of staging this moment. How will you show clearly to the audience what is happening between the two young people when there is so much other noise and action on stage? Be prepared to show or explain your solution to the class.

ROMEO AND JULIET ACT 1 SCENE 5
柔密欧与茱丽叶

Enter [CAPULET, LADY CAPULET, JULIET, TYBALT *and his* PAGE, NURSE, *and*] *all the* GUESTS *and* GENTLEWOMEN *to the Maskers*[1].

CAPULET   Welcome, gentlemen! Ladies that have their toes   15
              Unplagued with corns[2] will walk a bout[3] with you.
              Ah, my mistresses, which of you all
              Will now deny to dance? She that makes dainty[4],
              She I'll swear hath corns. Am I come near ye now?[5]
              Welcome, gentlemen! I have seen the day   20
              That I have worn a visor[6] and could tell
              A whispering tale in a fair lady's ear,
              Such as would please; 'tis gone, 'tis gone, 'tis gone.
              You are welcome, gentlemen. Come, musicians, play.
                            Music plays.
              A hall, a hall, give room! and foot it, girls.   25
                            And they dance.
              More light, you knaves[7], and turn the tables up[8];
              And quench the fire, the room is grown too hot.
              Ah, sirrah, this unlooked-for sport[9] comes well.
              Nay, sit, nay, sit, good Cousin Capulet,
              For you and I are past our dancing days.   30
              How long is't now since last yourself and I
              Were in a mask?
COUSIN CAPULET   Berlady[10], thirty years.
CAPULET   What, man, 'tis not so much, 'tis not so much:
              'Tis since the nuptial[11] of Lucentio,
              Come Pentecost[12] as quickly as it will,   35
              Some five and twenty years, and then we masked.
COUSIN CAPULET 'Tis more, 'tis more, his son is elder, sir;
              His son is thirty.
CAPULET   Will you tell me that?
              His son was but a ward[13] two years ago.
ROMEO   [*To a Servingman*] What lady's that which doth enrich the hand   40
              Of yonder[14] knight?
SERVINGMAN   I know not, sir.

Romeo is entranced by Juliet's beauty. Tybalt, recognising Romeo's voice, is outraged that a Montague should dare gatecrash Capulet's party. Capulet scolds Tybalt for wanting to pick a fight.

剧情简介： 茱丽叶的美貌令柔密欧为之倾倒。提巴尔辨出了柔密欧的声音，芒特鸠家的人竟然闯进卡普莱家的夜宴，这让他愤怒不已。卡普莱训斥责提巴尔想找碴儿打架。

Language in the play 剧中语言

'O she doth teach the torches to burn bright!'

Line 43 is an example of **hyperbole** (夸张) – extravagant and exaggerated language. Romeo makes other flamboyant (华丽) comparisons ('cheek'/'jewel', 'snowy dove' / 'crows'), all of which are contrasts of light versus dark.

a Turn to the 'Antithesis' page of the Language file that you began on page 2. Head up two columns 'Light' and 'Dark'. Make a note of the contrasts above. Continue to track similar language references as they feature in the play.

b Why do you think these images of light and dark spring so readily into Romeo's mind at this point?

1. Ethiop 埃塞俄比人（即今天的埃塞俄比亚人，在古希腊文里，这个词的意思是"黑脸"）
2. The measure done 等这场舞跳完
3. rude 粗糙
4. forswear it 打破你的誓言（指曾经对若泽兰发过的誓）
5. rapier 长剑
6. hither = to this place
7. antic face 古怪的面具
8. fleer and scorn 蔑视（fleer = scorn，这里使用了"重言法"）
9. solemnity 盛宴
10. stock and honour 血统和荣誉（stock和honour意义近似，这里用的也是"重言法"）
11. in spite 砸场子
12. portly 高贵，端庄
13. well-governed 有礼貌，行为端庄
14. disparagement 轻慢，无礼
15. ill-beseeming 不合时宜
16. semblance 样子
17. goodman boy 农民娃（两个词是对提巴尔的双重辱骂）
18. go to! 得了！别说了！（表示反对或厌恶）

1 Revealing character: Tybalt and Capulet (in pairs)

Lines 53–91 dramatise an episode in which Capulet is increasingly angered by Tybalt's intention to pick a fight with Romeo. The incident reveals much about the characters of the two men.

- Take parts and speak the lines. Then repeat, but this time speak only one word from each line. Simply say whichever word strikes you as being the most important in the line – for any reason.
- Try the exercise another time, changing roles, then write down a list of the single words you have chosen. Do you think there are 'typical' Tybalt words and 'typical' Capulet words? If so, what do they suggest about the character of each man?

ROMEO	O she doth teach the torches to burn bright!
	It seems she hangs upon the cheek of night
	As a rich jewel in an Ethiop's[1] ear – 45
	Beauty too rich for use, for earth too dear:
	So shows a snowy dove trooping with crows,
	As yonder lady o'er her fellows shows.
	The measure done[2], I'll watch her place of stand,
	And touching hers, make blessèd my rude[3] hand. 50
	Did my heart love till now? forswear it[4], sight!
	For I ne'er saw true beauty till this night.
TYBALT	This, by his voice, should be a Montague.
	Fetch me my rapier[5], boy.

[Exit Page]

	What dares the slave
	Come hither[6], covered with an antic face[7], 55
	To fleer and scorn[8] at our solemnity[9]?
	Now by the stock and honour[10] of my kin,
	To strike him dead I hold it not a sin.
CAPULET	Why, how now, kinsman, wherefore storm you so?
TYBALT	Uncle, this is a Montague, our foe: 60
	A villain that is hither come in spite[11],
	To scorn at our solemnity this night.
CAPULET	Young Romeo is it?
TYBALT	'Tis he, that villain Romeo.
CAPULET	Content thee, gentle coz, let him alone,
	'A bears him like a portly[12] gentleman; 65
	And to say truth, Verona brags of him
	To be a virtuous and well-governed[13] youth.
	I would not for the wealth of all this town
	Here in my house do him disparagement[14];
	Therefore be patient, take no note of him; 70
	It is my will, the which if thou respect,
	Show a fair presence, and put off these frowns,
	An ill-beseeming[15] semblance[16] for a feast.
TYBALT	It fits when such a villain is a guest:
	I'll not endure him.
CAPULET	He shall be endured. 75
	What, goodman boy[17], I say he shall, go to![18]
	Am I the master here, or you? go to!
	You'll not endure him? God shall mend my soul,

Tybalt, rebuked by Capulet, leaves the party. He threatens vengeance. Romeo and Juliet talk together for the first time. Romeo learns from the Nurse that Juliet is a Capulet.

 剧情简介：提巴尔受到卡普莱训斥后离开了宴会，威胁要报复。柔密欧和茱丽叶第一次说话。柔密欧从茱丽叶奶妈那里得知她是卡普莱家的人。

1 First meeting of Romeo and Juliet (in pairs)

The first fourteen lines (92–105) of the lovers' meeting are written in sonnet form (the first twelve lines rhyme alternately; the last two lines are a rhyming couplet). It is helpful to know that:

- sonnet writing was a popular and highly esteemed activity at Queen Elizabeth's court (see p. 216)
- to show their faith, pilgrims made long journeys to the shrines (神龛) of the Holy Land; they brought back palm leaves (棕榈叶) as proof of their visits, and so were known as 'palmers'
- Romeo compares Juliet to a shrine or saint – religious imagery runs through their conversation ('profane', 'holy shrine', 'sin', 'pilgrims', 'wrong', 'devotion' (虔诚), 'palmers', 'faith', 'despair', 'purged', 'trespass').

Take parts and sit facing each other. Speak your lines slowly, pointing at yourself or your partner (or to your own or your partner's hands or lips) on each appropriate mention. Use your imagination to perform actions you feel are appropriate to the words. Afterwards, talk together about this first meeting of Romeo and Juliet. For example, discuss:

- why you think Shakespeare gives Romeo this religious imagery
- how Romeo's language is different from that of earlier scenes
- whether you feel he is now genuinely in love
- how you think Juliet feels on this first meeting.

Stagecraft 导演技巧
The first kiss

Romeo first kisses Juliet after line 106. It is a very dramatic and iconic moment in the scene, but it can be played in a number of ways. Do the two lovers show hesitancy, embarrassment, carefree emotion, desire or other feelings? Is their second kiss (in line 109) the same as, or different to, their first? (Notice that Juliet's response to Romeo's kissing is ambiguous!)

- Based on your reading of the text, come up with some ideas for performing this episode and then explain them in a letter to a director who is working on a modern stage production.

1 set cock-a-hoop 搞得鸡飞狗跳
2 you'll be the man! 您想当大丈夫吗？
3 saucy 粗鲁无礼
4 chance = happen
5 scathe 害
6 contrary 作对，反对
7 Well said = Well done
8 hearts 朋友们
9 princox 小公鸡
10 perforce 强行
11 choler 怒气
12 gall 胆汁
13 profane 亵渎，玷污
14 shrine 神龛（指茱丽叶的手）
15 mannerly 得体，恰当
16 palmers = pilgrims
17 trespass 犯罪
18 by th'book 中规中矩
19 craves 要求
20 bachelor 小伙子

	You'll make a mutiny among my guests!		
	You will set cock-a-hoop[1]! you'll be the man![2]		80
TYBALT	Why, uncle, 'tis a shame.		
CAPULET	Go to, go to,		
	You are a saucy[3] boy. Is't so indeed?		
	This trick may chance[4] to scathe[5] you, I know what.		
	You must contrary[6] me! Marry, 'tis time. –		
	Well said[7], my hearts[8]! – You are a princox[9], go,		85
	Be quiet, or – More light, more light! – For shame,		
	I'll make you quiet, what! – Cheerly, my hearts!		
TYBALT	Patience perforce[10] with wilful choler[11] meeting		
	Makes my flesh tremble in their different greeting:		
	I will withdraw, but this intrusion shall,		90
	Now seeming sweet, convert to bitt'rest gall[12].	*Exit*	
ROMEO	[*To Juliet*] If I profane[13] with my unworthiest hand		
	This holy shrine[14], the gentle sin is this,		
	My lips, two blushing pilgrims, ready stand		
	To smooth that rough touch with a tender kiss.		95
JULIET	Good pilgrim, you do wrong your hand too much,		
	Which mannerly[15] devotion shows in this,		
	For saints have hands that pilgrims' hands do touch,		
	And palm to palm is holy palmers'[16] kiss.		
ROMEO	Have not saints lips, and holy palmers too?		100
JULIET	Ay, pilgrim, lips that they must use in prayer.		
ROMEO	O then, dear saint, let lips do what hands do:		
	They pray, grant thou, lest faith turn to despair.		
JULIET	Saints do not move, though grant for prayers' sake.		
ROMEO	Then move not while my prayer's effect I take.		105
	Thus from my lips, by thine, my sin is purged.		
	[*Kissing her.*]		
JULIET	Then have my lips the sin that they have took.		
ROMEO	Sin from my lips? O trespass[17] sweetly urged!		
	Give me my sin again.		
	[*Kissing her again.*]		
JULIET	You kiss by th'book[18].		
NURSE	Madam, your mother craves[19] a word with you.		110
ROMEO	What is her mother?		
NURSE	Marry, bachelor[20],		
	Her mother is the lady of the house,		
	And a good lady, and a wise and virtuous.		

Romeo realises with dismay that Juliet is a Capulet. The party ends and Juliet feels similar foreboding on learning Romeo's name. She has fallen in love with one of her family's hated enemies.

剧情简介：柔密欧得知茱丽叶是卡普莱家族的人后感到失落。宴会结束，茱丽叶得知柔密欧的名字后，同样预感不妙，她已经爱上了家族的一个仇人。

1 Romeo's dismay (in small groups)

At lines 116–17, Romeo learns the dreadful truth: Juliet is a Capulet.

- Try speaking Romeo's two lines in several different ways until you feel they match what you think he feels at this moment. Share your version with others in your group.

Language in the play 剧中语言

a 'My grave is like to be my wedding bed'

Line 134 is the first time that Juliet speaks in such a sombre mood, imagining Death as her bridegroom. You'll find that this **personification** (拟人) of Death marrying Juliet keeps appearing in the play (see Act 4 Scene 5, lines 35–40 and pp. 214–15).

- Start a new section in your Language file called 'Personification'. In this section, sketh an illustration of the line and caption (加说明文字) it with the quotation.

b 'My only love sprung from my only hate!'

Line 137 echoes line 166 in Act 1 Scene 1 ('Here's much to do with hate, but more with love'). Juliet's lines 137–40 contain examples of the many antitheses that run through the play: 'love'/'hate', 'early'/'late', 'unknown'/'known', 'love'/'loathèd'.

- Add these to the relevant section of your Language file. Why do you think Shakespeare gives Juliet so many antitheses at this point in the play?

Write about it 写作练习

Thinking about structure

The moods created in this final scene of the first act switch back and forth dramatically.

a Break down the scene into specific episodes, then explore each one and assign it a particular mood. For example, you might think that the opening fourteen lines involving the servants are full of energy and bustle.

b Produce a 'mood map' of the scene, showing the atmosphere that Shakespeare creates in each episode. Annotate the map with your thoughts about how Shakespeare structures this scene to highlight contrasts.

1 **withal** = with
2 **lay hold of** 抓住；娶
3 **chinks** 钱柜子
4 **O dear account!** 好一笔值钱的账！好一个天价尤物！
5 **my life ... debt** 我的命就是欠仇家的债
6 **the sport ... best** 戏的高潮已经过了
7 **by my fay** 真的，的确 (fay = faith)
8 **waxes** = grows
9 **yond** = that/those ... over there; over there
10 **Too early ... too late!** 不相识时见得太早，待相识时却已太晚！
11 **Prodigious** 不吉利

ROMEO AND JULIET ACT 1 SCENE 5
柔密欧与茱丽叶

	I nursed her daughter that you talked withal¹;	
	I tell you, he that can lay hold of² her	115
	Shall have the chinks³.	
ROMEO	Is she a Capulet?	
	O dear account!⁴ my life is my foe's debt⁵.	
BENVOLIO	Away, be gone, the sport is at the best⁶.	
ROMEO	Ay, so I fear, the more is my unrest.	
CAPULET	Nay, gentlemen, prepare not to be gone,	120
	We have a trifling foolish banquet towards.	

[*They whisper in his ear.*]

Is it e'en so? Why then I thank you all.
I thank you, honest gentlemen, good night.
More torches here, come on! then let's to bed.
Ah, sirrah, by my fay⁷, it waxes⁸ late,   125
I'll to my rest.

[*Exeunt all but Juliet and Nurse*]

JULIET	Come hither, Nurse. What is yond⁹ gentleman?	
NURSE	The son and heir of old Tiberio.	
JULIET	What's he that now is going out of door?	
NURSE	Marry, that I think be young Petruchio.	130
JULIET	What's he that follows here, that would not dance?	
NURSE	I know not.	
JULIET	Go ask his name. – If he be marrièd,	
	My grave is like to be my wedding bed.	
NURSE	His name is Romeo, and a Montague,	135
	The only son of your great enemy.	
JULIET	My only love sprung from my only hate!	
	Too early seen unknown, and known too late!¹⁰	
	Prodigious¹¹ birth of love it is to me,	
	That I must love a loathèd enemy.	140
NURSE	What's tis? what's tis?	
JULIET	A rhyme I learnt even now	
	Of one I danced withal.	

One calls within, 'Juliet!'

NURSE	Anon, anon!
	Come let's away, the strangers all are gone.

Exeunt

ROMEO AND JULIET
柔密欧与茱丽叶

Looking back at Act 1 第1幕回顾
Activities for groups or individuals

1 What is Tybalt like?

a Tybalt speaks only five lines in Act 1 Scene 1, and just seventeen more in Act 1 Scene 5. Yet each line helps create a strong impression of what he is like. Read through these lines again, then choose one key word from each line that you think clearly shows his character. Find a way of presenting these words strikingly on paper, then display them in class.

b Tybalt meets his friends as he leaves Capulet's party. Script the conversation he has with them, in modern English, telling his story of the party and his past experience of the Montagues.

2 Advising Romeo

Benvolio tells Romeo to cure his infatuation (迷恋) with Rosaline by looking at other girls ('Examine other beauties').

- Imagine you are an agony aunt (知心姐姐) for a magazine. Romeo writes to you with his problem. Using details from the script in Act 1 Scene 1, lines 154–227, write Romeo's letter and your advice in reply.

3 Rosaline's diary

Until he sees Juliet, Romeo believes he is in love with Rosaline. She never appears, so give her a voice.

- Write a few entries in Rosaline's diary. How does she feel about Romeo's infatuation? What did she say as she kept him at a distance (see Act 1 Scene 1, lines 199–215), refusing his advances (求爱)? How does she feel when she hears he has fallen for Juliet? Remember, Rosaline is Juliet's cousin, so she's a Capulet too.

4 Report the party

Imagine you have been sent by a television station to report on Capulet's party (Scene 5). Your news editor says: 'Don't forget to interview the servants – they're the ones who will really know. And "the lively Helena" is a real chatterbox (话匣子)! You'll be given a five-minute slot in tomorrow's news programme.'

- Work in groups to prepare and deliver your report.

5 Young love

Before the ball, Lady Capulet urged Juliet to marry. Later the same evening, Juliet will agree to marry Romeo the following day. In many countries today that would be seen as inappropriate behaviour for a thirteen-year-old girl.

- Carry out some further research into Elizabethan attitudes towards courtship and marriage. What might people at the time have thought about getting married at thirteen? What do you think? Discuss this in groups and suggest reasons why early marriage seems to be acceptable in Shakespeare's Verona. Have one person record your reasons as bullet points.

6 Parents and children

Several scenes in the first act explore the relationship between parents and children. For example, Montague tells of Romeo's strange behaviour in Scene 1; Capulet speaks of his daughter Juliet to Paris in Scene 2; Lady Capulet converses with Juliet and the Nurse in Scene 3.

- Remind yourself of each of these scenes, then write about how you think the parents are presented. Do they behave fairly and reasonably towards their children? Add to this essay as you read on.

7 The language of Act 1

Pick out two striking images from Shakespeare's language in Act 1. Explain clearly to a partner why you have chosen these particular images, why you think each one is effective and how it adds to the dramatic impact.

LOOKING BACK AT ACT 1

Compare how these two productions (film, above, and theatre, right) have staged the first meeting between Romeo and Juliet. What do you think the directors might have had in mind?

The Chorus reminds the audience that Romeo's infatuation with Rosaline has ended. Romeo now loves Juliet, who returns his love. But dangers beset the young lovers. Act 2 begins with Mercutio teasing the hidden Romeo.

 剧情简介：叙事人提醒观众柔密欧对若泽兰的迷恋结束了；柔密欧现在爱上了茱丽叶，茱丽叶也爱上了柔密欧。然而危险困扰着这对年轻恋人。莫丘休取笑不见踪影的柔密欧，由此拉开第2幕。

1 The Chorus speaks a sonnet (in groups of four to eight)

The words of the Chorus summarise much of the play so far and hint at the next scene. Sit in a circle. Read the Chorus's speech, each person speaking a line in turn. Then work on some or all of the following:

a Act out the story told in the fourteen lines. One person reads a line or two, then pauses. In that pause, other members of the group mime what is described. Two reminders: 'old desire' (line 144) is love for Rosaline, and the last two lines imply that the pleasures of Romeo and Juliet's meetings make their dangers and hardships bearable.

b Some critics have viewed the Chorus's lines more as a conclusion to Act 1 than an opening to Act 2 (as here). What do you think?

c These fourteen lines are often cut in performance. Imagine you are preparing to put on the play. Half of you want to include the Chorus's lines, half don't. Debate whether they should be left in or cut.

d All companies acting Shakespeare 'double' the parts (actors play more than one role). So the Chorus is spoken by someone with another role (or roles) in the play. Look at the list of characters on page 1 and decide who seems most likely to 'double' the Chorus.

1 young affection （对茱丽叶的）新爱情
2 fair 美人（指若泽兰）
3 matched 相比之下
4 fair 美丽
5 again = in return
6 foe supposed 本来的仇家（指茱丽叶）
7 complain 悲叹，哀叹
8 means 机会
9 Temp'ring extremities with 以……来抵消端的痛苦
10 dull earth 无精打采的身躯
11 centre 内心，心灵
12 conjure （用咒语或魔法）召唤
13 humours 奇思妙想

Stagecraft 导演技巧

a How to show the 'orchard wall'

In line 5, Benvolio refers to Romeo having 'leapt this orchard wall'. It is unlikely that a wall would have been used (or even represented) in the Globe Theatre.

- Look at the illustration on page 220. If you were directing the play at that time, how would you represent the orchard wall on that stage? Write down or draw your ideas.

b Romeo listens in

After line 2, the stage direction instructs Romeo to withdraw, remaining out of sight but eavesdropping (偷听) on the conversation between Benvolio and Mercutio.

- Annotate a photocopy of lines 3–42 with your thoughts about how Romeo might react to each of the personal comments that his friends make about him. Which ones do you think he would find amusing and which ones annoying or offensive?

[*Enter*] CHORUS.

Now old desire doth in his death-bed lie,
And young affection[1] gapes to be his heir; 145
That fair[2] for which love groaned for and would die,
With tender Juliet matched[3] is now not fair[4].
Now Romeo is beloved, and loves again[5],
Alike bewitchèd by the charm of looks;
But to his foe supposed[6] he must complain[7], 150
And she steal love's sweet bait from fearful hooks.
Being held a foe, he may not have access
To breathe such vows as lovers use to swear,
And she as much in love, her means[8] much less
To meet her new-belovèd any where: 155
But passion lends them power, time means, to meet,
Temp'ring extremities with[9] extreme sweet. [*Exit*]

Act 2 Scene 1
Outside Capulet's mansion

Enter ROMEO *alone*.

ROMEO Can I go forward when my heart is here?
Turn back, dull earth[10], and find thy centre[11] out.
[*Romeo withdraws*]

Enter BENVOLIO *with* MERCUTIO

BENVOLIO Romeo! my cousin Romeo! Romeo!
MERCUTIO   He is wise,
And on my life hath stol'n him home to bed.
BENVOLIO He ran this way and leapt this orchard wall. 5
Call, good Mercutio.
MERCUTIO   Nay, I'll conjure[12] too.
Romeo! humours[13]! madman! passion! lover!
Appear thou in the likeness of a sigh,

Mercutio, pretending to be a magician, uses much sexual innuendo as he mocks Romeo's love for Rosaline. Unable to get any response from Romeo, he goes off to sleep.

 剧情简介：莫丘休假装魔法师，口中满是淫词浪语，取笑柔密欧对若泽兰的爱恋。他见柔密欧没有反应，于是睡觉去了。

Language in the play 剧中语言
Mercutio's wordplay – very sexual puns

Mercutio, outrageous and imaginative as usual, teases Romeo, seizing every opportunity to make sexual puns:

demesnes	parklands for pleasure (or sexual parts)
spirit	ghost (or semen)
circle	magic circle (or vagina)
stand	ghost rising (or sexual erection)
down	ghost disappearing (or end of sexual intercourse)
honest	proper (and virginal)
mark	target (or sexual intercourse)
medlar (欧楂果)	apple-like fruit (or female sexual organ)
open-arse	slang for medlar (or female sexual organ)
pop'rin pear	pear from Poperinghe in Flanders (产自古代弗兰德斯的一种梨) (shaped like a penis)

- On page 30, you began a Character file to collect evidence of Mercutio's clever use of language. Now add examples from the script opposite, especially his use of puns.

Themes 主题分析
The conflicts of love (in pairs)

The play continues to explore the complexities of love.

a Talk together about why you think Shakespeare makes Mercutio speak as he does in the script opposite. For example, one reason may be that his sexual joking opposes and highlights the true love that Romeo and Juliet share (notice that Mercutio assumes Romeo is still in love with Rosaline). What other reasons can you come up with?

b Look back to Act 1 Scene 3, in which the Nurse speaks about love and relationships. On a piece of paper draw two columns, one for the Nurse and one for Mercutio. Fill these in with examples of the 'love' language each character uses. Are there similarities in their viewpoints and the ways they express them?

c Benvolio describes Romeo's new-found love: 'Blind is his love, and best befits the dark.' What do you think he means by this and why do you think he says it?

1 **gossip** 老相好（莫丘休开玩笑）
2 **Venus** 维纳斯（罗马神话中的爱神）
3 **purblind** 几乎眼瞎
4 **Abraham** 亚伯拉罕（该词有不同典故，指不同的人，这里指神射手丘比特）
5 **trim** （射得）准
6 **King Cophetua** 科菲多亚王（英格兰一首古代歌谣中的人物，被丘比特的箭射中，爱上了一位乞丐姑娘）
7 **The ape is dead** 这只猴子死了（把好友柔密欧戏称为一只猴子）
8 **demesnes** 部位；地带
9 **raise** 唤起，召唤出
10 **invocation** 符咒
11 **consorted with** 与……为伴
12 **humorous** 潮湿；变化无常
13 **truckle-bed** 带轮的床（指舒适的床）

	Speak but one rhyme, and I am satisfied;	
	Cry but 'Ay me!', pronounce but 'love' and 'dove',	10
	Speak to my gossip[1] Venus[2] one fair word,	
	One nickname for her purblind[3] son and heir,	
	Young Abraham[4] Cupid, he that shot so trim[5]	
	When King Cophetua[6] loved the beggar-maid.	
	He heareth not, he stirreth not, he moveth not,	15
	The ape is dead[7], and I must conjure him.	
	I conjure thee by Rosaline's bright eyes,	
	By her high forehead and her scarlet lip,	
	By her fine foot, straight leg, and quivering thigh,	
	And the demesnes[8] that there adjacent lie,	20
	That in thy likeness thou appear to us.	
BENVOLIO	And if he hear thee, thou wilt anger him.	
MERCUTIO	This cannot anger him; 'twould anger him	
	To raise[9] a spirit in his mistress' circle,	
	Of some strange nature, letting it there stand	25
	Till she had laid it and conjured it down:	
	That were some spite. My invocation[10]	
	Is fair and honest: in his mistress' name	
	I conjure only but to raise up him.	
BENVOLIO	Come, he hath hid himself among these trees	30
	To be consorted with[11] the humorous[12] night:	
	Blind is his love, and best befits the dark.	
MERCUTIO	If love be blind, love cannot hit the mark.	
	Now will he sit under a medlar tree,	
	And wish his mistress were that kind of fruit	35
	As maids call medlars, when they laugh alone.	
	O Romeo, that she were, O that she were	
	An open-arse, thou a pop'rin pear!	
	Romeo, good night, I'll to my truckle-bed[13],	
	This field-bed is too cold for me to sleep.	40
	Come, shall we go?	
BENVOLIO	Go then, for 'tis in vain	
	To seek him here that means not to be found.	

Exit [with Mercutio]

Romeo, hidden from Juliet, sees her at an upstairs window. He compares her beauty to that of the sun, brighter than the stars, as glorious as an angel.

剧情简介：柔密欧藏在茱丽叶看不见的地方，却能抬头望着楼上窗户里的她。他将茱丽叶与太阳媲美，比星星还明亮，跟天使一样光彩夺目。

Write about it 写作练习

'He jests at scars that never felt a wound'

Romeo is now becoming more isolated from his two friends Mercutio and Benvolio. His first line is a dismissive (不屑一顾) comment on Mercutio's joking about love. Just as someone who has never been wounded can make light of a soldier's battle scars, so someone who has never been in love finds it easy to joke about the sufferings of a person deeply in love.

- In modern English prose, write a short interior monologue for Romeo (what he's thinking rather than saying) at this moment in the play. How does he feel about the dramatic changes in his life?

1 **Be not her maid** 不要做她的侍女（"她"指贞洁女神荻阿娜 [Diana]，月亮也被视为荻阿娜）

2 **vestal livery** 处女的制服（指贞洁）

3 **sick and green** （即所谓的 **green sickness** [黄萎病]，婚龄处女所患的一种贫血症）

4 **fools** （指那些不结婚的"傻瓜"，因此保留处女之身）

5 **discourses** 说话

6 **entreat** 恳求

7 **spheres** 轨道（根据希腊天文学家托勒密的地心说，日月星辰都绕着地球转动，轨道是环绕地球的透明球体）

8 **wingèd messenger** 有翅膀的信使（即天使）

9 **white-upturnèd** （指人仰视的时候显出眼白）

1 Romeo's view of Juliet (in pairs)

To help you understand how Romeo feels about Juliet, try this 'echoing' activity. Sit facing each other. One person reads lines 1–32 aloud. The other listens (or follows in the script) and quietly echoes certain words or phrases:

- to do with light (such as 'sun') or brightness or eyesight
- that refer to something overhead.

As you echo each 'upward' word, point your finger upward. Change roles and repeat. Afterwards, talk together about what those 'light-giving' words and 'upward' words tell you about Romeo's view of Juliet.

2 Thinking about Juliet?

Lines 1–32 are virtually a **soliloquy** (独白) (see p. 218). Juliet speaks at line 25, but she does not know that Romeo is there.

a Go through Romeo's speech again and divide it into sense units (see p. 24). Alongside each sense unit, indicate whether you think Romeo is speaking directly to Juliet or whether he is addressing his thoughts to the audience.

b Does your version show that Romeo is thinking more about what it feels like to be in love or about Juliet herself? Write a paragraph explaining your verdict.

Act 2 Scene 2
Capulet's orchard

ROMEO advances.

ROMEO　　He jests at scars that never felt a wound.
　　　　　But soft, what light through yonder window breaks?
　　　　　It is the east, and Juliet is the sun.
　　　　　Arise, fair sun, and kill the envious moon,
　　　　　Who is already sick and pale with grief　　　　　　　5
　　　　　That thou, her maid, art far more fair than she.
　　　　　Be not her maid[1], since she is envious;
　　　　　Her vestal livery[2] is but sick and green[3],
　　　　　And none but fools[4] do wear it; cast it off.

[JULIET appears aloft as at a window.]

　　　　　It is my lady, O it is my love:　　　　　　　　　　10
　　　　　O that she knew she were!
　　　　　She speaks, yet she says nothing; what of that?
　　　　　Her eye discourses[5], I will answer it.
　　　　　I am too bold, 'tis not to me she speaks:
　　　　　Two of the fairest stars in all the heaven,　　　　　15
　　　　　Having some business, do entreat[6] her eyes
　　　　　To twinkle in their spheres[7] till they return.
　　　　　What if her eyes were there, they in her head?
　　　　　The brightness of her cheek would shame those stars,
　　　　　As daylight doth a lamp; her eyes in heaven　　　　20
　　　　　Would through the airy region stream so bright
　　　　　That birds would sing and think it were not night.
　　　　　See how she leans her cheek upon her hand!
　　　　　O that I were a glove upon that hand,
　　　　　That I might touch that cheek!
JULIET　　　　　　　　　　　　Ay me!
ROMEO　　[*Aside*]　　　　　　　　　　She speaks.　　　　25
　　　　　O speak again, bright angel, for thou art
　　　　　As glorious to this night, being o'er my head,
　　　　　As is a wingèd messenger[8] of heaven
　　　　　Unto the white-upturnèd[9] wond'ring eyes

Juliet declares her love for Romeo in spite of his belonging to the hated Montagues. He is his own perfect self, whatever he is called. When Romeo reveals himself, she fears for his safety.

 剧情简介：即使柔密欧是仇敌芒特鸠家族的人，茱丽叶仍宣布爱他。他不管姓什么，自身都是一个完人。柔密欧出现在自己面前时，茱丽叶担心起他的安危来。

Stagecraft 导演技巧
The 'balcony' scene

Scene 2 is always known as the 'balcony' scene, even though the word is never used by Shakespeare and does not appear in the stage directions. Many productions take their inspiration from Romeo's opening lines, which suggest he is looking upwards.

a Look at the two images below. One shows a traditional representation (left), the other a symbolic one (right). Write down what you think are the merits of each. Focus on how they would work for the opening exchanges in Scene 2 (the first 70 lines or so).

b Study the images on pages vii, viii, 204 and 215, and then try to create your own set design for this scene.

1 lazy puffing clouds 懒洋洋飘在天上的大块云朵
2 wherefore = why
3 though = even if
4 owes = owns
5 doff 抛弃
6 new baptised 重新受洗（有了新的名字）
7 Henceforth 从此以后
8 bescreened 隐藏
9 stumblest on my counsel 碰巧听到我的告白
10 the place death 死亡之地
11 o'erperch 飞跃

1 What's in a name? (in small groups)

When Juliet declares 'That which we call a rose / By any other word would smell as sweet', she points out that what really matters is the object itself, not the name we use to label it. Whatever it were called, its essential quality would remain unchanged.

• Identify all the 'names' you can find between lines 33 and 61. What dramatic effects does Shakespeare achieve by using so many names in this episode?

	Of mortals that fall back to gaze on him,	30
	When he bestrides the lazy puffing clouds¹,	
	And sails upon the bosom of the air.	
JULIET	O Romeo, Romeo, wherefore² art thou Romeo?	
	Deny thy father and refuse thy name;	
	Or if thou wilt not, be but sworn my love,	35
	And I'll no longer be a Capulet.	
ROMEO	[*Aside*] Shall I hear more, or shall I speak at this?	
JULIET	'Tis but thy name that is my enemy;	
	Thou art thyself, though³ not a Montague.	
	What's Montague? It is nor hand nor foot,	40
	Nor arm nor face, nor any other part	
	Belonging to a man. O be some other name!	
	What's in a name? That which we call a rose	
	By any other word would smell as sweet;	
	So Romeo would, were he not Romeo called,	45
	Retain that dear perfection which he owes⁴	
	Without that title. Romeo, doff⁵ thy name,	
	And for thy name, which is no part of thee,	
	Take all myself.	
ROMEO	I take thee at thy word:	
	Call me but love, and I'll be new baptised⁶;	50
	Henceforth⁷ I never will be Romeo.	
JULIET	What man art thou that thus bescreened⁸ in night	
	So stumblest on my counsel⁹?	
ROMEO	By a name	
	I know not how to tell thee who I am.	
	My name, dear saint, is hateful to myself,	55
	Because it is an enemy to thee;	
	Had I it written, I would tear the word.	
JULIET	My ears have yet not drunk a hundred words	
	Of thy tongue's uttering, yet I know the sound.	
	Art thou not Romeo, and a Montague?	60
ROMEO	Neither, fair maid, if either thee dislike.	
JULIET	How cam'st thou hither, tell me, and wherefore?	
	The orchard walls are high and hard to climb,	
	And the place death¹⁰, considering who thou art,	
	If any of my kinsmen find thee here.	65
ROMEO	With love's light wings did I o'erperch¹¹ these walls,	
	For stony limits cannot hold love out,	

Juliet warns Romeo that her family will kill him if they find him. Admitting embarrassment at being overheard telling of her love, she asks if he loves her.

 剧情简介：茱丽叶警告柔密欧如果被她的家人发现，他们会杀了他。她因为柔密欧偷听到自己对他的告白感到难堪，追问他是否爱自己。

1 Imagery: life as a hazardous voyage

In lines 82–4, Romeo uses the image of himself as a merchant adventurer who would brave any dangerous sea journey to gain the reward of Juliet herself at the end of it ('pilot' is a sailor).

a Life as a perilous sea is a tragic theme that runs throughout the play. As you continue reading, look out for other examples of this image.

b Why do you think this image would have such a powerful impact on an audience watching the play in Shakespeare's day? Can you think of an equivalent image for the twenty-first century?

c What do you think of Romeo's comparison of Juliet to 'merchandise'? Is it complimentary (称赞) or condescending (居高临下)? Write a paragraph giving your response to this image.

Language in the play 剧中语言

Juliet's language – simple and true? (in small groups)

Juliet's 'Fain would I dwell on form' (line 88) suggests she would gladly stick to speaking and behaving with ceremony and politeness. But her 'farewell compliment' (line 89) shows her rejecting pompous (华而不实), artificial ways of behaving and speaking. To find out if she succeeds in her wish to speak simply and truly, without affectation, try the following activities.

a Read lines 90–106. The first group member begins, but reads only to a punctuation mark (the first is a question mark). The second group member then reads to the next punctuation mark, and stops. The third does the same, and so on round the group. Read the lines several times in this way.

b After the readings, talk together about Juliet's language. Write down examples of where she speaks directly and simply, without formality. Then find some individual words and lines from earlier scenes that you think are 'typical' of the way the men in the play speak. For example, you might focus on aspects of their aggressive or coarse language. Look at speeches by the brawling servants, Benvolio, Tybalt, Lords Montague and Capulet, Mercutio and Romeo.

c Display your collected language extracts visually in ways that highlight any key differences you have noticed between the two sexes.

---

1 proof　能防范
2 but thou　如果你不
3 proroguèd　延迟
4 wanting of　缺少
5 Love　爱神（丘比特）
6 bepaint　上色
7 Fain　乐意
8 dwell on form　恪守礼仪
9 compliment　外表
10 perjuries　谎言
11 Jove = Jupiter（乔武，即朱庇特，罗马神话中的主神，也是掌管誓言的神，但是不太在乎恋人是否遵守誓言）
12 perverse　执拗，任性
13 So thou wilt = If that will make you
14 fond　愚蠢；痴情
15 light　轻浮
16 coying to be strange　故作矜持
17 ere I was ware　在我意识到之前
18 impute　把……归于
19 light love　轻佻的爱情

	And what love can do, that dares love attempt:
	Therefore thy kinsmen are no stop to me.
JULIET	If they do see thee, they will murder thee.
ROMEO	Alack, there lies more peril in thine eye
	Than twenty of their swords. Look thou but sweet,
	And I am proof[1] against their enmity.
JULIET	I would not for the world they saw thee here.
ROMEO	I have night's cloak to hide me from their eyes,
	And but thou[2] love me, let them find me here;
	My life were better ended by their hate,
	Than death proroguèd[3], wanting of[4] thy love.
JULIET	By whose direction found'st thou out this place?
ROMEO	By Love[5], that first did prompt me to enquire:
	He lent me counsel, and I lent him eyes.
	I am no pilot, yet wert thou as far
	As that vast shore washed with the farthest sea,
	I should adventure for such merchandise.
JULIET	Thou knowest the mask of night is on my face,
	Else would a maiden blush bepaint[6] my cheek
	For that which thou hast heard me speak tonight.
	Fain[7] would I dwell on form[8], fain, fain deny
	What I have spoke, but farewell compliment[9].
	Dost thou love me? I know thou wilt say 'Ay';
	And I will take thy word; yet if thou swear'st,
	Thou mayst prove false: at lovers' perjuries[10]
	They say Jove[11] laughs. O gentle Romeo,
	If thou dost love, pronounce it faithfully;
	Or if thou think'st I am too quickly won,
	I'll frown and be perverse[12], and say thee nay,
	So thou wilt[13] woo, but else not for the world.
	In truth, fair Montague, I am too fond[14],
	And therefore thou mayst think my behaviour light[15]:
	But trust me, gentleman, I'll prove more true
	Than those that have more coying to be strange[16].
	I should have been more strange, I must confess,
	But that thou overheard'st, ere I was ware[17],
	My true-love passion; therefore pardon me,
	And not impute[18] this yielding to light love[19],
	Which the dark night hath so discoverèd.

Romeo and Juliet exchange vows of love, but both are fearful. Juliet fears the suddenness of their love. Romeo fears because what is happening seems dream-like and unreal.

剧情简介：柔密欧和茱丽叶相互发誓爱对方，但是两个人都很害怕——茱丽叶害怕爱情来得快也去得快，柔密欧害怕是因为他觉得发生的事情如梦如幻不真实。

▼ How effectively does this image convey the relationship between the two lovers as you think it is presented in this scene? Give your reasons. Then have a go at writing thought bubbles (思想泡泡) in modern English for Romeo and Juliet that match this moment.

1 circled orb 环绕地球的轨道
2 likewise variable （像月亮盈亏圆缺）一样不停变化
3 idolatry 崇拜
4 contract 山盟海誓
5 But = Only
6 frank 大方，慷慨
7 bounty 慷慨
8 adieu 再见
9 Anon 一会儿见
10 substantial 有实质内容

Language in the play 剧中语言

Juliet describes love (in sixes)

There are at least five significant images connected with love in the script opposite:

- Lines 109–11 make reference to the moon as a symbol of inconstancy (反复无常) in love.
- Juliet (line 114) uses the word 'idolatry' to suggest that she worships Romeo like a god.
- In lines 118–20, Juliet likens the love she shares with Romeo to 'lightning'.
- Lines 121–2 compare their young love to a bud that has yet to flower.
- Juliet's lines 133–5 suggest that her love is as 'infinite' and 'boundless' as the sea.

Take each image in turn and depict it as a tableau for others to look at. Afterwards, talk together in your group about how Juliet's use of imagery adds to your understanding of what she feels about being in love.

ROMEO	Lady, by yonder blessèd moon I vow,
	That tips with silver all these fruit-tree tops –
JULIET	O swear not by the moon, th'inconstant moon,
	That monthly changes in her circled orb[1], 110
	Lest that thy love prove likewise variable[2].
ROMEO	What shall I swear by?
JULIET	Do not swear at all;
	Or if thou wilt, swear by thy gracious self,
	Which is the god of my idolatry[3],
	And I'll believe thee.
ROMEO	If my heart's dear love – 115
JULIET	Well, do not swear. Although I joy in thee,
	I have no joy of this contract[4] tonight,
	It is too rash, too unadvised, too sudden,
	Too like the lightning, which doth cease to be
	Ere one can say 'It lightens'. Sweet, good night: 120
	This bud of love, by summer's ripening breath,
	May prove a beauteous flower when next we meet.
	Good night, good night! as sweet repose and rest
	Come to thy heart as that within my breast.
ROMEO	O wilt thou leave me so unsatisfied? 125
JULIET	What satisfaction canst thou have tonight?
ROMEO	Th'exchange of thy love's faithful vow for mine.
JULIET	I gave thee mine before thou didst request it;
	And yet I would it were to give again.
ROMEO	Wouldst thou withdraw it? for what purpose, love? 130
JULIET	But[5] to be frank[6] and give it thee again,
	And yet I wish but for the thing I have:
	My bounty[7] is as boundless as the sea,
	My love as deep; the more I give to thee
	The more I have, for both are infinite. 135
	[*Nurse calls within.*]
	I hear some noise within; dear love, adieu[8]! –
	Anon[9], good Nurse! – Sweet Montague, be true.
	Stay but a little, I will come again. [*Exit above*]
ROMEO	O blessèd, blessèd night! I am afeard,
	Being in night, all this is but a dream, 140
	Too flattering-sweet to be substantial[10].

Juliet, promising marriage, says she will send a messenger tomorrow to ask the time and place of the wedding. At the Nurse's call, Juliet goes inside the house. Returning, she calls Romeo back.

剧情简介：茱丽叶答应跟柔密欧结婚，她说明天派信使去打听婚礼的时间和地点。听到奶妈叫她，茱丽叶回到房间，然后又转身把柔密欧唤了回来。

1 Responding to the Nurse's calls (in threes)

The Nurse does not appear in this scene but, between the stage direction after line 135 and line 157, the audience hears her voice 'within' summoning Juliet three times. Juliet is torn between her desire to continue talking to Romeo and the need to respond to the Nurse's calls. Romeo is reluctant to leave, even though he knows there is a danger that he'll be discovered.

- Take parts as Juliet, the Nurse and Romeo, and read the exchange aloud in a way that creates as much dramatic impact as you can. Other groups should comment on your interpretation and the kind of atmosphere you have created.

Characters 人物分析

Juliet's journey

By line 144 of this scene, Juliet is clearly thinking about becoming Romeo's wife. Yet in Act 1, Shakespeare emphasises several times that she is still very young and naive. Juliet first appears in Act 1 Scene 3, meets Romeo in Act 1 Scene 5 and here in Act 2 Scene 2, she pledges to marry him. These three scenes chart her voyage from the 'innocent' daughter of the strong-minded Capulets to independence and the adult responsibilities of a marriage against her parents' wishes.

a Look back through Juliet's lines in the play so far and then think about the point she has reached in the script opposite. Much has happened to change the way she might think about herself and her relationship with her parents and the Nurse. Most significantly, she has fallen deeply in love with Romeo.

b Step into role as Juliet, and in a piece of creative writing reflect on the dramatic and momentous ways your life has altered. Challenge yourself by looking into the future. What problems and difficulties might await? What are your greatest fears and anxieties? Choose the format that you think works best. A series of diary entries, for example, would allow you to chart some of the stages of Juliet's emotional journey. But you could equally choose to express your thoughts in a blog or as a monologue.

1 **bent** 目的，意图
2 **one that I'll procure** 我会选一个人
3 **perform the rite** 举行婚礼
4 **By and by** 马上，立刻
5 **cease thy strife** 别再费力气（向我求爱了）
6 **worse** （这是对good night里的good进行比较；柔密欧的意思是：没有你哪里来的good night，只有worse night）
7 **want** 缺少
8 **Hist** 嘘（驯鹰人 [即后文的falc'ner = falconer] 呼唤鹰时发出的声音）
9 **tassel-gentle** 雄性游隼，雄鹰（茱丽叶把柔密欧比作雄鹰）
10 **Bondage is hoarse** 囚犯只能轻声细语（茱丽叶在家被严格管束）
11 **Echo** 回声女神艾蔻（希腊和罗马神话中的一位山间仙女。在罗马神话《变形记》中，天后朱诺 [Juno] 追逐天王朱庇特，被艾蔻唠唠叨叨地干扰，未能追上，于是诅咒艾蔻，使她只能重复别人刚说过的话。后来艾蔻爱上了自恋的美男子纳悉瑟 [Narcissus]，却遭拒绝，最后憔悴而死）
12 **niësse** 雏鹰
13 **a'clock** 时间

[Enter Juliet above.]

JULIET   Three words, dear Romeo, and good night indeed.
         If that thy bent[1] of love be honourable,
         Thy purpose marriage, send me word tomorrow,
         By one that I'll procure[2] to come to thee,   145
         Where and what time thou wilt perform the rite[3],
         And all my fortunes at thy foot I'll lay,
         And follow thee my lord throughout the world.

NURSE   [*Within*] Madam!

JULIET   I come, anon. – But if thou meanest not well,   150
         I do beseech thee –

NURSE   [*Within*]   Madam!

JULIET   By and by[4] I come –
         To cease thy strife[5], and leave me to my grief.
         Tomorrow will I send.

ROMEO   So thrive my soul –

JULIET   A thousand times good night!

         [*Exit above*]

ROMEO   A thousand times the worse[6], to want[7] thy light.   155
         Love goes toward love as schoolboys from their books,
         But love from love, toward school with heavy looks.
         [*Retiring slowly.*]

         Enter Juliet again [*above*].

JULIET   Hist[8], Romeo, hist! O for a falc'ner's voice,
         To lure this tassel-gentle[9] back again:
         Bondage is hoarse[10], and may not speak aloud,   160
         Else would I tear the cave where Echo[11] lies,
         And make her airy tongue more hoarse than mine
         With repetition of my Romeo's name.

ROMEO   It is my soul that calls upon my name.
         How silver-sweet sound lovers' tongues by night,   165
         Like softest music to attending ears!

JULIET   Romeo!

ROMEO   My niësse[12]?

JULIET   What a'clock[13] tomorrow
         Shall I send to thee?

ROMEO   By the hour of nine.

JULIET   I will not fail, 'tis twenty year till then.
         I have forgot why I did call thee back.   170

Romeo and Juliet reluctantly part. She compares him to a captive bird that can never escape from its owner. Romeo promises to seek Friar Lawrence's help.

 剧情简介：柔密欧和茱丽叶依依惜别。茱丽叶把柔密欧比作一只被捕获的鸟，再也飞不出主人的手掌。柔密欧答应去找劳润修士帮忙。

Write about it 写作练习

Plan a movie pitch (电影推介) (by yourself)

The 'balcony' scene is one of the most famous in the play. A lot happens here and by the end of the scene, Romeo is rushing off to begin planning his marriage to Juliet.

Imagine that you are making a film pitch to a group of media moguls (传媒大亨). These people have the money to finance a new movie version of the play – if you can convince them of the merits of your concept. Part of your pitch will be based on your original ideas for this key scene.

- Write an account of how think the 'balcony' scene could be filmed to maximise dramatic effect. You will need to persuade your audience that your ideas are fresh, striking and well-matched to the medium of film. Describe how you would set the scene and how you think different sections of it could be played. Add further ideas about how lighting, costume and music could contribute to the overall effect.
- Pick your ideal cast (演员阵容) (you can choose any actors you think would suit the roles of Romeo and Juliet), then identify several lines you think are particularly important and write instructions on how they should be delivered. Remember that your production can be big-budget! You could include this pitch in the Director's Journal that you began on page 22.

1 **wanton's bird** 假小子玩的鸟（她会用绳子绑住鸟腿防止它飞走）
2 **gyves** 镣铐
3 **loving-jealous** 深爱而嫉妒
4 **kill thee with much cherishing** 用珍爱来爱死你
5 **morrow** 次日，明天
6 **ghostly sire** 神父（指劳润修士）
7 **close cell** 密室
8 **dear hap** 好运

ROMEO	Let me stand here till thou remember it.	
JULIET	I shall forget, to have thee still stand there,	
	Rememb'ring how I love thy company.	
ROMEO	And I'll still stay, to have thee still forget,	
	Forgetting any other home but this.	175
JULIET	'Tis almost morning, I would have thee gone:	
	And yet no farther than a wanton's bird[1],	
	That lets it hop a little from his hand,	
	Like a poor prisoner in his twisted gyves[2],	
	And with a silken thread plucks it back again,	180
	So loving-jealous[3] of his liberty.	
ROMEO	I would I were thy bird.	
JULIET	Sweet, so would I,	
	Yet I should kill thee with much cherishing[4].	
	Good night, good night! Parting is such sweet sorrow,	
	That I shall say good night till it be morrow[5]. [*Exit above*]	185
ROMEO	Sleep dwell upon thine eyes, peace in thy breast!	
	Would I were sleep and peace, so sweet to rest!	
	Hence will I to my ghostly sire's[6] close cell[7],	
	His help to crave, and my dear hap[8] to tell. *Exit*	

At daybreak, Friar Lawrence is gathering flowers and herbs. He reflects that, like people, they contain both healing medicine and poison – both good and evil.

剧情简介：黎明时分，劳润修士在采集鲜花和药草。他若有所思地说，这些花草与人类一样，既有能治病的好花草，又有毒害人的坏花草。

Characters 人物分析

Focus on Friar Lawrence

This is the first appearance of Friar Lawrence in the play. Romeo comes to the Friar to tell him of his good fortune in falling in love with Juliet – and to ask him for help.

a Read quickly through the Friar's lines in the script opposite, then think about how closely the image below matches your own impression of the Friar.

b Why do you think that the first time we see the Friar he is gathering herbs at daybreak? Try to come up with at least two symbolic reasons for this.

c Romeo decides to talk to the Friar, rather than his own father, about his relationship with Juliet. Suggest reasons why this might be.

1 A world at odds with itself (by yourself)

Friar Lawrence will play a vital (but unfortunate) part in what happens to Romeo and Juliet.

- Read lines 1–30 to yourself, but quietly emphasise each antithesis. They are: 'morn smiles' / 'frowning night', 'day' / 'night's', 'baleful weeds' / 'precious-juicèd flowers', 'mother' / 'tomb', 'grave' / 'womb', 'vile' / 'good', 'fair use' / 'abuse', 'Virtue' / 'vice', 'Poison' / 'medicine', 'cheers each part' / 'stays all senses', 'grace' / 'rude will'.

- Why do you think Friar Lawrence voices so many antitheses (mainly focused on good things versus bad things) when he first appears in the play? Write down a few ideas of your own, then compare your notes with your neighbour. Add your notes on this to the 'Antithesis' section of your Language file.

1 Check'ring = Checkering （画横竖道）
2 fleckled 斑驳
3 reels 摇摇晃晃地走
4 Titan 泰坦（希腊神话中奥林匹斯诸神出现之前那些神的统称。这里的泰坦指太阳神赫利俄斯 [Helios]，他驾驭一辆燃烧的战车（即太阳）驰过天空）
5 osier cage 柳编篮子
6 baleful 有毒
7 divers 各种各样
8 None but for some 没有一种花草没有一点儿优秀品质
9 mickle 很多，巨大
10 For nought so vile 因为没有一种如此卑劣
11 ought = aught/anything
12 strained 被迫，被逼
13 Revolts … abuse 违背其本性加以滥用
14 vice sometime by action dignified 罪恶加以巧用也会有光彩
15 infant rind 稚嫩的外皮
16 part 部分（这里指这一部分的香味）
17 stays 使停止，麻痹
18 with = together with
19 encamp them still 永远扎营
20 In … will = grace and rude （文雅与粗野）will still encamp in man as well …
21 canker 尺蠖（一种专食花苞和嫩叶的害虫）

Act 2 Scene 3
Outside Friar Lawrence's cell

Enter FRIAR LAWRENCE *alone, with a basket.*

FRIAR LAWRENCE The grey-eyed morn smiles on the frowning night,
Check'ring[1] the eastern clouds with streaks of light;
And fleckled[2] darkness like a drunkard reels[3]
From forth day's path and Titan's[4] fiery wheels:
Now ere the sun advance his burning eye, 5
The day to cheer, and night's dank dew to dry,
I must upfill this osier cage[5] of ours
With baleful[6] weeds and precious-juicèd flowers.
The earth that's nature's mother is her tomb;
What is her burying grave, that is her womb; 10
And from her womb children of divers[7] kind
We sucking on her natural bosom find:
Many for many virtues excellent,
None but for some[8], and yet all different.
O mickle[9] is the powerful grace that lies 15
In plants, herbs, stones, and their true qualities:
For nought so vile[10], that on the earth doth live,
But to the earth some special good doth give;
Nor ought[11] so good but, strained[12] from that fair use,
Revolts from true birth, stumbling on abuse[13]. 20
Virtue itself turns vice, being misapplied,
And vice sometime by action dignified[14].

Enter ROMEO.

Within the infant rind[15] of this weak flower
Poison hath residence, and medicine power:
For this, being smelt, with that part[16] cheers each part, 25
Being tasted, stays[17] all senses with[18] the heart.
Two such opposèd kings encamp them still[19]
In man as well as herbs, grace and rude will[20];
And where the worser is predominant,
Full soon the canker[21] death eats up that plant. 30

Friar Lawrence fears that Romeo has spent the night with Rosaline. But Romeo, telling of his and Juliet's mutual love, asks the Friar to marry them.

 剧情简介：劳润修士担心柔密欧已经跟若泽兰一起过夜了，但是柔密欧说他和茱丽叶已经互诉衷肠，还请修士为他们主婚。

1 Should the actors emphasise the rhymes?

Read the last word in each line aloud from line 31 ('Benedicite!', pronounced 'beneedissitee') to the end of the scene. What do you discover? Find out if the whole scene is written in this way. Then step into role as director and write a note for your actors advising them, with reasons, whether or not to strongly emphasise the rhymes.

Themes 主题分析

Youth versus age (in pairs)

One of the themes of the play is youth versus age (see pp. 210–11), most obviously in how the two young lovers are trapped in the web of hate of the older generation. In lines 35–8, Friar Lawrence's image identifies another contrast between young and old: elderly men with worries on their minds will never sleep as soundly as innocent, inexperienced young men.

a Look at exactly how the Friar expresses this contrast, then work out a physical way of illustrating what the lines say about the difference between old men and young men.

b As you read the rest of this scene, look out for the ways in which Shakespeare highlights the differences in attitude between Romeo and Friar Lawrence.

2 Romeo – facing up to the truth? (in pairs)

Friar Lawrence does not find Romeo's explanation in lines 48–54 at all clear. He tells the young man that ambiguous, unclear confessions will only be given similarly unsatisfactory absolution ('riddling shrift'). As a Franciscan priest, Friar Lawrence could give absolution to those who confessed (told him confidentially about) their sins. To clarify Romeo's explanation, try the following activity.

- One person reads lines 48–54. But only read up to a punctuation mark, then pause. In each pause, the other person makes clear Romeo's veiled ('riddling') meaning. The explanations given in the glossary to the right will help you (and remember that 'foe' in line 54 is ambiguous: it could mean Juliet – or possibly the Capulets).

---

1 **Benedicite!** 祝福你！
2 **distempered** 心烦意乱
3 **bid … bed** 起床
4 **unbruisèd** 没有跌过跤
5 **unstuffed** 空空如也
6 **couch** 躺下休息
7 **uproused** 早起
8 **distemp'rature** 心绪不宁
9 **ghostly father** 神父
10 **holy physic** 仙丹妙药（指结婚仪式）
11 **lo** = look
12 **intercession** 恳求，诉求
13 **steads** 有助于
14 **foe** 仇家（指茱丽叶或卡普莱家族）
15 **homely in thy drift** 有什么想法就说什么
16 **Riddling** 晦涩，含糊
17 **shrift** 宽恕
18 **pass** 一边走（一边说）

ROMEO	Good morrow, father.
FRIAR LAWRENCE	Benedicite![1]
	What early tongue so sweet saluteth me?
	Young son, it argues a distempered[2] head
	So soon to bid good morrow to thy bed[3]:
	Care keeps his watch in every old man's eye,
	And where care lodges, sleep will never lie;
	But where unbruisèd[4] youth with unstuffed[5] brain
	Doth couch[6] his limbs, there golden sleep doth reign.
	Therefore thy earliness doth me assure
	Thou art uproused[7] with some distemp'rature[8];
	Or if not so, then here I hit it right,
	Our Romeo hath not been in bed tonight.
ROMEO	That last is true, the sweeter rest was mine.
FRIAR LAWRENCE	God pardon sin! wast thou with Rosaline?
ROMEO	With Rosaline, my ghostly father[9]? no;
	I have forgot that name, and that name's woe.
FRIAR LAWRENCE	That's my good son, but where hast thou been then?
ROMEO	I'll tell thee ere thou ask it me again:
	I have been feasting with mine enemy,
	Where on a sudden one hath wounded me
	That's by me wounded; both our remedies
	Within thy help and holy physic[10] lies.
	I bear no hatred, blessèd man; for lo[11],
	My intercession[12] likewise steads[13] my foe[14].
FRIAR LAWRENCE	Be plain, good son, and homely in thy drift[15],
	Riddling[16] confession finds but riddling shrift[17].
ROMEO	Then plainly know, my heart's dear love is set
	On the fair daughter of rich Capulet;
	As mine on hers, so hers is set on mine,
	And all combined, save what thou must combine
	By holy marriage. When and where and how
	We met, we wooed, and made exchange of vow,
	I'll tell thee as we pass[18], but this I pray,
	That thou consent to marry us today.

After chiding Romeo for his fickleness in love, Friar Lawrence agrees to marry Romeo and Juliet because he believes their marriage will end the feuding of the Montagues and Capulets.

剧情简介：劳润修士责备柔密欧恋爱浮躁后，答应为他和茱丽叶主婚，因为他相信他们俩的婚姻会结束芒特鸠和卡普莱两家的世仇。

Themes 主题分析
Fast versus slow (in pairs)

The final two lines (93–4) suggest a lot about the characters of Romeo and Friar Lawrence. Romeo is impetuous (冲动，鲁莽), full of urgency: he wants to rush into marriage with Juliet. Friar Lawrence, like the advice he gives, is cautious and thoughtful. He is all too aware that acting with speed and rashness can result in accidents.

- Taking parts, read from line 31 to the end of the scene in the style these last two lines suggest (Romeo – hasty; Friar Lawrence – wise and slow).
- Afterwards, decide if you think those speaking styles are appropriate to the characters. Keep the idea of hasty/slow in your mind as you read on.

1 Question Friar Lawrence (in large groups)

Friar Lawrence criticises Romeo for his fickleness and inconstancy in love: the 'dear' love he had for Rosaline has quickly been transferred to Juliet. Yet the Friar agrees to marry Romeo and Juliet, seeing it as an opportunity to mend the feud between the Montague and Capulet households.

- One student plays the Friar in the **hot-seat***. The others question him to test out the wisdom of his decision and explore any possible risks.

Write about it 写作练习
Romeo fills in the details

In his haste, Romeo only offers Friar Lawrence a brief explanation of his love for Juliet. He leaves out many details of their first meeting at the Capulet ball and his subsequent visit to her garden (the 'balcony' scene).

a Imagine that Romeo sits down with the Friar and updates him with all the missing information. What questions might the Friar ask? How would Romeo describe the events that have occurred so far and his feelings about the situation?

b Write their dialogue as a script that captures the close relationship between the two men. Shakespeare did not include stage directions in this scene, but you could put them in your version.

1. Holy Saint Francis 圣方济各（天主教方济各会创始人；劳润借此表示惊讶）
2. Young … eyes 年轻人的爱情不在心里，而是在眼睛里
3. Jesu Maria = Jesus and Mary（表示惊讶）
4. brine 咸水，盐水（指眼泪）
5. sallow 苍白
6. season 加味
7. that … taste 平淡无味
8. wast thyself 做你自己
9. sentence 谚语，警句
10. chid'st = chided（责备）
11. doting 痴情
12. bad'st 要求
13. grace 善意，感谢
14. O … spell 哦，她看透了你的爱情，只不过是照本宣科，不是口说心声
15. waverer 动摇分子
16. In one respect 出于一个考虑
17. rancour 仇恨
18. stand on 坚决要求

* hot seat 热座位，一种课堂游戏，玩法是请一位同学坐到讲台的一把椅子上，其他同学轮番给他/她出难题，哪个问题回答不出就算输。

FRIAR LAWRENCE   Holy Saint Francis[1], what a change is here!
                 Is Rosaline, that thou didst love so dear,
                 So soon forsaken? Young men's love then lies
                 Not truly in their hearts, but in their eyes[2].
                 Jesu Maria[3], what a deal of brine[4]
                 Hath washed thy sallow[5] cheeks for Rosaline!
                 How much salt water thrown away in waste,
                 To season[6] love, that of it doth not taste[7]!
                 The sun not yet thy sighs from heaven clears,
                 Thy old groans yet ringing in mine ancient ears;
                 Lo here upon thy cheek the stain doth sit
                 Of an old tear that is not washed off yet.
                 If e'er thou wast thyself[8], and these woes thine,
                 Thou and these woes were all for Rosaline.
                 And art thou changed? Pronounce this sentence[9] then:
                 Women may fall, when there's no strength in men.
ROMEO   Thou chid'st[10] me oft for loving Rosaline.
FRIAR LAWRENCE   For doting[11], not for loving, pupil mine.
ROMEO   And bad'st[12] me bury love.
FRIAR LAWRENCE   Not in a grave,
                 To lay one in, another out to have.
ROMEO   I pray thee chide me not. Her I love now
                 Doth grace[13] for grace and love for love allow;
                 The other did not so.
FRIAR LAWRENCE   O she knew well
                 Thy love did read by rote, that could not spell[14].
                 But come, young waverer[15], come go with me,
                 In one respect[16] I'll thy assistant be:
                 For this alliance may so happy prove
                 To turn your households' rancour[17] to pure love.
ROMEO   O let us hence, I stand on[18] sudden haste.
FRIAR LAWRENCE   Wisely and slow, they stumble that run fast.

                                                              Exeunt

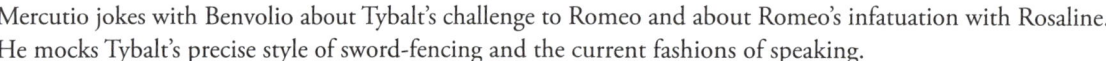

Mercutio jokes with Benvolio about Tybalt's challenge to Romeo and about Romeo's infatuation with Rosaline. He mocks Tybalt's precise style of sword-fencing and the current fashions of speaking.

剧情简介：莫丘休和本沃琉说笑，议论提巴尔对柔密欧的挑战，嘲笑柔密欧对若泽兰的痴情；他还嘲弄提巴尔循规蹈矩的剑法和当时的时髦词语。

1 Friendship under pressure? (in pairs)

Act 2 Scene 4 opens with Mercutio questioning Benvolio about what Romeo has been up to the previous night. He still thinks that Romeo is in love with Rosaline. Shakespeare uses this scene to emphasise once again how Romeo has withdrawn from his friends.

- Take parts and read aloud lines 1–5. Notice that Mercutio and Benvolio speak to each other in prose rather than the heightened language and style of poetry. Try different methods of reading these lines to explore the best way of conveying the growing frustration these characters feel at Romeo's continued absence. In your Director's Journal, write down your ideas for staging Mercutio's and Benvolio's entrances to enhance the impact of the opening exchange.

Write about it 写作练习

Tybalt's challenge (by yourself)

Tybalt has sent a letter challenging Romeo to a duel. Look back at Act 1 and remind yourself of the type of language that Tybalt uses, the type of character he is and the source of his grievances.

- Write the letter that Tybalt sends to Romeo. Use appropriate modern English, but try to match the style and expression to your impressions of Tybalt so far.

Characters 人物分析

Mercutio's mockery (in small groups)

As usual, Mercutio is quick to use language as a weapon. In lines 13–31 he targets:

- Romeo (lines 13–16) and how his being in love renders him hopeless as a man and thus unable to take up Tybalt's challenge
- Tybalt (lines 18–23) and his pretentious way of fencing ('passado' = lunge [突刺]; 'punto reverso' = backhanded thrust [反手刺]; 'hay' = hit [猛击])
- the affected ways of speaking that young men adopt (lines 25–31).

Use the glossary to help you understand the details of Mercutio's verbal onslaught (猛攻), then talk together about what these three speeches reveal about Mercutio's view of the world. Write your ideas in the Character file you are compiling on Mercutio.

1. should = can
2. wench 妞
3. answer it （指接受挑战）
4. dares 挑战
5. pin = centre
6. cleft … butt-shaft 被瞎眼弓箭男孩（丘比特）的无头箭射穿
7. Prince of Cats 猫王（中世纪的民间传说中有个猫王叫Tybert，Tybalt即对Tybert的模仿）
8. captain of compliments 花架子队长（compliment：外表）
9. sing prick-song 照谱唱歌（讽刺提巴尔击剑时如同照着乐谱唱歌一样循规蹈矩）
10. rests his minim rests 在微停处停顿
11. the third in your bosom 第三处刺入您的胸膛
12. butcher of a silk button 残杀一颗丝纽扣
13. duellist 剑客
14. very first house 一流击剑学校
15. of … cause 有第一和第二动因（当时有一本名为 The Book of Honour and Honourable Quarrels 的决斗法典，里面说决斗的第一和第二动因都是荣誉，荣誉高于生命）
16. immortal 不朽
17. pox 天花（The pox of … 意思是"遭瘟的……"，是一种比较温和的诅咒语）
18. lisping 拿腔拿调
19. phantasimes = fantasticoes （狂人）
20. new tuners of accent 说话洋腔洋调的人
21. grandsire 老爷爷
22. flies 飞虫
23. these pardon-me's 这些张嘴就是 pardon-me 的人
24. O … bones! 噢，骨头好疼啊！

Act 2 Scene 4
A street in Verona

Enter BENVOLIO *and* MERCUTIO.

MERCUTIO Where the dev'l should[1] this Romeo be?
Came he not home tonight?

BENVOLIO Not to his father's, I spoke with his man.

MERCUTIO Why, that same pale hard-hearted wench[2], that Rosaline,
Torments him so, that he will sure run mad.

BENVOLIO Tybalt, the kinsman to old Capulet,
Hath sent a letter to his father's house.

MERCUTIO A challenge, on my life.

BENVOLIO Romeo will answer it[3].

MERCUTIO Any man that can write may answer a letter.

BENVOLIO Nay, he will answer the letter's master, how he dares[4], being dared.

MERCUTIO Alas, poor Romeo, he is already dead, stabbed with a white wench's black eye, run through the ear with a love-song, the very pin[5] of his heart cleft with the blind bow-boy's butt-shaft[6]; and is he a man to encounter Tybalt?

BENVOLIO Why, what is Tybalt?

MERCUTIO More than Prince of Cats[7]. O, he's the courageous captain of compliments[8]: he fights as you sing prick-song[9], keeps time, distance, and proportion; he rests his minim rests[10], one, two, and the third in your bosom[11]; the very butcher of a silk button[12], a duellist[13], a duellist; a gentleman of the very first house[14], of the first and second cause[15]. Ah, the immortal[16] 'passado', the 'punto reverso', the 'hay'!

BENVOLIO The what?

MERCUTIO The pox[17] of such antic, lisping[18], affecting phantasimes[19], these new tuners of accent[20]! 'By Jesu, a very good blade! a very tall man! a very good whore!' Why, is not this a lamentable thing, grandsire[21], that we should be thus afflicted with these strange flies[22], these fashion-mongers, these pardon-me's[23], who stand so much on the new form, that they cannot sit at ease on the old bench? O their bones, their bones![24]

Mercutio (thinking Romeo loves Rosaline) teases Romeo about his love, saying that many beautiful women in history cannot compare with Rosaline. The two men joke together, trying to outdo each other's puns.

 剧情简介：莫丘休以为柔密欧还爱着若泽兰，取笑他一片痴情，说历史上很多美貌的女子都比不过若泽兰。两个人都拿对方打趣，看谁说的双关语高明。

1 Tragic ladies – fateful forecasts (in small groups)

Mercutio teases Romeo, accusing him of writing love poetry ('numbers') to Rosaline like that of the fourteenth-century Italian poet Petrarch (彼特拉克) to his love, Laura. But the women he names ominously predict the tragic fate that will befall Romeo and Juliet:

- **Dido** was queen of Carthage. When her lover Aeneas deserted her, she killed herself.
- **Cleopatra** (pictured below) was queen of Egypt, loved by both Julius Caesar and Mark Antony. She and Mark Antony committed suicide.
- **Helen**, the wife of Menelaus, king of Sparta, was stolen by the Trojan, Paris. Her abduction led to the siege (围攻) and destruction of Troy.
- **Hero** was loved by Leander, who swam the Hellespont (the Dardanelles) to meet her every night. He drowned and she committed suicide.
- **Thisbe** loved Pyramus, but their families were bitter enemies. Thinking her killed by a lion, he killed himself. She then committed suicide.

Each person in the group takes one or more of these tragic love stories and finds out more about it, before creating a poster to illustrate the tale. View all the posters and then discuss what they add to your understanding of *Romeo and Juliet*.

2 Romeo: one of the young men? (in pairs)

In this scene, many productions show Romeo consciously re-engaging with the world of his young male friends. He is about to marry Juliet but he still takes part in racy (不雅), 'laddish' banter with Mercutio – and he certainly seems a match for his friend as they trade insults.

- Read through lines 32–82 and then talk about how you would present this exchange in a production of your own. What effects would you hope to create?

1 roe 鱼子（没了鱼子的鱼干瘪而无活力；另一种解释是Romeo没了Ro仅剩下Meo = Me, oh! [我啊!]，即只会无病呻吟）
2 fishified 化成鱼
3 numbers 诗
4 to 与……比起来
5 berhyme 为……唱赞美诗
6 dowdy 浪荡婆娘
7 hildings 野女人
8 harlots 娼妓
9 French slop 法式灯笼裤
10 You … night 昨晚您把我们给耍了
11 slip 假币 / 偷偷溜走（双关）
12 conceive 理解
13 case 情况 / 女性生殖器（双关）
14 bow in the hams 勾腿 / 苟合（hams指膝关节；双关）
15 cur'sy = curtsy（行屈膝礼）
16 hit it (说) 到点子上 / 到位（双关）
17 pink 完美 / 花 / 鞋饰
18 pump 鞋 / 阴茎（双关）
19 Sure wit! 真聪明!
20 solely singular 磨破
21 Swits and spurs 马鞭和马刺（指快马加鞭让脑子动起来）
22 cry a match (比赛结束) 宣布胜利
23 wild-goose chase 徒劳的追求
24 goose 蠢鸟 / 妓女 / 笨蛋
25 I … ear 咬你耳朵（表示亲密）
26 sharp sauce 酸苦的酱
27 cheverel 狍皮（一种非常柔软的皮革，暗指阴茎）
28 ell = 45英寸（旧时计量单位）

ROMEO AND JULIET ACT 2 SCENE 4
柔密欧与茱丽叶

Enter ROMEO.

BENVOLIO Here comes Romeo, here comes Romeo.

MERCUTIO Without his roe[1], like a dried herring: O flesh, flesh, how art thou fishified[2]! Now is he for the numbers[3] that Petrarch flowed in. Laura to[4] his lady was a kitchen wench (marry, she had a better love to berhyme[5] her), Dido a dowdy[6], Cleopatra a gipsy, Helen and Hero hildings[7] and harlots[8], Thisbe a grey eye or so, but not to the purpose. Signior Romeo, 'bon jour'! there's a French salutation to your French slop[9]. You gave us the counterfeit fairly last night[10].

ROMEO Good morrow to you both. What counterfeit did I give you?

MERCUTIO The slip[11], sir, the slip, can you not conceive[12]?

ROMEO Pardon, good Mercutio, my business was great, and in such a case as mine a man may strain courtesy.

MERCUTIO That's as much as to say, such a case[13] as yours constrains a man to bow in the hams[14].

ROMEO Meaning to cur'sy[15].

MERCUTIO Thou hast most kindly hit it[16].

ROMEO A most courteous exposition.

MERCUTIO Nay, I am the very pink[17] of courtesy.

ROMEO Pink for flower.

MERCUTIO Right.

ROMEO Why then is my pump[18] well flowered.

MERCUTIO Sure wit![19] Follow me this jest now, till thou hast worn out thy pump, that when the single sole of it is worn, the jest may remain, after the wearing, solely singular[20].

ROMEO O single-soled jest, solely singular for the singleness!

MERCUTIO Come between us, good Benvolio, my wits faints.

ROMEO Swits and spurs[21], swits and spurs, or I'll cry a match[22].

MERCUTIO Nay, if our wits run the wild-goose chase[23], I am done; for thou hast more of the wild goose in one of thy wits than, I am sure, I have in my whole five. Was I with you there for the goose[24]?

ROMEO Thou wast never with me for any thing when thou wast not there for the goose.

MERCUTIO I will bite thee by the ear[25] for that jest.

ROMEO Nay, good goose, bite not.

MERCUTIO Thy wit is a very bitter sweeting, it is a most sharp sauce[26].

ROMEO And is it not then well served in to a sweet goose?

MERCUTIO O here's a wit of cheverel[27], that stretches from an inch narrow to an ell[28] broad!

Mercutio's joking becomes more and more sexual. When the Nurse appears, seeking Romeo, Mercutio directs his sexual teasing at her. Romeo identifies himself.

剧情简介：莫丘休的荤段子越来越不堪入耳。茱丽叶的奶妈上场找柔密欧，莫丘休转而戏弄起她来。柔密欧亮明了身份。

Language in the play 剧中语言
Should Mercutio add actions to words?

Mercutio relishes his sexual puns. After his fairly conventional use of 'art' five times in lines 73–4 (meaning 'are' or 'skill'), his imagination takes over. Here are just some of his puns: 'bauble' = stick carried by a fool, or penis; 'hole' = hole or vagina; 'tale' = story or penis; 'against the hair' = against my wishes or against pubic hair. In Elizabethan times, even the word 'occupy' (line 80) had a sexual double meaning.

- How actively do you think Mercutio should bring out the sexual meanings in a stage performance? Write a paragraph explaining whether you feel that adding actions to the 'sexual' words would increase an audience's enjoyment and understanding, or whether you think such actions are unnecessary. Give reasons for your preference.

▶ What kind of relationship between Mercutio (left) and Romeo (right) is portrayed in this image? From your reading of this scene, do you think this is the correct portrayal?

1 I … goose （之前的 broad 意思是"粗"，柔密欧说他要抻一抻这个词的意思；即加在 goose "[笨]鹅"前面时，broad 表示"明白无误"，far and wide 表示"远近四方"）
2 by art … nature 既先天造化，又后天修炼
3 drivelling … natural 傻乎乎的爱就像个大白痴
4 lolling 伸着舌头
5 bauble 玩意儿
6 stop … hair 在我针对毛的故事中停下来（tale: 尾巴/故事，暗指阴茎）
7 else = otherwise
8 Here's goodly gear! 来好事了！
9 A sail 一面帆（奶妈穿的裙子肥大蓬松，给人感觉像是驶来一艘鼓着帆的船）
10 a shirt and a smock 一件衬衫和一件裙子
11 good den = good evening （伊丽莎白时代用这句话作午后的问候语）
12 for … noon 日晷上的咸猪手现正落在正午的点点上
13 Out upon you 您说
14 mar 伤害；毁灭
15 troth = truth （实话）
16 quoth'a = he said
17 took 理解
18 confidence 悄悄话
19 indite （本是 invite，本沃琉模仿、嘲弄奶妈的用词错误）
20 bawd 老鸨
21 So ho! 嘿嗬！（猎人发现猎物时的吼声）

ROMEO	I stretch it out for that word 'broad', which, added to the goose, proves thee far and wide a broad goose[1].	70
MERCUTIO	Why, is not this better now than groaning for love? Now art thou sociable, now art thou Romeo; now art thou what thou art, by art as well as by nature[2], for this drivelling love is like a great natural[3] that runs lolling[4] up and down to hide his bauble[5] in a hole.	75
BENVOLIO	Stop there, stop there.	
MERCUTIO	Thou desirest me to stop in my tale against the hair[6].	
BENVOLIO	Thou wouldst else[7] have made thy tale large.	
MERCUTIO	O thou art deceived; I would have made it short, for I was come to the whole depth of my tale, and meant indeed to occupy the argument no longer.	80
ROMEO	Here's goodly gear![8]	

Enter NURSE *and her man* [PETER].

	A sail[9], a sail!	
MERCUTIO	Two, two: a shirt and a smock[10].	
NURSE	Peter!	85
PETER	Anon.	
NURSE	My fan, Peter.	
MERCUTIO	Good Peter, to hide her face, for her fan's the fairer face.	
NURSE	God ye good morrow, gentlemen.	
MERCUTIO	God ye good den[11], fair gentlewoman.	90
NURSE	Is it good den?	
MERCUTIO	'Tis no less, I tell ye, for the bawdy hand of the dial is now upon the prick of noon[12].	
NURSE	Out upon you[13], what a man are you?	
ROMEO	One, gentlewoman, that God hath made, himself to mar[14].	95
NURSE	By my troth[15], it is well said: 'for himself to mar', quoth'a[16]? Gentlemen, can any of you tell me where I may find the young Romeo?	
ROMEO	I can tell you, but young Romeo will be older when you have found him than he was when you sought him: I am the youngest of that name, for fault of a worse.	100
NURSE	You say well.	
MERCUTIO	Yea, is the worst well? Very well took[17], i'faith, wisely, wisely.	
NURSE	If you be he, sir, I desire some confidence[18] with you.	105
BENVOLIO	She will indite[19] him to some supper.	
MERCUTIO	A bawd[20], a bawd, a bawd! So ho![21]	

Mercutio sings a song full of indecent meaning. He leaves, continuing to mock the Nurse. She protests against his sauciness to her, then cautions Romeo not to deceive Juliet.

剧情简介：莫丘休唱了一首很不雅的歌，临别前还不停地嘲弄奶妈。奶妈因莫丘休对自己厚颜无耻而愤愤不平，接着告诫柔密欧不要欺骗茱丽叶。

Language in the play 剧中语言
Mercutio's song – obscene (淫秽) (but obscure) humour

In his song, lines 111–16, Mercutio is playing his usual language game, seizing every opportunity for sexual punning. His 'So ho!' (line 107) sets him off on a hunting **metaphor** (隐喻): chasing the hare. In his song, 'stale', 'hare' and 'hoar' can mean or sound like 'whore': a prostitute. Superficially, the song means that any old dish is good to eat when you're hungry, but if it goes mouldy (发霉), it's not worth paying for ('too much for a score'). Modern audiences and readers are often puzzled by the song, because both its surface meaning and its indecent meaning are obscure.

- If you were directing the play, would you cut the song from the performance? Why, or why not? Be prepared to justify your answer to your classmates. (For more information about metaphors in the play, see p. 214.)

Write about it 写作练习
How does the Nurse respond?

The Nurse makes a comment about Mercutio directly after he leaves (lines 121–2). She calls the young man 'saucy' and acknowledges that his language is full of 'ropery' (dirty jokes). But what is she thinking privately about Mercutio? Note that she must have *understood* the jokes in order to point out publicly that they are rude!

- Write a few sentences outlining the Nurse's unspoken thoughts in the moments after she delivers line 122.

1 But is it fair? (in pairs)

In the patriarchal, male-dominated world of the play, the young men seem to think it's acceptable to treat the Nurse (who is probably much older than they are) without much respect. But the Nurse shows real concern for Juliet's well-being, warning Romeo that he should not seduce Juliet ('lead her in a fool's paradise', lines 136–7).

- Do you think that the Nurse deserves the mockery she receives? One person should argue 'yes' and the other 'no'.
- Would you have a different view about her treatment in today's society?

1. **lenten pie** 斋饼（基督徒大斋节 [Lent] 期间吃的素饼）
2. **stale and hoar** 陈旧并发霉（hoar用作动作谓词时意思是"长白毛"）
3. **spent** 吃完
4. **hare hoar** 白毛兔子（hoar与 whore [妓女] 谐音）
5. **score** 账单
6. **saucy merchant** 厚颜无耻的家伙
7. **ropery** = roguery（意思是"混账话"；奶妈说话常用错词）
8. **stand to** 坚持；坚挺
9. **And 'a** = If he（也可用来表示 even if）
10. **take him down** 放倒他
11. **Jacks** 流氓
12. **Scurvy knave** 臭无赖
13. **flirt-gills** = flirtatious girls（风骚女）
14. **skains-mates** 小刀友（skains = skeans/skeins [小刀，匕首]，这是奶妈的特色语言）
15. **use me at his pleasure** 调戏我取乐
16. **weapon** 家伙
17. **lead … paradise** 引诱她进入傻子乐园
18. **deal double with her** 对她两面三刀
19. **weak dealing** 卑劣行为
20. **protest** 发誓

| ROMEO | What hast thou found? |
| MERCUTIO | No hare, sir, unless a hare, sir, in a lenten pie[1], that is something stale and hoar[2] ere it be spent[3]. |

[*He walks by them and sings.*]

> An old hare hoar[4],
> And an old hare hoar,
> Is very good meat in Lent;
> But a hare that is hoar
> Is too much for a score[5],
> When it hoars ere it be spent.

Romeo, will you come to your father's? We'll to dinner thither.

| ROMEO | I will follow you. |
| MERCUTIO | Farewell, ancient lady, farewell, lady, [*Singing.*] 'lady, lady'. |

Exeunt [Mercutio and Benvolio]

NURSE	I pray you, sir, what saucy merchant[6] was this that was so full of his ropery[7]?
ROMEO	A gentleman, Nurse, that loves to hear himself talk, and will speak more in a minute than he will stand to[8] in a month.
NURSE	And 'a[9] speak any thing against me, I'll take him down[10], and 'a were lustier than he is, and twenty such Jacks[11]; and if I cannot, I'll find those that shall. Scurvy knave[12], I am none of his flirt-gills[13], I am none of his skains-mates[14]. [*She turns to Peter, her man.*] And thou must stand by too and suffer every knave to use me at his pleasure[15]!
PETER	I saw no man use you at his pleasure; if I had, my weapon[16] should quickly have been out. I warrant you, I dare draw as soon as another man, if I see occasion in a good quarrel, and the law on my side.
NURSE	Now afore God, I am so vexed that every part about me quivers. Scurvy knave! Pray you, sir, a word: and as I told you, my young lady bid me enquire you out; what she bid me say, I will keep to myself. But first let me tell ye, if ye should lead her in a fool's paradise[17], as they say, it were a very gross kind of behaviour, as they say; for the gentlewoman is young; and therefore, if you should deal double with her[18], truly it were an ill thing to be offered to any gentlewoman, and very weak dealing[19].
ROMEO	Nurse, commend me to thy lady and mistress. I protest[20] unto thee –
NURSE	Good heart, and i'faith I will tell her as much. Lord, Lord, she will be a joyful woman.

Romeo arranges to marry Juliet that afternoon at Friar Lawrence's cell. He will send a rope ladder to the Nurse so that he may climb to Juliet's room in Capulet's house.

  剧情简介： 柔密欧安排当天下午到劳润修士的修道室跟茱丽叶结婚。他将给奶妈送一个软梯，这样他就能爬上卡普莱家的房子，进到茱丽叶的卧室。

1 Decisions about the Nurse (in pairs)

a Does the Nurse take the money? In lines 151–3, Romeo offers money to the Nurse. The episode can be made very funny on stage, and can add to the audience's understanding of the Nurse's character. Work out a staging of the three lines that you feel will amuse the audience.

b 'As pale as any clout in the versal world' In lines 168–72, the Nurse says that Juliet would as happily set eyes on a 'toad' as Paris, and that when she tells Juliet that Paris is a handsomer ('properer') man than Romeo, Juliet looks as white as a sheet ('clout' = washed-out rag, 'versal' = universal). But is she just making up a story that she thinks Romeo wishes to hear? From your experience of the Nurse so far, suggest whether or not you think she is telling the truth.

Language in the play 剧中语言
Verse and prose (in pairs)

Most of this scene is in prose, but a few short sections are in verse.

- Identify the verse sections, then read the information about verse and prose in the 'Language' section on page 216. Suggest why Shakespeare switched between prose and verse in this scene. Write down your answer and pass it to a partner for discussion.

Write about it 写作练习
A mixture of moods?

In most productions, this scene is full of comic atmosphere. It is rich in racy language, which is often accompanied by strikingly funny 'stage business' (戏台动作) (actions and gestures that complement the words).

a Look back through the scene and identify all the different opportunities to showcase the comic features. Then see if you can highlight any elements of the scene that might be used to suggest a different mood. Is this scene entirely about making the audience laugh, or could parts of it be played in other ways?

b Write your findings in a critical essay in which you explore the variety of moods and dramatic effects that could be achieved in this scene. Remember to use embedded quotations to support your points.

1 mark me   听我说
2 shrift   坦白，忏悔
3 shrived   赦免（忏悔的罪孽）
4 tackled stair   软梯
5 top-gallant   桅杆顶
6 be my convoy   指引我
7 quit   报答
8 Hark = Listen
9 Is your man secret?   您的人能保守秘密吗？
10 Two … away   两个人要想保密，就要把一个人收拾了（谚语）
11 prating   叽叽喳喳
12 would fain lay knife aboard   想先下刀为强（伊丽莎白时代酒馆的客人们把刀放在桌子上占位置）
13 as lieve   宁可
14 properer   更英俊
15 clout   抹布
16 dog-name   狗名（字母R被称为"狗字母"，因为它的发音像狗吠）
17 sententious   (奶妈可能想说 sentences)
18 apace   快走

ROMEO AND JULIET ACT 2 SCENE 4
柔密欧与茱丽叶

ROMEO   What wilt thou tell her, Nurse? thou dost not mark me[1].   145
NURSE   I will tell her, sir, that you do protest, which, as I take it, is a gentleman-like offer.
ROMEO   Bid her devise
Some means to come to shrift[2] this afternoon,
And there she shall at Friar Lawrence' cell   150
Be shrived[3] and married. Here is for thy pains.
NURSE   No truly, sir, not a penny.
ROMEO   Go to, I say you shall.
NURSE   This afternoon, sir? Well, she shall be there.
ROMEO   And stay, good Nurse, behind the abbey wall: 155
Within this hour my man shall be with thee,
And bring thee cords made like a tackled stair[4],
Which to the high top-gallant[5] of my joy
Must be my convoy[6] in the secret night.
Farewell, be trusty, and I'll quit[7] thy pains.   160
Farewell, commend me to thy mistress.
NURSE   Now God in heaven bless thee! Hark[8] you, sir.
ROMEO   What say'st thou, my dear Nurse?
NURSE   Is your man secret?[9] Did you ne'er hear say,
'Two may keep counsel, putting one away[10]'?   165
ROMEO   'Warrant thee, my man's as true as steel.
NURSE   Well, sir, my mistress is the sweetest lady – Lord, Lord! when 'twas a little prating[11] thing – O, there is a nobleman in town, one Paris, that would fain lay knife aboard[12]; but she, good soul, had as lieve[13] see a toad, a very toad, as see him. I anger her sometimes,   170
and tell her that Paris is the properer[14] man, but I'll warrant you, when I say so, she looks as pale as any clout[15] in the versal world. Doth not rosemary and Romeo begin both with a letter?
ROMEO   Ay, Nurse, what of that? Both with an R.
NURSE   Ah, mocker, that's the dog-name[16]. R is for the – no, I know it   175
begins with some other letter – and she hath the prettiest sententious[17] of it, of you and rosemary, that it would do you good to hear it.
ROMEO   Commend me to thy lady.
NURSE   Ay, a thousand times.
[Exit Romeo]
Peter!
PETER   Anon.   180
NURSE   [Handing him her fan.] Before and apace[18].
Exit [after Peter]

Juliet is impatient for the Nurse's return. She compares the speed of love and young people with the slowness of the old. The Nurse finally arrives, grumbling of her aches and pains.

 剧情简介：茱丽叶急切盼望奶妈回来，她对比年轻人相爱的速度和老年人的缓慢。奶妈终于到了，牢骚满腹，抱怨腰酸背痛。

1 Get on with it! (in pairs)

Juliet is eagerly awaiting the Nurse's return with a message from Romeo. She cannot wait to hear the news.

a Take turns to read Juliet's lines 1–19 to each other, speaking them with Juliet's impatience in mind. After your readings, work together to write a set of notes for the actor playing Juliet, advising her how to deliver different sections of the soliloquy. Include these in your Director's Journal.

b Look at lines 1–19 again. From each line, say out loud just one word connected with movement (for example, line 1 – 'send', line 2 – 'return'). How many of these 'movement' words can you find? Talk together about how they create a sense of urgency.

1 Perchance　或许，大概
2 lame　跛子；行走缓慢
3 heralds　信使
4 low'ring　阴沉沉
5 nimble-pinioned doves　快速飞翔的白鸽（pinion 有"羽毛"的意思，pinioned 表示"长着翅膀"；为爱神维纳斯 [Venus] 拉天车的是白鸽）
6 bandy　噼里啪啦地打
7 feign　假装
8 Unwieldy　笨拙
9 Fie　呸（表示厌恶或愤怒）
10 jaunce　颠簸劳累的行程
11 stay a while　稍等一下

Themes 主题分析

Fast versus slow

Juliet sent the Nurse at nine o'clock, but she met Romeo at twelve (see Scene 4, lines 92–3). No one knows what the Nurse was doing during that time, but it has served to increase Juliet's eagerness for news. In this scene, Shakespeare builds up a sense of urgency in Juliet's soliloquy. He then has the Nurse use all kinds of delaying tricks that frustrate Juliet and increase her impatience.

- Come up with two delaying tactics of your own to add to the dramatic effectiveness of this scene. Select your strongest idea to share with the class.

Write about it 写作练习

The missing three hours (by yourself)

The Nurse has 'gone missing' for the three hours (see above). What has she been up to in this time?

- Use your knowledge of the Nurse so far – and your imagination – to write a short story that sheds light on the mystery. Use this opportunity to 'flesh out' the Nurse's character and lifestyle. You might follow Shakespeare's lead in highlighting some of the comic aspects of her personality and behaviour. Or perhaps you'd like to explore a more serious side to this character – after all, the Nurse is clearly very fond of Juliet and takes her responsibilities towards her young charge seriously.

Act 2 Scene 5
Capulet's mansion

Enter JULIET.

JULIET	The clock struck nine when I did send the Nurse;
	In half an hour she promised to return.
	Perchance[1] she cannot meet him: that's not so.
	O, she is lame[2]! Love's heralds[3] should be thoughts,
	Which ten times faster glides than the sun's beams,	5
	Driving back shadows over low'ring[4] hills;
	Therefore do nimble-pinioned doves[5] draw Love,
	And therefore hath the wind-swift Cupid wings.
	Now is the sun upon the highmost hill
	Of this day's journey, and from nine till twelve	10
	Is three long hours, yet she is not come.
	Had she affections and warm youthful blood,
	She would be as swift in motion as a ball;
	My words would bandy[6] her to my sweet love,
	And his to me.	15
	But old folks, many feign[7] as they were dead,
	Unwieldy[8], slow, heavy, and pale as lead.

Enter NURSE [*with* PETER].

	O God, she comes! O honey Nurse, what news?
	Hast thou met with him? Send thy man away.
NURSE	Peter, stay at the gate.	20

[*Exit Peter*]

JULIET	Now, good sweet Nurse – O Lord, why look'st thou sad?
	Though news be sad, yet tell them merrily;
	If good, thou shamest the music of sweet news
	By playing it to me with so sour a face.
NURSE	I am a-weary, give me leave a while.	25
	Fie[9], how my bones ache! What a jaunce[10] have I!
JULIET	I would thou hadst my bones, and I thy news.
	Nay, come, I pray thee speak, good, good Nurse, speak.
NURSE	Jesu, what haste! can you not stay a while[11]?
	Do you not see that I am out of breath?	30

Juliet is increasingly frustrated by the Nurse's irrelevant replies. At last, Juliet hears the longed-for news: Romeo is waiting to marry her at Friar Lawrence's cell.

剧情简介：茱丽叶对奶妈回答自己的问题时东拉西扯越来越烦，但她终于听到了期盼已久的消息：柔密欧在劳润修士的修道室里等着跟她完婚呢。

Stagecraft 导演技巧

Stage the scene (in pairs)

a Read through the whole scene, one person as Juliet, the other as the Nurse. Just enjoy how the Nurse keeps Juliet waiting until she finally tells the news of Romeo.

b After reading it, work out how to stage the scene. Where in the Capulet mansion do you think this exchange should take place? Write notes for the actors, suggesting how they should reflect the changing moods of Juliet and the Nurse. Best of all – act it out!

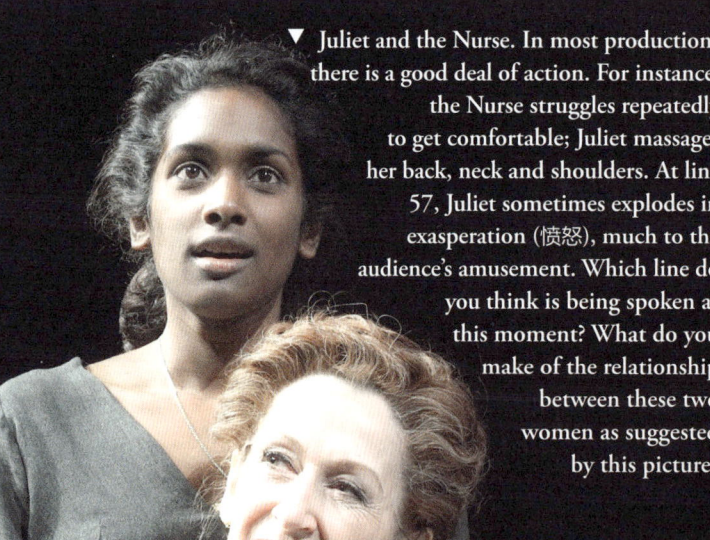

▼ Juliet and the Nurse. In most productions there is a good deal of action. For instance, the Nurse struggles repeatedly to get comfortable; Juliet massages her back, neck and shoulders. At line 57, Juliet sometimes explodes in exasperation (愤怒), much to the audience's amusement. Which line do you think is being spoken at this moment? What do you make of the relationship between these two women as suggested by this picture?

1 **in** = about
2 **stay the circumstance** 等待详情
3 **simple** 傻
4 **be not … on** 不值一提
5 **Beshrew** 挨刀的（语气柔和的诅咒）
6 **God's lady** = Virgin Mary（圣母马利亚）
7 **Marry come up, I trow** 圣母快来吧（表示不耐烦；trow = trust）
8 **poultice** 膏药
9 **Here's such as coil!** 你太小题大做了！
10 **leave** 许可
11 **hie** 赶快

JULIET	How art thou out of breath, when thou hast breath	
	To say to me that thou art out of breath?	
	The excuse that thou dost make in¹ this delay	
	Is longer than the tale thou dost excuse.	
	Is thy news good or bad? Answer to that.	35
	Say either, and I'll stay the circumstance²:	
	Let me be satisfied, is't good or bad?	
NURSE	Well, you have made a simple³ choice, you know not how to choose a man: Romeo? no, not he; though his face be better than any man's, yet his leg excels all men's, and for a hand and a foot and a body, though they be not to be talked on⁴, yet they are past compare. He is not the flower of courtesy, but I'll warrant him, as gentle as a lamb. Go thy ways, wench, serve God. What, have you dined at home?	40
JULIET	No, no! But all this did I know before.	45
	What says he of our marriage, what of that?	
NURSE	Lord, how my head aches! what a head have I!	
	It beats as it would fall in twenty pieces.	
	My back a't'other side – ah, my back, my back!	
	Beshrew⁵ your heart for sending me about	50
	To catch my death with jauncing up and down!	
JULIET	I'faith, I am sorry that thou art not well.	
	Sweet, sweet, sweet Nurse, tell me, what says my love?	
NURSE	Your love says, like an honest gentleman,	
	And a courteous, and a kind, and a handsome,	55
	And I warrant a virtuous – Where is your mother?	
JULIET	Where is my mother? why, she is within,	
	Where should she be? How oddly thou repliest:	
	'Your love says, like an honest gentleman,	
	"Where is your mother?"'	
NURSE	O God's lady⁶ dear,	60
	Are you so hot? Marry come up, I trow⁷;	
	Is this the poultice⁸ for my aching bones?	
	Henceforward do your messages yourself.	
JULIET	Here's such a coil!⁹ Come, what says Romeo?	
NURSE	Have you got leave¹⁰ to go to shrift today?	65
JULIET	I have.	
NURSE	Then hie¹¹ you hence to Friar Lawrence' cell,	
	There stays a husband to make you a wife.	

The Nurse, with a sexual joke, sends Juliet off to her marriage with Romeo. In Scene 6, Friar Lawrence and Romeo await Juliet. Romeo longs for marriage, but his words have an ominous ring.

剧情简介：奶妈开着性爱玩笑，催促茱丽叶快去找柔密欧结婚。第6场，劳润修士和柔密欧等待茱丽叶。柔密欧渴望结婚，但他的话里有一些不吉利的意味。

1 How embarrassing! (in pairs)

'Now comes the wanton blood up in your cheeks'. The Nurse's vivid image is a way of saying 'You're blushing!' In Act 2 Scene 2, lines 85–6, there is another example of Juliet blushing. She appears to be quickly embarrassed, so how does she respond to the sexual jokes in the Nurse's lines 72–5?

- What movements and expressions might Juliet use as she hears the Nurse talk of 'bird's nest' and 'bear the burden'?

1 wanton　激情澎湃
2 a bird's nest　一只鸟的巢（茱丽叶的卧室 / 私处）
3 drudge　奴仆
4 bear the burden　承受负担（柔密欧的体重）
5 That … not　日后不用悲哀来斥责我们
6 countervail　比得上
7 close our hands　让我们双手紧握（结为夫妻）

Stagecraft 导演技巧

Appropriate exits and entrances (in fours)

a Take parts (the Nurse, Juliet, Friar Lawrence, Romeo). Work out how Juliet and the Nurse would deliver the final four lines of Scene 5, and how they would leave the stage. The way they leave should match their language and feelings.

b Explore how you might stage the opening eight lines of Act 2 Scene 6. What similarities or contrasts would you seek to highlight as one scene moves into the next?

c Learn your few lines and run the action! Ask other groups to watch your performance and comment on what they observe. Can they pick out all the key dramatic features that you were looking to draw their attention to?

Language in the play 剧中语言

'Love-devouring Death' and other personification (in small groups)

'Love-devouring Death' is a personification – turning death into a person and giving it human feelings and actions (see p. 44). Friar Lawrence also personifies 'the heavens' (Scene 6, line 1) when he imagines the heavens smiling. In the next line, he imagines 'after-hours' (the future) sorrowfully telling off himself and Romeo.

- In each case, after discussion in your group, suggest two reasons why Shakespeare might have chosen to give the Friar these particular images at this point in the play.
- Compare your reasons with those of other groups and write your findings in the 'Personification' section of your Language file.

柔密欧与茱丽叶

	Now comes the wanton[1] blood up in your cheeks,	
	They'll be in scarlet straight at any news.	70
	Hie you to church, I must another way,	
	To fetch a ladder, by the which your love	
	Must climb a bird's nest[2] soon when it is dark.	
	I am the drudge[3], and toil in your delight;	
	But you shall bear the burden[4] soon at night.	75
	Go, I'll to dinner, hie you to the cell.	
JULIET	Hie to high fortune! Honest Nurse, farewell.	

Exeunt

Act 2 Scene 6
Friar Lawrence's cell

Enter FRIAR LAWRENCE *and* ROMEO.

FRIAR LAWRENCE	So smile the heavens upon this holy act,	
	That after-hours with sorrow chide us not[5].	
ROMEO	Amen, amen! but come what sorrow can,	
	It cannot countervail[6] the exchange of joy	
	That one short minute gives me in her sight.	5
	Do thou but close our hands[7] with holy words,	
	Then love-devouring Death do what he dare,	
	It is enough I may but call her mine.	

The Friar advises moderation in love, not violent excess. In reply to Romeo's elaborate language asking her to give an ornate description of their happiness, Juliet speaks of her true love. They leave to be married.

 剧情简介：劳润修士告诫爱情要有节制，不可过于激烈。柔密欧妙语连珠表达幸福，而茱丽叶拒绝用华丽辞藻描述他们的幸福，而是倾诉了内心的真爱。他们离开去举行婚礼。

Language in the play 剧中语言

Imagery – the Friar warns and praises

Friar Lawrence's first speech opposite is rich in imagery. He begins with an image of joyous love as fire and gunpowder, which destroy ('consume') at the very moment ('triumph') of meeting ('kiss'). His next image is of how over-sweet honey can become revolting and can destroy the appetite. His image of Juliet is of how someone in love seems to float on air.

- Match these images with the lines opposite. Then write a paragraph on each image, explaining what it shows about the Friar's attitude towards Romeo and Juliet's love.

1 Can true love be measured? (in pairs)

Romeo, in elaborate language, invites Juliet to tell of their love like a rich description ('blazon') of a coat of arms. But Juliet argues ('Conceit, more rich in matter than in words', line 30) that true love does not need words. It is so rich, it cannot be measured, nor can it ever be fully described. Some argue that here Shakespeare shows Romeo and Juliet speaking to each other as if they are mature and experienced lovers, not youthful and impulsive ones.

- What do you think? Talk together about how much you feel their relationship has developed since their meeting at the end of Act 1.

Stagecraft 导演技巧

A pause in the action? (in threes)

Nearly all modern productions of *Romeo and Juliet* insert an interval (幕间休息). In most cases, that break is placed here at the end of Act 2.

a Why do you think directors see this as a good moment to pause the action?

b If you were directing the play and had decided to place the interval here, how would you close Act 2? Create a tableau of the final moment of the scene that would stay firmly in the audience's mind as the curtain comes down.

c As you read on into Act 3, consider other possible choices for the interval break and how they might leave the audience with different impressions.

1 powder 火药
2 loathsome 令人作呕
3 confounds 破坏
4 tardy 晚，迟
5 Will … flint 永远不会磨坏永久的石板（因为茱丽叶脚步轻盈）
6 bestride the gossamers 在蛛丝上行走
7 wanton 欢愉
8 so light is vanity 虚荣又如此之少
9 ghostly confessor 灵魂忏悔师
10 As much to him 对他的谢意也同样多
11 measure 程度，多少
12 heaped 堆在一起
13 blazon 描绘
14 rich music's tongue 如音乐般动听的话语
15 Unfold the imagined 展现所能想象的
16 Conceit, more rich in matter 内涵更丰富的观念
17 his = its
18 worth 财产，财富
19 sum up 数得清
20 Till … one 直到神圣教会将二合为一

ROMEO AND JULIET ACT 2 SCENE 6
柔密欧与茱丽叶

FRIAR LAWRENCE These violent delights have violent ends,
And in their triumph die like fire and powder[1], 10
Which as they kiss consume. The sweetest honey
Is loathsome[2] in his own deliciousness,
And in the taste confounds[3] the appetite.
Therefore love moderately, long love doth so;
Too swift arrives as tardy[4] as too slow. 15

Enter JULIET.

Here comes the lady. O, so light a foot
Will ne'er wear out the everlasting flint[5];
A lover may bestride the gossamers[6]
That idles in the wanton[7] summer air,
And yet not fall, so light is vanity[8]. 20

JULIET Good even to my ghostly confessor[9].
FRIAR LAWRENCE Romeo shall thank thee, daughter, for us both.
[*Romeo kisses Juliet.*]
JULIET As much to him[10], else is his thanks too much.
[*Juliet returns his kiss.*]
ROMEO Ah, Juliet, if the measure[11] of thy joy
Be heaped[12] like mine, and that thy skill be more 25
To blazon[13] it, then sweeten with thy breath
This neighbour air, and let rich music's tongue[14]
Unfold the imagined[15] happiness that both
Receive in either by this dear encounter.
JULIET Conceit, more rich in matter[16] than in words, 30
Brags of his[17] substance, not of ornament;
They are but beggars that can count their worth[18],
But my true love is grown to such excess
I cannot sum up[19] sum of half my wealth.
FRIAR LAWRENCE Come, come with me, and we will make short work, 35
For by your leaves, you shall not stay alone
Till Holy Church incorporate two in one[20].

[*Exeunt*]

ROMEO AND JULIET 柔密欧与茱丽叶

Looking back at Act 2 第2幕回顾
Activities for groups or individuals

1 Headlines from Act 2

Imagine you are a newspaper sub-editor (助理编辑). Is your paper a tabloid (小报) or a broadsheet (大报)? Your job is to write brief, memorable headlines for each of the six scenes in Act 2. Make your headlines as accurate as possible. Try to use some of Shakespeare's own words.

2 What is your image of the Nurse?

Throughout this edition there are several photographs showing different portrayals of the Nurse.

- Look at the images of the Nurse on pages 24, 82, 106 and 207. Which comes closest to your imagining of what the Nurse is like? Write a paragraph giving reasons why you have chosen that picture – and why some others do not match your impression.

3 Cast (选派角色) the play

You are a director about to film the play. Who would you sign up to play some of the characters you've met so far? Choose anyone you like: movie or television actors, singers or other public figures. Say why you think each person is suitable. Remember, Juliet is only thirteen!

4 Research malapropisms (文字误用)

The Nurse uses many **malapropisms**. 'Confidence' (Act 2 Scene 4, line 105) is her mistake for 'conference'. Benvolio, replying, uses 'indite' (line 106) for 'invite' (presumably mockingly). Malapropisms are named after Mrs Malaprop, who mixed up her words, in Sheridan's play *The Rivals*.

- Find out more about Mrs Malaprop. Shakespeare would have known malapropisms as 'cacozelia'. Why do you think he gives malapropisms to the Nurse?

5 Verse and prose

Glance through Scenes 1–6. Five are written in verse, one in prose. Why do you think Shakespeare changed his style from verse to prose in that particular scene?

6 Hints about tragedy?

Although there are many potentially comic moments in Act 2, Shakespeare also underlines the ever-present threat of death. For example, Romeo knows that he will die if he is discovered in Juliet's garden. Friar Lawrence gathers flowers that can kill as well as heal. Tybalt's letter to Romeo challenges him to a deadly duel.

- See what other references to death you can discover in Act 2, and display your findings visually.

7 Gathering momentum (蓄势待发)

Things happen quickly in Act 2. Shakespeare gives us precise information about exactly when each scene and episode takes place. Flick back through the act and then produce a detailed timeline showing how Act 2 unfolds.

8 Show the marriage ceremony

Shakespeare does not show the wedding of Romeo and Juliet.

- In pairs, talk about whether the dramatic effect of the play would be increased by adding a wedding scene. To help your thinking, rehearse and perform a scene showing Romeo and Juliet getting married, to see how well it works.

9 Truly, madly, deeply?

By the time Act 3 opens, Romeo and Juliet are married.

a Look back through Act 2 and gather examples of how Shakespeare presents their blossoming relationship. Explore what they say and do, and think about their views of and relationships with other characters.

b What do you think this act has to say about the nature of 'young love'? Using quotations to back up your points, write an essay in answer to the question.

Compare these two images of the closing moment of Act 2. Which do you think more effectively captures the mood that the text creates? Explain your thinking.

Benvolio fears meeting the Capulets, knowing a fight will surely follow. Mercutio laughs at his fears, accusing Benvolio of being a quick-tempered quarreller.

剧情简介： 本沃琉害怕碰到卡普莱家的人，知道一场争斗在所难免。莫丘休笑话他胆子小，还指责他性子急、爱吵架。

Themes 主题分析

Public versus private (in small groups)

Act 2 ended with the intense intimacy of Romeo and Juliet's secret marriage plans. In contrast, Shakespeare sets the opening of Act 3 in a very public place. Just like at the start of the play, the characters are in the open air and the tension is building. Benvolio fears that a meeting with the Capulets will spark another street fight: the weather is hot and the 'mad blood stirring'.

a Read quickly through the next few pages to get a sense of what happens. Then talk together about where you would set this scene if you were filming it. Although Shakespeare notionally locates the play in Verona, Italy, you have free choice. In what country would you shoot it? What kind of outdoor space would you choose? Give your production designer some ideas to work with.

b Discuss why Shakespeare might have emphasised the contrast between events that take place in public and those that occur in private. Fill in a table marked 'Public Action' and 'Private Action' with information from Acts 1 and 2. What similarities or differences do you notice between the kinds of action that take place in these two different arenas? Annotate the table with your answer.

1 To fight or not to fight? (in threes)

a Mercutio (who is probably describing his own behaviour rather than Benvolio's), gives five examples of Benvolio getting into arguments (lines 15–25). Every quarrel was caused by something trivial. Work out some actions that Mercutio might use to accompany each quarrel. For example, does he pat Benvolio's chin for the first?

b Take parts as Benvolio, Mercutio and Tybalt. Have a go at staging the episode directly after Tybalt's entrance up to line 48. Speak and act in a style that matches what you know of these characters. Remember that Benvolio has played the peacekeeper in previous scenes. Do you think he is still looking to avoid trouble?

1 **Capels** = Capulets
2 **are abroad** = are about（到处都是）
3 **scape** = escape（避免）
4 **claps … table** 把剑"啪"的一声拍在桌子上（me没有实际意义）
5 **operation** 作用，影响
6 **draws him on** 对……抽刀相向（him也没有实际意义）
7 **drawer** 酒保
8 **hot a Jack** 暴躁家伙
9 **moody** 生气
10 **what to** = what then（接下来莫丘休故意把这个to曲解为two）
11 **hazel** 榛子色
12 **meat** 瓤（指蛋清和蛋黄）
13 **beaten … egg** 打得糊里糊涂像鸡蛋一样（分不出蛋清和蛋黄）
14 **doublet** 小双衣（流行于伊丽莎白时代的男士紧身上衣，有的带短裙）
15 **Easter** 复活节（复活节前40天为大斋期，基督徒在此期间斋戒、忏悔，不穿新衣服）
16 **riband** = ribbon（丝带）
17 **tutor me from** 教导我不要……
18 **And I were** = If I were
19 **apt** 倾向于，愿意
20 **buy … life** 买下我生命的绝对所有权（即要了我的小命）

Act 3 Scene 1
Verona, a public place

Enter MERCUTIO *and his* PAGE, BENVOLIO, *and* MEN.

BENVOLIO I pray thee, good Mercutio, let's retire:
The day is hot, the Capels[1] are abroad[2],
And if we meet we shall not scape[3] a brawl,
For now, these hot days, is the mad blood stirring.

MERCUTIO Thou art like one of these fellows that, when he enters the confines of a tavern, claps me his sword upon the table[4], and says 'God send me no need of thee!'; and by the operation[5] of the second cup draws him on[6] the drawer[7], when indeed there is no need.

BENVOLIO Am I like such a fellow?

MERCUTIO Come, come, thou art as hot a Jack[8] in thy mood as any in Italy, and as soon moved to be moody[9], and as soon moody to be moved.

BENVOLIO And what to[10]?

MERCUTIO Nay, and there were two such, we should have none shortly, for one would kill the other. Thou? why, thou wilt quarrel with a man that hath a hair more or a hair less in his beard than thou hast; thou wilt quarrel with a man for cracking nuts, having no other reason but because thou hast hazel[11] eyes. What eye but such an eye would spy out such a quarrel? Thy head is as full of quarrels as an egg is full of meat[12], and yet thy head hath been beaten as addle as an egg[13] for quarrelling. Thou hast quarrelled with a man for coughing in the street, because he hath wakened thy dog that hath lain asleep in the sun. Didst thou not fall out with a tailor for wearing his new doublet[14] before Easter[15]? with another for tying his new shoes with old riband[16]? and yet thou wilt tutor me from[17] quarrelling?

BENVOLIO And I were[18] so apt[19] to quarrel as thou art, any man should buy the fee-simple of my life[20] for an hour and a quarter.

MERCUTIO The fee-simple? O simple!

Mercutio taunts Tybalt, but Tybalt ignores his insults, because he is seeking Romeo. However, Romeo refuses to accept Tybalt's challenge to fight and tries to placate him, much to Mercutio's disgust.

 剧情简介： 莫丘休奚落提巴尔，但提巴尔不理睬他的侮辱，因为他在寻找柔密欧。然而柔密欧拒绝接受提巴尔的决斗挑战并试图安抚他，这让莫丘休大为反感。

Write about it 写作练习
Romeo's point of view

When Romeo arrives (line 48) and looks around, what does he make of what he sees? His mind is probably racing as he understands the dangerous situation developing. Don't forget that Romeo is now a married man – the last thing he wants is a fight, especially with Tybalt (a Capulet, like Juliet). Should he get involved?

- In role as Romeo, write a few paragraphs in modern English weighing up your options and considering the consequences of stepping in.

Language in the play 剧中语言
Mercutio's wordplay as a weapon (in pairs)

a Mercutio can't help twisting language into insults against Tybalt. In the lines between Tybalt's arrival and Romeo's entrance, he tries at least four times to bat Tybalt's language back at him with attitude! Practise reading aloud Mercutio's lines and then record them in a way that you think reflects how Mercutio feels about Tybalt.

b At line 49, Tybalt says that Romeo is the man he intends to fight. Mercutio, who has already made double meanings out of Tybalt's 'consortest', now pretends that 'man' means servant or 'follower'. He says Romeo will never wear the uniform of Tybalt's servants. Only if Tybalt invites Romeo to meet at a duelling place ('field') will Romeo be Tybalt's 'man'. Explain clearly to a partner how Mercutio uses his lines 50–2 to try to insult Tybalt – and why Tybalt might take offence. Record your ideas in your Character file on Mercutio.

1 'be satisfied' (in groups of four or more)

Line 65 is an electric moment in the play. Tybalt has deeply insulted Romeo ('villain', 'boy'). But because he is now married to Juliet, Romeo wants only to make peace with Tybalt, who is now one of his family. Everyone on stage will react dramatically to Romeo's two words.

- Prepare a tableau to show all characters at the moment when Romeo says 'be satisfied'. Hold the frozen moment for thirty seconds. Other groups identify who's who in your tableau. Then allow each member to come to life and speak the precise thoughts in their character's head at that moment.

1 and … occasion 如果您给我个缘由
2 consortest 是……的跟班（作为动词谓词，consort的意思是"陪伴"）
3 Consort 乐班（作为名词，consort有"乐班"的意思）
4 minstrels 卖唱的（莫丘休出身高贵，认为这是对他的侮辱）
5 discords 不中听的乐曲
6 fiddlestick 琴弓（指剑）
7 'Zounds = By God's wounds （以基督的伤口起誓）
8 not … pleasure 不为讨任何人的欢心而让步（not和no是用双重否定来强调否定，不可按"负负得正"来理解）
9 I'll be hanged 我敢以性命起誓
10 livery 制服
11 Your worship 阁下，老爷（讽刺语气）
12 appertaining 适当，恰如其分
13 devise 想象
14 tender 珍视

Enter TYBALT, PETRUCHIO, *and others.*

BENVOLIO   By my head, here comes the Capulets. 30
MERCUTIO   By my heel, I care not.
TYBALT   Follow me close, for I will speak to them.
Gentlemen, good den, a word with one of you.
MERCUTIO   And but one word with one of us? couple it with something, make it a word and a blow. 35
TYBALT   You shall find me apt enough to that, sir, and you will give me occasion¹.
MERCUTIO   Could you not take some occasion without giving?
TYBALT   Mercutio, thou consortest² with Romeo.
MERCUTIO   Consort³? what, dost thou make us minstrels⁴? And thou make minstrels of us, look to hear nothing but discords⁵. Here's my fiddlestick⁶, here's that shall make you dance. 'Zounds⁷, consort! 40
BENVOLIO   We talk here in the public haunt of men:
Either withdraw unto some private place,
Or reason coldly of your grievances, 45
Or else depart; here all eyes gaze on us.
MERCUTIO   Men's eyes were made to look, and let them gaze;
I will not budge for no man's pleasure⁸, I.

Enter ROMEO.

TYBALT   Well, peace be with you, sir, here comes my man.
MERCUTIO   But I'll be hanged⁹, sir, if he wear your livery¹⁰. 50
Marry, go before to field, he'll be your follower;
Your worship¹¹ in that sense may call him man.
TYBALT   Romeo, the love I bear thee can afford
No better term than this: thou art a villain.
ROMEO   Tybalt, the reason that I have to love thee 55
Doth much excuse the appertaining¹² rage
To such a greeting. Villain am I none;
Therefore farewell, I see thou knowest me not.
TYBALT   Boy, this shall not excuse the injuries
That thou hast done me, therefore turn and draw. 60
ROMEO   I do protest I never injuried thee,
But love thee better than thou canst devise¹³,
Till thou shalt know the reason of my love;
And so, good Capulet, which name I tender¹⁴
As dearly as mine own, be satisfied. 65
MERCUTIO   O calm, dishonourable, vile submission!

Mercutio, angered by Romeo's refusal to fight, challenges Tybalt. Romeo tries to make peace, but his intervention is fatal for Mercutio, who, mortally wounded, curses Montagues and Capulets alike.

剧情简介：柔密欧拒绝应战让莫丘休感到气愤，他向提巴尔发起挑战。柔密欧想讲和，结果他调停不成，反而让莫丘休受了致命伤，莫丘休临终前同时诅咒了芒特鸠和卡普莱两个家族。

Characters 人物分析
Mercutio: always the joker? (in pairs)

a Even though he knows he is about to die, Mercutio continues to make jokes: 'Ask for me tomorrow, and you shall find me a grave man.' One person reads all of Mercutio's lines in the script opposite, but stops at the end of each sentence. The other person says to whom the sentence is probably spoken, and describes Mercutio's tone of voice (mocking, angry, serious and so on).

b Mercutio's last two words in the play ('Your houses!') suggest that he blames the feud between the Montagues and the Capulets for his impending death (垂死). Fatally wounded, he leaves with Benvolio; we do not see him again. Imagine that Mercutio is able to speak more to Benvolio before he dies. What would he say about the way things have turned out? Talk about likely topics (Romeo's refusal to fight? Tybalt's escape? His own misfortune?) and then write Mercutio's additional lines. Use modern English if you wish.

Stagecraft 导演技巧
Mercutio's final moments (in small groups)

In every production, the director and actors have to decide how to play lines 82–99. For example, exactly when do Mercutio's friends realise that he isn't joking, merely scratched, but mortally wounded?

- Talk together about how you think this part of the scene should be played. What kind of performance will have the greatest effect on the audience? Afterwards, take roles (as director, Mercutio, Benvolio, Romeo and others) and stage your version.

1 'Alla stoccata' 突刺（意大利剑术语，用来指代提巴尔，表示对他的蔑视）
2 carries it away 获胜，占上风
3 dry-beat 干打（不是手持武器打出血来，而是徒手打）
4 pilcher 剑鞘
5 by the ears 揪着耳朵（剑柄也叫ear）
6 'passado' 突刺（参见第70页；这里说明莫丘休知道提巴尔的招数，表示蔑视）
7 forbear 克制
8 bandying 打架斗殴
9 sped 不行了
10 hath nothing 未受伤
11 villain 小子（伊丽莎白时代以此称呼下人；注意本场第54行、第57行和第92行的villain意思是"恶棍、混蛋"）
12 peppered 到头了
13 book of arithmetic 算术书（这里指剑法书，参见第70页）
14 A plague a'both your houses!
  = A plague on both your houses!
  （愿瘟疫降临你们两家！）

Romeo and Juliet Act 3 Scene 1
柔密欧与茱丽叶

	'Alla stoccata'¹ carries it away². [*Draws.*]	
	Tybalt, you rat-catcher, will you walk?	
TYBALT	What wouldst thou have with me?	
MERCUTIO	Good King of Cats, nothing but one of your nine lives that	70
	I mean to make bold withal, and as you shall use me hereafter,	
	dry-beat³ the rest of the eight. Will you pluck your sword out of	
	his pilcher⁴ by the ears⁵? Make haste, lest mine be about your ears	
	ere it be out.	
TYBALT	I am for you. [*Drawing.*]	75
ROMEO	Gentle Mercutio, put thy rapier up.	
MERCUTIO	Come, sir, your 'passado'⁶.	
	[*They fight.*]	
ROMEO	Draw, Benvolio, beat down their weapons.	
	Gentlemen, for shame forbear⁷ this outrage!	
	Tybalt, Mercutio, the Prince expressly hath	80
	Forbid this bandying⁸ in Verona streets.	
	[*Romeo steps between them.*]	
	Hold, Tybalt! Good Mercutio!	
	[*Tybalt under Romeo's arm thrusts Mercutio in.*]	
	Away Tybalt [*with his followers*]	
MERCUTIO	I am hurt.	
	A plague a'both houses! I am sped⁹.	
	Is he gone and hath nothing¹⁰?	
BENVOLIO	What, art thou hurt?	
MERCUTIO	Ay, ay, a scratch, a scratch, marry, 'tis enough.	85
	Where is my page? Go, villain¹¹, fetch a surgeon.	
	[*Exit Page*]	
ROMEO	Courage, man, the hurt cannot be much.	
MERCUTIO	No, 'tis not so deep as a well, nor so wide as a church-door,	
	but 'tis enough, 'twill serve. Ask for me tomorrow, and you shall	
	find me a grave man. I am peppered¹², I warrant, for this world. A	90
	plague a'both your houses! 'Zounds, a dog, a rat, a mouse, a cat,	
	to scratch a man to death! a braggart, a rogue, a villain, that fights	
	by the book of arithmetic¹³. Why the dev'l came you between us?	
	I was hurt under your arm.	
ROMEO	I thought all for the best.	95
MERCUTIO	Help me into some house, Benvolio,	
	Or I shall faint. A plague a'both your houses!¹⁴	
	They have made worms' meat of me. I have it,	
	And soundly too. Your houses!	
	Exit [*with Benvolio*]	

95

Romeo, blaming himself for Mercutio's wound, and resentful of Tybalt's insults, fears that his love for Juliet has weakened his courage. Learning that Mercutio is dead, he vows to kill Tybalt, slays him, then flees.

 剧情简介：柔密欧因莫丘休受伤而自责，对提巴尔的辱骂怒不可遏，他担心他对茱丽叶的爱已经削弱了自己的勇气。听说莫丘休死了，柔密欧发誓要杀死提巴尔，得手后逃走。

Themes 主题分析

Male pride and honour

Lines 105–6 suggest that Romeo is angry with himself for allowing Juliet's beauty to make him 'effeminate' and to diminish his bravery. Tybalt's slaughter of Mercutio seems to reawaken Romeo's 'manliness'.

a Study all Romeo's lines in the script opposite, then pick out words and phrases that strike you as belonging to a code of male pride and honour. Choose a visual image or symbol to represent the theme. Print or draw it at the centre of a spider diagram (蜘蛛网图), then surround it with quotations and your own explanations of what each word or phrase reveals about Romeo and the world of the young men in the play.

b Tybalt re-enters at line 111, but Shakespeare gives him no words. Write a short aside in Shakespearean style for Tybalt to speak to the audience. How is he feeling? Remember, he has just fatally wounded Mercutio, and Benvolio describes him as 'furious'.

c How important do you think 'manliness' is for young men today? What modern examples of this quality can you think of? How do they compare with the ideals of manliness in the play?

Stagecraft 导演技巧

Staging the fight (in pairs)

In Zeffirelli's film of *Romeo and Juliet*, Romeo pursues Tybalt and kills him in a savage brawl. There is a similarly vicious struggle in Baz Luhrmann's movie. Both versions were intended to show that violence lies just below Verona's glamorous surface appearance.

Should the fight be staged as a dignified, formal fencing match, rather like the illustrations on pages 94 and 221? Or should it be brutal, dirty and painful?

- Talk together about how Tybalt's death (lines 121–2) might be staged and decide on your version. Arrange the movements of the fight, but be very careful. The first rule of all stage-fighting is that no one must be hurt. Try everything out in slow motion first.
- As you run through your final version, think about adding a 'soundscape' (音景) to the actions. What kinds of 'non-language' noises will accompany your actors' movements? What kind of music?

1 **ally** 亲戚
2 **very friend** = true friend
3 **slander** 污蔑
4 **effeminate** 阴柔（无男子气概）
5 **temper** 性格
6 **softened valour's steel** 软化了钢铁的勇猛
7 **aspired** 升至，抵达
8 **untimely** 过早
9 **black fate** 恶果，噩运
10 **on moe days doth depend** 有待来日 (moe = more)
11 **respective lenity** 彬彬有礼的宽宏大量
12 **but … heads** 离开我们头顶仅一小段距离（意思是莫丘休的灵魂刚离开我们升入天堂）
13 **Staying for thine** 等待你的灵魂
14 **doom thee death** 判你死刑
15 **fortune's fool** 命运的玩物

ROMEO	This gentleman, the Prince's near ally[1],	100
	My very friend[2], hath got this mortal hurt	
	In my behalf; my reputation stained	
	With Tybalt's slander[3] – Tybalt, that an hour	
	Hath been my cousin. O sweet Juliet,	
	Thy beauty hath made me effeminate[4],	105
	And in my temper[5] softened valour's steel[6]!	

Enter Benvolio.

BENVOLIO	O Romeo, Romeo, brave Mercutio is dead.	
	That gallant spirit hath aspired[7] the clouds,	
	Which too untimely[8] here did scorn the earth.	
ROMEO	This day's black fate[9] on moe days doth depend[10],	110
	This but begins the woe others must end.	

[Enter Tybalt.]

BENVOLIO	Here comes the furious Tybalt back again.	
ROMEO	Again, in triumph, and Mercutio slain?	
	Away to heaven, respective lenity[11],	
	And fire-eyed fury be my conduct now!	115
	Now, Tybalt, take the 'villain' back again	
	That late thou gavest me, for Mercutio's soul	
	Is but a little way above our heads[12],	
	Staying for thine[13] to keep him company:	
	Either thou or I, or both, must go with him.	120
TYBALT	Thou wretched boy, that didst consort him here,	
	Shalt with him hence.	
ROMEO	This shall determine that.	

They fight; Tybalt falls.

BENVOLIO	Romeo, away, be gone!	
	The citizens are up, and Tybalt slain.	
	Stand not amazed, the Prince will doom thee death[14]	125
	If thou art taken. Hence be gone, away!	
ROMEO	O, I am fortune's fool[15].	
BENVOLIO	Why dost thou stay?	

Exit Romeo

Enter Citizens [as OFFICERS *of the Watch].*

OFFICER	Which way ran he that killed Mercutio?
	Tybalt, that murderer, which way ran he?

Lady Capulet demands that Romeo must die. Her demand for Montague blood reveals the depth of hatred between the two families. Benvolio tells the story of how Mercutio and Tybalt died.

剧情简介：卡普莱夫人要求柔密欧必须偿命。血债要用芒特鸠家的血偿还，她的这一要求彰显了两家的深仇大恨。本沃琉讲述莫丘休和提巴尔是怎么死的。

1 Lady Capulet grieves for Tybalt

Lady Capulet's words suggest extreme emotion as she mourns over Tybalt and calls for Romeo's death. However, she has been absent from the play for some time, and the audience may need to reconnect with this character. How would you increase the dramatic impact of her words and add power to her display of grief?

- In your Director's Journal, write bullet points (项目符号) of advice to an actor playing Lady Capulet on how to deliver her five lines opposite (think about tone, expressions, actions, and so on).

Write about it 写作练习

What happened in the fight?

You are one of the Officers of the Watch – the force of law and order in Verona. The Prince charges you with the task of writing up clearly and objectively an official account of the brawl.

- Use material from the first 127 lines of the scene to construct your formal report of what has happened. Then consider Benvolio as a material witness. Use lines 133–66 as his witness statement.
- Compare your own account of the fight with Benvolio's version. How closely do they match? Produce a final version for the Prince, in which you explain clearly how you have conflated (合并) the two accounts to arrive at the definitive report.

Language in the play 剧中语言

Imagery: a sword by any other name (in small groups)

Benvolio uses metaphors in place of 'swords' and 'sword-fighting': 'piercing steel' (line 150); 'deadly point to point' (line 151); 'Cold death' (line 153); 'fatal points' (line 157); 'envious thrust' (line 159).

a Suggest a few other such images for a sword, then try to come up with one or two reasons why Shakespeare has Benvolio use such metaphors in his account of the brawl.

b Take any everyday object (such as a mobile phone or a pen) and make up similarly vivid metaphors to represent it. (See pp. 214–15 in the 'Language' section for more information.)

1 fray 斗殴
2 discover 讲述
3 manage 过程
4 spoke him fair 对他说话很客气
5 bethink 好好想想
6 nice 微不足道
7 take truce 停战
8 unruly spleen 控制不住的脾气（伊丽莎白时代人们认为怒气生于脾脏 [spleen]）
9 tilts 用剑刺
10 martial 好战
11 dexterity 灵活，敏捷
12 Retorts 反击
13 agile 敏捷
14 'twixt = between
15 envious 狠毒
16 stout 果敢
17 entertained 有了……想法

| BENVOLIO | There lies that Tybalt. |
| OFFICER | Up, sir, go with me; 130
I charge thee in the Prince's name obey. |

Enter PRINCE, *old* MONTAGUE, CAPULET, *their* WIVES, *and all.*

| PRINCE | Where are the vile beginners of this fray[1]? |
| BENVOLIO | O noble Prince, I can discover[2] all
The unlucky manage[3] of this fatal brawl;
There lies the man, slain by young Romeo, 135
That slew thy kinsman, brave Mercutio. |
| LADY CAPULET | Tybalt, my cousin! O my brother's child!
O Prince! O husband! O, the blood is spilled
Of my dear kinsman. Prince, as thou art true,
For blood of ours, shed blood of Montague. 140
O cousin, cousin! |
| PRINCE | Benvolio, who began this bloody fray? |
| BENVOLIO | Tybalt, here slain, whom Romeo's hand did slay.
Romeo, that spoke him fair[4], bid him bethink[5]
How nice[6] the quarrel was, and urged withal 145
Your high displeasure; all this, utterèd
With gentle breath, calm look, knees humbly bowed,
Could not take truce[7] with the unruly spleen[8]
Of Tybalt deaf to peace, but that he tilts[9]
With piercing steel at bold Mercutio's breast, 150
Who, all as hot, turns deadly point to point,
And with a martial[10] scorn, with one hand beats
Cold death aside, and with the other sends
It back to Tybalt, whose dexterity[11]
Retorts[12] it. Romeo he cries aloud, 155
'Hold, friends! friends, part!' and swifter than his tongue,
His agile[13] arm beats down their fatal points,
And 'twixt[14] them rushes; underneath whose arm
An envious[15] thrust from Tybalt hit the life
Of stout[16] Mercutio, and then Tybalt fled; 160
But by and by comes back to Romeo,
Who had but newly entertained[17] revenge,
And to't they go like lightning, for, ere I
Could draw to part them, was stout Tybalt slain; |

Lady Capulet, accusing Benvolio of lying, again demands Romeo's death. But Prince Escales orders that, for killing Tybalt, Romeo will be banished from Verona.

  剧情简介：卡普莱夫人指控本沃琉撒谎，再次要求柔密欧偿命。但是艾斯克勒亲王下令，柔密欧因杀死了提巴尔而将被逐出维罗纳。

1 Ending in rhyme (in pairs)

The scene ends with all the speeches in the script opposite spoken in rhyme.

- Do you think the actors should emphasise the rhymes? Decide by thinking about and then discussing what such emphasis would contribute to the closing dramatic atmosphere of the scene. Try it out!

Write about it 写作练习
Storyboard the action

- Imagine you are going to produce a photo-strip of the action in this scene. Before you begin your photoshoot, plan exactly what images you want to include. Don't be too ambitious: consider about ten frames.
- Draw your storyboard template (模板) and sketch in an outline of your selected shots. Make sure you include notes for each photo that clearly identify what you intend each one to show. Then write a caption for each photo, using your own words and a quotation from the script.
- Have a go at shooting your version, using classmates as the actors.

1	Affection	亲情
2	have an interest	有利害关系
3	hearts' proceeding	冲动的行为（指流血斗殴）
4	My blood	我的血亲（指莫丘休）
5	amerce	惩罚
6	purchase out	买光；救赎
7	Mercy ... kill	赦免杀人者，仅是对谋杀的慈悲

▼ The death of Tybalt. Choose a line from Act 3 Scene 1 as a suitable caption for this image.

                        And as he fell, did Romeo turn and fly.   165
                        This is the truth, or let Benvolio die.
LADY CAPULET   He is a kinsman to the Montague,
                        Affection[1] makes him false, he speaks not true:
                        Some twenty of them fought in this black strife,
                        And all those twenty could but kill one life.   170
                        I beg for justice, which thou, Prince, must give:
                        Romeo slew Tybalt, Romeo must not live.
PRINCE   Romeo slew him, he slew Mercutio;
                        Who now the price of his dear blood doth owe?
MONTAGUE   Not Romeo, Prince, he was Mercutio's friend;   175
                        His fault concludes but what the law should end,
                        The life of Tybalt.
PRINCE   And for that offence
                        Immediately we do exile him hence.
                        I have an interest[2] in your hearts' proceeding[3]:
                        My blood[4] for your rude brawls doth lie a-bleeding; 180
                        But I'll amerce[5] you with so strong a fine
                        That you shall all repent the loss of mine.
                        I will be deaf to pleading and excuses,
                        Nor tears nor prayers shall purchase out[6] abuses:
                        Therefore use none. Let Romeo hence in haste,   185
                        Else, when he is found, that hour is his last.
                        Bear hence this body, and attend our will:
                        Mercy but murders, pardoning those that kill[7].

                                                                                    Exeunt

Juliet, unaware of the murderous events of the day, and filled with love for Romeo, longs for the night to come. She thinks of Romeo, after her death, as like a star in the night sky.

 剧情简介：茱丽叶对当天的杀人事件一无所知，心里充满对柔密欧的爱，盼望着夜晚的到来。她想象柔密欧在她死后会变作夜空中的一颗星。

1 Juliet longs for the night (in small groups)

Juliet passionately reveals the depth of her longing for Romeo. Critics call her thirty-one lines an *epithalamium* (新婚颂歌) or wedding song. Use the following activities to help you experience and understand her feelings.

a **An insight into Juliet's mind** Sit closely together. One person quietly reads the speech. On the first read-through, the others echo aloud all words that seem to be commands. On the second, echo words concerned with speed or haste (e.g. 'Gallop', 'fiery-footed', 'whip', and so on). On the final read-through, echo all words connected with night or darkness. Afterwards, talk together about how the patterns created by such words convey what Juliet is thinking and feeling.

b **Trouble ahead?** Although Juliet is incredibly happy as she awaits her wedding night, her soliloquy contains at least three references to death: the image of the youthful, headstrong (任性) Phaëton; her own death; and her imagining of Romeo's body in the heavens. Find these quotations in the script opposite, write them down and explain what they add to the overall mood of Juliet's soliloquy.

c **Embarrassing?** Juliet is only thirteen but some lines of her speech are quite sexual. In previous centuries, some productions even cut these lines. Identify the words and phrases you think might prove challenging for an actor playing Juliet. As director, write advice for her.

1 **Gallop … steeds** 飞驰吧，你们这些四蹄燃着火焰的骏马
2 **Phoebus' lodging** 福玻斯的住所（即西方，因太阳在西方落下。在希腊神话中，太阳神是赫利俄斯[Helios]，又称福玻斯，后来与另一位名叫阿波罗[Apollo]的神混淆）
3 **Phaëton** 法厄同（英文现一般写作Phaethon，福玻斯之子，有一次他架着父亲的太阳战车在天上驰骋，结果难以驾驭，被宙斯用雷电劈死）
4 **close** 密闭
5 **That runaways' eyes may wink** 可以让路上行人的眼睛闭上
6 **amorous rites** 男欢女爱之礼
7 **civil** 文雅
8 **learn** = teach
9 **stainless maidenhoods** 纯洁无瑕的少男少女
10 **Hood … cheeks** 给我未碰过男人、在面颊里扑腾的热血套上罩（hood和bating是驯鹰术语，参见第60页）
11 **strange love grow bold** 羞涩的爱情变得大胆
12 **modesty** 贞洁
13 **garish** 耀眼，夺目

Stagecraft 导演技巧

The setting for Juliet's speech

Most productions set this speech in the intimacy of Juliet's bedroom, but the picture here shows a different idea.

- What do you think the director had in mind in this production? What ideas do you have for different settings?

Act 3 Scene 2
Juliet's room in Capulet's mansion

Enter JULIET *alone.*

JULIET Gallop apace, you fiery-footed steeds[1],
Towards Phoebus' lodging[2]; such a waggoner
As Phaëton[3] would whip you to the west,
And bring in cloudy night immediately.
Spread thy close[4] curtain, love-performing Night,   5
That runaways' eyes may wink[5], and Romeo
Leap to these arms, untalked of and unseen:
Lovers can see to do their amorous rites[6]
By their own beauties, or if love be blind,
It best agrees with night. Come, civil[7] Night,   10
Thou sober-suited matron all in black,
And learn[8] me how to lose a winning match,
Played for a pair of stainless maidenhoods[9].
Hood my unmanned blood, bating in my cheeks[10],
With thy black mantle, till strange love grow bold[11],   15
Think true love acted simple modesty[12].
Come, Night, come, Romeo, come, thou day in night,
For thou wilt lie upon the wings of night,
Whiter than new snow upon a raven's back.
Come, gentle Night, come, loving, black-browed Night,   20
Give me my Romeo, and when I shall die,
Take him and cut him out in little stars,
And he will make the face of heaven so fine
That all the world will be in love with night,
And pay no worship to the garish[13] sun.   25
O, I have bought the mansion of a love,
But not possessed it, and though I am sold,
Not yet enjoyed. So tedious is this day
As is the night before some festival
To an impatient child that hath new robes   30
And may not wear them. O, here comes my Nurse,

Juliet, alarmed by the Nurse's mourning for Tybalt's death, thinks that Romeo has died. She wishes that she too could die, and lie beside Romeo in death.

 剧情简介：茱丽叶看到奶妈哀悼提巴尔的死，心慌意乱，以为柔密欧死了。她但愿自己也可以死，躺在柔密欧身边。

Language in the play 剧中语言
'I', 'ay' and 'eyes' (in pairs)

Elizabethans not only enjoyed joking puns (of which Mercutio was a master), but also appreciated them in tragic situations. In lines 45–52, Juliet and the Nurse repeatedly use one vowel sound: 'I'. However, this repetitive wordplay can appear forced and contrived to a modern audience at such a serious moment in the play.

- Read the lines aloud to each other, in any manner you think appropriate. Then talk about the challenges of creating just the right mood in performance. Listen to other pairs and find out whether they identified the same challenges.

Themes 主题分析
Death

In line 59, Juliet wishes that her body ('Vile earth') should be buried ('to earth resign'), ending her life ('end motion here'). Between lines 36 and 60, Shakespeare repeatedly uses words that stress the theme of death and suffering in the play.

a Catch the mood of this part of the scene by looking through the lines and picking out just one word from each line that emphasises death or disaster. How many lines lack such words?

b Write down your chosen words, then compare your choices with those of other students. Talk together about how these words add to the atmosphere of this passage.

1 Ask the Nurse … and Juliet (in pairs)

It is only at line 69 that the Nurse lets Juliet know that she has been talking about Tybalt's death, not Romeo's. Why does the Nurse mislead Juliet for so long?

- One of you plays the Nurse, in the hot-seat. The other person asks her about her actions here.
- Afterwards, change roles and put Juliet in the hot-seat. How does she feel about what the Nurse has just put her through? Is she angry or just relieved to discover that Romeo is unharmed?

1 heavenly eloquence 天籁之音
2 cords 绳索（这里指软梯）
3 weraday = welladay（哎；哀叹语）
4 dismal 凄凉，阴森
5 cockatrice 鸡蛇怪（中世纪传说中的鸡头蛇身怪，人被它看一眼即可丧命）
6 weal or woe 是福是祸
7 God save the mark! = God have mercy!
8 corse = corpse（尸体；奶妈特色语言）
9 bedaubed 涂抹，弄污
10 gore blood 淤血，凝血
11 sounded = swounded = swoon（晕过去）
12 bankrout = bankrupt（指茱丽叶对柔密欧"爱的投资"输了个精光）
13 Vile earth 卑贱的泥土（指茱丽叶自己的身体）
14 press one heavy bier 睡在同一个沉重的棺材里
15 so contrary 朝着如此相反的方向

Enter NURSE, *with [the ladder of] cords [in her lap].*

And she brings news, and every tongue that speaks
But Romeo's name speaks heavenly eloquence[1].
Now, Nurse, what news? What hast thou there? the cords[2]
That Romeo bid thee fetch?

NURSE	Ay, ay, the cords.	35

[Throws them down.]

JULIET Ay me, what news? Why dost thou wring thy hands?

NURSE Ah weraday[3], he's dead, he's dead, he's dead!
We are undone, lady, we are undone.
Alack the day, he's gone, he's killed, he's dead!

JULIET Can heaven be so envious?

NURSE   Romeo can, 40
Though heaven cannot. O Romeo, Romeo!
Who ever would have thought it? Romeo!

JULIET What devil art thou that dost torment me thus?
This torture should be roared in dismal[4] hell.
Hath Romeo slain himself? Say thou but 'ay', 45
And that bare vowel 'I' shall poison more
Than the death-darting eye of cockatrice[5].
I am not I, if there be such an 'ay',
Or those eyes shut, that makes thee answer 'ay'.
If he be slain, say 'ay', or if not, 'no': 50
Brief sounds determine my weal or woe[6].

NURSE I saw the wound, I saw it with mine eyes
(God save the mark![7]), here on his manly breast:
A piteous corse[8], a bloody piteous corse,
Pale, pale as ashes, all bedaubed[9] in blood, 55
All in gore blood[10]; I sounded[11] at the sight.

JULIET O break, my heart, poor bankrout[12], break at once!
To prison, eyes, ne'er look on liberty!
Vile earth[13], to earth resign, end motion here,
And thou and Romeo press one heavy bier[14]! 60

NURSE O Tybalt, Tybalt, the best friend I had!
O courteous Tybalt, honest gentleman,
That ever I should live to see thee dead!

JULIET What storm is this that blows so contrary[15]?
Is Romeo slaughtered? and is Tybalt dead? 65
My dearest cousin, and my dearer lord?

Juliet learns that Tybalt is dead and Romeo banished. She begins to accuse Romeo of seeming beautiful but acting vilely, but then rebukes the Nurse for wishing shame on Romeo.

剧情简介：茱丽叶得知提巴尔死了而且柔密欧被流放，开始指控柔密欧外表美丽而行为险恶，但是接着责怪奶妈说什么但愿柔密欧知耻。

Language in the play 剧中语言
Appearance and reality (in small groups)

The theme of appearance versus reality is important in all Shakespeare's plays. Hearing that Romeo has killed Tybalt, Juliet uses oxymorons to lament that a beautiful appearance can hide an evil reality ('beautiful tyrant', 'damnèd saint', and so on). Romeo also uses oxymorons (see p. 14). The characters use antitheses to similar effect ('O serpent heart, hid with a flow'ring face!', line 73).

a How many oxymorons and antitheses can you count in lines 73–85? Add them to the 'Antithesis' section of your Language file.

b Choose one antithesis or oxymoron and prepare a tableau involving every member of the group. Each group shows its tableau. The other groups guess which oxymorons or antitheses are being portrayed. Afterwards, display all the examples you have used imaginatively on a whole-class poster.

1 the general doom 最后审判日，世界末日（这一天到来会奏响最后的号角）
2 keep 居住于；守卫
3 fiend angelical 天使般的魔鬼
4 Despisèd substance of divinest show! 最神圣的外表下的卑鄙内容！
5 justly 恰恰
6 bower 容纳
7 perjured 说谎
8 forsworn 不守誓言
9 naught 邪恶
10 dissemblers 伪君子，假善人
11 aqua-vitae 生命之水（拉丁文，指酒）
12 chide at 责怪
13 mangled 损毁，践踏
14 tributary drops 悼念的泪珠

1 What does the Nurse think about men? (in pairs)

- Identify the seven things the Nurse says about men in lines 85–7. What do they have in common?
- Talk together about possible reasons why Shakespeare gives her such a list at this point in the play. Is it because of what she has experienced in Verona? Don't be afraid to speculate about her reasons. You'll find it helpful to talk about each characteristic in turn ('no trust', 'No faith', and so on).

▶ What effect do the revelations in this scene have on Juliet?

	Then, dreadful trumpet, sound the general doom[1],
	For who is living, if those two are gone?
NURSE	Tybalt is gone and Romeo banishèd,
	Romeo that killed him, he is banishèd.
JULIET	O God, did Romeo's hand shed Tybalt's blood?
NURSE	It did, it did, alas the day, it did!
JULIET	O serpent heart, hid with a flow'ring face!
	Did ever dragon keep[2] so fair a cave?
	Beautiful tyrant, fiend angelical[3]!
	Dove-feathered raven, wolvish-ravening lamb!
	Despisèd substance of divinest show![4]
	Just opposite to what thou justly[5] seem'st,
	A damnèd saint, an honourable villain!
	O nature, what hadst thou to do in hell
	When thou didst bower[6] the spirit of a fiend
	In mortal paradise of such sweet flesh?
	Was ever book containing such vile matter
	So fairly bound? O that deceit should dwell
	In such a gorgeous palace!
NURSE	There's no trust,
	No faith, no honesty in men, all perjured[7],
	All forsworn[8], all naught[9], all dissemblers[10].
	Ah, where's my man? Give me some aqua-vitae[11];
	These griefs, these woes, these sorrows make me old.
	Shame come to Romeo!
JULIET	Blistered be thy tongue
	For such a wish! he was not born to shame:
	Upon his brow shame is ashamed to sit;
	For 'tis a throne where honour may be crowned
	Sole monarch of the universal earth.
	O what a beast was I to chide at[12] him!
NURSE	Will you speak well of him that killed your cousin?
JULIET	Shall I speak ill of him that is my husband?
	Ah, poor my lord, what tongue shall smooth thy name,
	When I, thy three-hours wife, have mangled[13] it?
	But wherefore, villain, didst thou kill my cousin?
	That villain cousin would have killed my husband.
	Back, foolish tears, back to your native spring,
	Your tributary drops[14] belong to woe,
	Which you mistaking offer up to joy.

Juliet is devastated by the thought of Romeo's banishment. She threatens to kill herself. But she is cheered by the Nurse's promise to find Romeo and send him to her bedchamber that night.

 剧情简介：一想到柔密欧要被流放，茱丽叶悲痛欲绝。她威胁要寻短见，但是奶妈答应帮她去找柔密欧，叫他当晚来她的卧房，她于是高兴起来。

1 Juliet's emotional rollercoaster (in pairs)

Throughout this scene, Juliet's feelings fluctuate (上下波动) rapidly.

- Consider the whole scene. Together, draw a mood graph similar to the one pictured below. First, establish what you think is Juliet's 'normal' emotional state. Then split the scene into key 'episodes' and allocate each one a number (+10 for extreme happiness; -10 for deep distress).
- Plot the episodes on the graph. Tag each point on the graph to a key quotation. What do you notice when you connect up all the points?
- Pin the final version to the wall for others to look at. In what ways are the graphs similar or different?

1	fellowship 陪伴（祸不单行）
2	needly 必然，必定
3	modern lamentation 习以为常的悲痛
4	rear-ward 最后一个词
5	that word's death 那个词（指 **banishèd**）的杀伤力
6	sound 准确表达
7	beguiled 被骗，上当
8	wot 知道

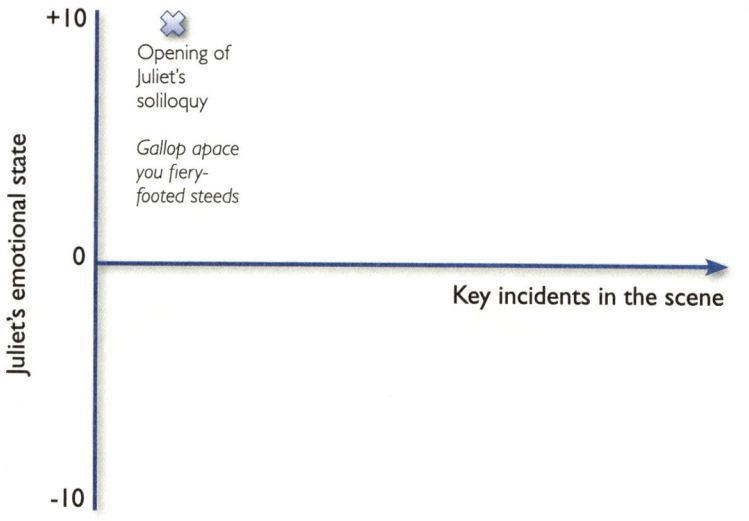

Language in the play 剧中语言

Juliet's powerful language (in pairs)

Look through Juliet's words between line 97 and the end of the scene. She is absolutely devastated by the thought of Romeo's banishment, and her language reflects her mood.

- With a partner, note down the words and phrases that most powerfully express her feelings. For example, not for the first time, we hear Juliet *repeating* language that is very important to her. The word 'banishèd' is repeated five times. And in her final couplet, Juliet uses the language of chivalry ('my true knight'). Add your choices to these two examples, then explore some of the reasons why you think Juliet's language is so powerful and dramatic. Join up with other pairs to explain your thinking.

	My husband lives that Tybalt would have slain,	105
	And Tybalt's dead that would have slain my husband:	
	All this is comfort, wherefore weep I then?	
	Some word there was, worser than Tybalt's death,	
	That murdered me; I would forget it fain,	
	But O, it presses to my memory,	110
	Like damnèd guilty deeds to sinners' minds:	
	'Tybalt is dead, and Romeo banishèd.'	
	That 'banishèd', that one word 'banishèd',	
	Hath slain ten thousand Tybalts. Tybalt's death	
	Was woe enough if it had ended there;	115
	Or if sour woe delights in fellowship¹,	
	And needly² will be ranked with other griefs,	
	Why followed not, when she said 'Tybalt's dead',	
	'Thy father' or 'thy mother', nay, or both,	
	Which modern lamentation³ might have moved?	120
	But with a rear-ward⁴ following Tybalt's death,	
	'Romeo is banishèd': to speak that word,	
	Is father, mother, Tybalt, Romeo, Juliet,	
	All slain, all dead. 'Romeo is banishèd!'	
	There is no end, no limit, measure, bound,	125
	In that word's death⁵, no words can that woe sound⁶.	
	Where is my father and my mother, Nurse?	
NURSE	Weeping and wailing over Tybalt's corse.	
	Will you go to them? I will bring you thither.	
JULIET	Wash they his wounds with tears? mine shall be spent,	130
	When theirs are dry, for Romeo's banishment.	
	Take up those cords. Poor ropes, you are beguiled⁷,	
	Both you and I, for Romeo is exiled.	
	He made you for a highway to my bed,	
	But I, a maid, die maiden-widowèd.	135
	Come, cords, come, Nurse, I'll to my wedding bed,	
	And death, not Romeo, take my maidenhead!	
NURSE	Hie to your chamber. I'll find Romeo	
	To comfort you, I wot⁸ well where he is.	
	Hark ye, your Romeo will be here at night.	140
	I'll to him, he is hid at Lawrence' cell.	
JULIET	O find him! Give this ring to my true knight,	
	And bid him come to take his last farewell.	

Exeunt

Friar Lawrence tells Romeo of the Prince's sentence: he is to be banished. The news appals Romeo. Life, for him, exists only in Verona with Juliet. Exile is the same as death.

  剧情简介：劳润修士向柔密欧转告了亲王放逐他的判决。这消息令柔密欧惊愕不已。对于他来讲，离开了维罗纳和茱丽叶，生活将毫无意义；流放意味着死亡。

Stagecraft 导演技巧

Romeo enters (in pairs)

Romeo is in hiding, having fled after killing Tybalt. One production showed him cowering under a table. The audience laughed as Friar Lawrence dragged him out.

a   Do you think that was an appropriate 'entrance' for Romeo? One of you argues that it is; the other argues against that view. Which argument is the more convincing?

b   Work together to decide how you would stage Romeo's entrance in order to reflect your understanding of his state of mind at this point in the play.

1   fearful   担惊受怕
2   Affliction   苦难，苦恼
3   enamoured of thy parts   眷恋你的方方面面
4   doom   判决
5   craves acquaintance at my hand   与我结交
6   sour company   悲哀
7   tidings   音信，消息
8   vanished   说出
9   without = outside
10 purgatory   炼狱
11 mistermed   误称

1 Romeo and the Friar

Read quickly through this scene to establish the way that Romeo and the Friar speak to and behave with each other. Then study the picture below and describe the kind of relationship depicted between the two men. How far do you think it is backed up by the text? Write thought bubbles for each character that fit the moment shown here.

Act 3 Scene 3
Friar Lawrence's cell

Enter FRIAR LAWRENCE.

FRIAR LAWRENCE Romeo, come forth, come forth, thou fearful[1] man:
Affliction[2] is enamoured of thy parts[3],
And thou art wedded to calamity.

[*Enter*] ROMEO.

ROMEO Father, what news? What is the Prince's doom[4]?
What sorrow craves acquaintance at my hand[5], 5
That I yet know not?

FRIAR LAWRENCE   Too familiar
Is my dear son with such sour company[6]!
I bring thee tidings[7] of the Prince's doom.

ROMEO What less than doomsday is the Prince's doom?

FRIAR LAWRENCE A gentler judgement vanished[8] from his lips: 10
Not body's death, but body's banishment.

ROMEO Ha, banishment? be merciful, say 'death':
For exile hath more terror in his look,
Much more than death. Do not say 'banishment'!

FRIAR LAWRENCE Here from Verona art thou banishèd. 15
Be patient, for the world is broad and wide.

ROMEO There is no world without[9] Verona walls,
But purgatory[10], torture, hell itself:
Hence 'banishèd' is banished from the world,
And world's exile is death; then 'banishèd' 20
Is death mistermed[11]. Calling death 'banishèd',
Thou cut'st my head off with a golden axe,
And smilest upon the stroke that murders me.

Friar Lawrence condemns Romeo's ingratitude, and claims that the Prince is merciful. Romeo, distraught because banishment will mean he can no longer be with Juliet, refuses to be comforted.

 剧情简介：劳润修士批评柔密欧不感恩戴德，称亲王很宽容。柔密欧感到心烦意乱，因为放逐意味着不能跟茱丽叶厮守，他无法平静。

Language in the play 剧中语言
Audiences – then and now

Once again, Shakespeare has written lines that his Elizabethan audiences enjoyed, but that modern audiences are likely to find strange or artificial. When Romeo talks of 'every cat and dog / And little mouse' being able to look on Juliet (lines 30–1), and flies being able to kiss her (lines 35–7), his words can sound bizarre today. But Elizabethans relished the comparisons and liked the punning ('Flies may do this, but I from this must fly'). Perhaps Shakespeare wrote the lines to highlight Romeo's immaturity. Or he may have written them to emphasise the depth of Romeo's grief, in which even the smallest, most trivial things are hugely important.

a What do you think of these ideas? Write down your reactions to them.

b The speech presents a challenge to the actor. So help Romeo by writing your advice on how he might speak lines 29–51 in your Director's Journal.

1 Thy … death   你的罪过依照我们的法律要判死罪
2 rushed aside the law   法外开恩
3 validity   价值，实惠
4 courtship   殷勤，求爱
5 carrion flies   食腐肉的苍蝇
6 vestal   处女的
7 Still … sin   想到自己的吻，总是泛起红潮
8 sudden mean of death   快速致死的手段
9 mean   卑劣
10 divine   神职人员
11 sin-absolver   宽恕罪孽的人
12 Displant   迁移
13 prevails   获胜，成功

1 Is action better than thought? (in small groups)

'Adversity's sweet milk, philosophy'. Friar Lawrence argues that philosophy (thinking, reasoning) will comfort someone in adversity (beset by problems). Romeo angrily dismisses that advice ('Hang up philosophy!') because thinking without action is no help.

• Do you favour the Friar's argument or Romeo's? Take sides and argue your case. Use Romeo's situation, or examples from your own experience.

2 Is banishment better than death? (in small groups)

Friar Lawrence tells Romeo that he should be thankful that the 'kind Prince' has ignored the law of Verona, shown mercy and commuted (减刑) the death sentence that he should have imposed on Romeo to banishment. But Romeo disagrees.

• Try a group reading of Romeo's lines 29–51, in which he speaks about the 'torture' of banishment. After a careful consideration of his arguments, discuss whether you think he is right to believe that banishment is far worse than death.

112

FRIAR LAWRENCE	O deadly sin! O rude unthankfulness!	
	Thy fault our law calls death[1], but the kind Prince,	25
	Taking thy part, hath rushed aside the law[2],	
	And turned that black word 'death' to 'banishment'.	
	This is dear mercy, and thou seest it not.	
ROMEO	'Tis torture, and not mercy. Heaven is here	
	Where Juliet lives, and every cat and dog	30
	And little mouse, every unworthy thing,	
	Live here in heaven, and may look on her,	
	But Romeo may not. More validity[3],	
	More honourable state, more courtship[4] lives	
	In carrion flies[5] than Romeo; they may seize	35
	On the white wonder of dear Juliet's hand,	
	And steal immortal blessing from her lips,	
	Who even in pure and vestal[6] modesty	
	Still blush, as thinking their own kisses sin[7];	
	But Romeo may not, he is banishèd.	40
	Flies may do this, but I from this must fly;	
	They are free men, but I am banishèd:	
	And sayest thou yet that exile is not death?	
	Hadst thou no poison mixed, no sharp-ground knife,	
	No sudden mean of death[8], though ne'er so mean[9],	45
	But 'banishèd' to kill me? 'Banishèd'?	
	O Friar, the damnèd use that word in hell;	
	Howling attends it. How hast thou the heart,	
	Being a divine[10], a ghostly confessor,	
	A sin-absolver[11], and my friend professed,	50
	To mangle me with that word 'banishèd'?	
FRIAR LAWRENCE	Thou fond mad man, hear me a little speak.	
ROMEO	O thou wilt speak again of banishment.	
FRIAR LAWRENCE	I'll give thee armour to keep off that word:	
	Adversity's sweet milk, philosophy,	55
	To comfort thee though thou art banishèd.	
ROMEO	Yet 'banishèd'? Hang up philosophy!	
	Unless philosophy can make a Juliet,	
	Displant[12] a town, reverse a prince's doom,	
	It helps not, it prevails[13] not; talk no more.	60
FRIAR LAWRENCE	O then I see that mad men have no ears.	
ROMEO	How should they when that wise men have no eyes?	

Romeo, bewailing all that's happened, falls weeping to the ground and ignores the Friar's pleas to stand up. The Nurse arrives and also begs him to stand.

 剧情简介：发生的一切让柔密欧忍不住悲伤，倒地放声痛哭，劳润修士劝他站起来，他置之不理。这时候奶妈来了，也求他站起来。

1 Can the Friar understand? (in fours)

Romeo accuses the Friar (who has taken a vow never to have a relationship with a woman) of not being able to understand how a young person in love feels: 'Thou canst not speak of that thou dost not feel' (line 64).

- Does Romeo have a point? Can a celibate (独身禁欲) priest (or person) ever really understand what it's like to love another human being? Take sides and present your arguments for and against.

2 Action-packed language (in pairs)

Friar Lawrence's lines 74–80 show his agitation (焦虑不安) as he responds to the repeated knocking.

- In pairs, one person reads the Friar's lines. The other accompanies them with gestures and actions. Change roles and repeat the exercise. How can you fill these seven lines with tension and uncertainty?

1. dispute 分析；讨论
2. estate 处境
3. Taking ... grave 为自己丈量尚未挖掘的坟墓
4. infold 遮蔽
5. taken 被捕
6. errand 差事
7. case 情形（后面的case指带有性暗示的"盒包"）
8. predicament 困境
9. Blubb'ring = Blubbering （又哭又闹）
10. so deep an O 如此痛苦（O 也有性暗示）

Language in the play 剧中语言

Is the Nurse being sexual? (in pairs)

Some people feel uncomfortable because, even at this serious moment, the Nurse uses words with sexual double meanings ('case', 'stand', 'rise', 'O').

- In pairs, discuss whether you think the Nurse is aware of the double meanings of her words. Give a reason for your answer.

Characters 人物分析

Do you feel sorry for Romeo? (in small groups)

a Read Romeo's lines 64–70 quietly around your group several times. Write down a list of the things that Romeo says have happened to him.

b Romeo reaches breaking point and falls to the floor. Talk in your group about whether you think he is being immature and melodramatic (过于夸张), or whether he deserves genuine sympathy and understanding.

c After reading through the rest of the scene, return to this question. What does he go on to do and say that might affect your judgement about his behaviour?

FRIAR LAWRENCE	Let me dispute¹ with thee of thy estate².
ROMEO	Thou canst not speak of that thou dost not feel.
	Wert thou as young as I, Juliet thy love,	65
	An hour but married, Tybalt murderèd,
	Doting like me, and like me banishèd,
	Then mightst thou speak, then mightst thou tear thy hair,
	And fall upon the ground as I do now,
	Taking the measure of an unmade grave³.	70

Enter Nurse [within] and knock.

FRIAR LAWRENCE	Arise, one knocks. Good Romeo, hide thyself.
ROMEO	Not I, unless the breath of heart-sick groans
	Mist-like infold⁴ me from the search of eyes.

Knock.

| FRIAR LAWRENCE | Hark how they knock! – Who's there? – Romeo, arise, |
| | Thou wilt be taken⁵. – Stay a while! – Stand up; | 75 |

Loud knock.

| | Run to my study. – By and by! – God's will, |
| | What simpleness is this? – I come, I come! |

Knock.

	Who knocks so hard? whence come you? what's your will?
NURSE	[*Within*] Let me come in, and you shall know my errand⁶:
	I come from Lady Juliet.
FRIAR LAWRENCE	Welcome then. [*Unlocks the door.*]	80

Enter NURSE.

NURSE	O holy Friar, O tell me, holy Friar,
	Where's my lady's lord? where's Romeo?
FRIAR LAWRENCE	There on the ground, with his own tears made drunk.
NURSE	O he is even in my mistress' case⁷,
	Just in her case. O woeful sympathy!	85
	Piteous predicament⁸! even so lies she,
	Blubb'ring⁹ and weeping, weeping and blubb'ring.
	Stand up, stand up, stand, and you be a man;
	For Juliet's sake, for her sake, rise and stand;
	Why should you fall into so deep an O¹⁰?	90

On hearing the Nurse tell of Juliet's sorrow, Romeo tries to stab himself. The Nurse seizes his dagger and Friar Lawrence rebukes him for his suicide attempt.

 剧情简介：柔密欧听奶妈说茱丽叶悲伤落泪，就想拔剑自尽。奶妈赶紧夺下他的短剑，劳润修士也斥责他企图自杀没出息。

1 More problems with a 'name' (in pairs)

Hearing of Juliet's sorrow, Romeo angrily condemns his own name and threatens to cut it from his body. His lines 102–8 echo those of Juliet in Act 2 Scene 2, lines 38–49.

- Turn back to that earlier speech and explore the relationship between these two sets of lines on 'names'. You could, for example, work on a dramatic presentation of the two speeches by 'intercutting' (interweaving) words and phrases from each one in order to highlight key similarities and differences.

Stagecraft 导演技巧

Who snatches the dagger? (in threes)

Some people believe that Shakespeare did not include the stage direction at line 108, but that the actor playing the Nurse added it. Would it make any difference if the Friar, rather than the Nurse, snatched the dagger from Romeo? For example, does being disarmed by a woman increase Romeo's sense of self-loathing (自我厌恶)?

- Decide how you would stage the 'snatch', then join up with two other students to have a go at acting it out.

Write about it 写作练习

The Friar tells Romeo off (in pairs)

a Sharing the lines between you, speak the Friar's lines 108–34. They are a long condemnation of Romeo's attempt at suicide. Afterwards, select and write down only one or two words from each line – words you think will have most effect on Romeo. For each of your chosen words, explain why you think they will have a real impact on the young man.

b The Friar says that Romeo shames his good looks ('shape'), his declarations of love ('love') and his intelligence ('wit'). He's like a stingy money-lender ('usurer') because, although he possesses those excellent qualities in abundance, he doesn't use them properly. Read what the Friar says about each quality (lines 126–34), and then describe them in your own words.

1	old murderer	杀人惯犯
2	With … own	用距离她自己血亲不远的血
3	concealed lady	隐秘的妻子（concealed这里重读第一个音节con，与后文的cancelled [无效] 谐音）
4	level of a gun	枪口（level的本义是"端枪瞄准"）
5	anatomy	身体（与后文的mansion同义）
6	sack	摧毁；攻破
7	form	外形
8	ill-beseeming	不男不女
9	tempered	历练
10	rail'st	抱怨
11	usurer	高利贷者
12	bedeck	装扮
13	shape	形体（上帝依自己的形体所造）
14	form of wax	蜡像（易熔化）
15	Digressing	偏离
16	valour	英勇

ROMEO   Nurse! [*He rises.*]
NURSE   Ah, sir, ah, sir, death's the end of all.
ROMEO   Spakest thou of Juliet? how is it with her?
                     Doth not she think me an old murderer[1],
                     Now I have stained the childhood of our joy   95
                     With blood removed but little from her own[2]?
                     Where is she? and how doth she? and what says
                     My concealed lady[3] to our cancelled love?
NURSE   O she says nothing, sir, but weeps and weeps,
                     And now falls on her bed, and then starts up,   100
                     And Tybalt calls, and then on Romeo cries,
                     And then down falls again.
ROMEO   As if that name,
                     Shot from the deadly level of a gun[4],
                     Did murder her, as that name's cursèd hand
                     Murdered her kinsman. O tell me, Friar, tell me,   105
                     In what vile part of this anatomy[5]
                     Doth my name lodge? Tell me, that I may sack[6]
                     The hateful mansion.
                     [*He offers to stab himself, and Nurse snatches the dagger away.*]
FRIAR LAWRENCE   Hold thy desperate hand!
                     Art thou a man? thy form[7] cries out thou art;
                     Thy tears are womanish, thy wild acts denote   110
                     The unreasonable fury of a beast.
                     Unseemly woman in a seeming man,
                     And ill-beseeming[8] beast in seeming both,
                     Thou hast amazed me. By my holy order,
                     I thought thy disposition better tempered[9].   115
                     Hast thou slain Tybalt? wilt thou slay thyself,
                     And slay thy lady that in thy life lives,
                     By doing damnèd hate upon thyself?
                     Why rail'st[10] thou on thy birth? the heaven and earth?
                     Since birth, and heaven, and earth, all three do meet   120
                     In thee at once, which thou at once wouldst lose.
                     Fie, fie, thou sham'st thy shape, thy love, thy wit,
                     Which like a usurer[11] abound'st in all,
                     And usest none in that true use indeed
                     Which should bedeck[12] thy shape[13], thy love, thy wit: 125
                     Thy noble shape is but a form of wax[14],
                     Digressing[15] from the valour[16] of a man;

Friar Lawrence rebukes Romeo for his lack of love and intelligence. He reminds Romeo of his good fortune and plans how he can eventually be recalled from exile.

剧情简介：劳润修士责备柔密欧爱情与脑子都欠缺，提醒柔密欧有好运眷顾他，跟他策划如何最终可以免遭放逐。

1 The Friar's long speech (in small groups)

The Friar's long speech (lines 108–58) has three sections. He first tells Romeo off, then tries to cheer him up, then sets out a plan of action. The following activities will help your understanding of the speech.

a One person reads the Friar's lines aloud, pausing frequently. In each pause, everyone else mimes appropriate expressions and movements for what they have heard. Freeze occasionally for everyone to compare each other's actions. (You will find it fascinating to see the different ways of representing the same line or image.)

b The condemnation (lines 108–34). Take turns to speak this section, using a critical tone of voice.

c Cheering up Romeo (lines 135–45). Speak the section in a good-humoured, positive tone. Emphasise the repetitions of 'there art thou happy'. (But notice the section ends with three lines of criticism.)

d The Friar's plan (lines 146–58). One person slowly speaks the lines; the others act out what the Friar advises. Try to show every action he describes. Might the Friar hesitate as he thinks up different parts of his plan?

1 perjury　打破誓言
2 flask　火药桶（劳润把柔密欧比作笨手笨脚自戕的士兵）
3 dismembered　被肢解
4 wast but lately dead　刚刚试图自杀
5 happy　幸运
6 courts　献殷勤
7 array　衣服
8 mishavèd　举止乖张
9 sullen　阴沉，愤懑
10 pouts　噘嘴，闷闷不乐
11 Take heed　注意，当心
12 decreed　约定，同意
13 Watch be set　布置了巡夜
　　（参见第182页对 **Watch** 的解释）
14 blaze　宣布
15 reconcile　使和解
16 apt unto　容易……

Write about it 写作练习

Explaining the Friar's complicated plan

In lines 146–58, the Friar suggests an ambitious plan to help Romeo.

- Write a version of the Friar's ideas that a group of younger students studying Shakespeare could easily understand. Use pictures or drawings to help illustrate key points if it helps. Try to keep as much detail as possible from the original speech.

Thy dear love sworn but hollow perjury[1],
Killing that love which thou hast vowed to cherish;
Thy wit, that ornament to shape and love, 130
Misshapen in the conduct of them both,
Like powder in a skilless soldier's flask[2],
Is set afire by thine own ignorance,
And thou dismembered[3] with thine own defence.
What, rouse thee, man! thy Juliet is alive, 135
For whose dear sake thou wast but lately dead[4]:
There art thou happy[5]. Tybalt would kill thee,
But thou slewest Tybalt: there art thou happy.
The law that threatened death becomes thy friend,
And turns it to exile: there art thou happy. 140
A pack of blessings light upon thy back,
Happiness courts[6] thee in her best array[7],
But like a mishavèd[8] and sullen[9] wench,
Thou pouts[10] upon thy fortune and thy love:
Take heed[11], take heed, for such die miserable. 145
Go get thee to thy love as was decreed[12],
Ascend her chamber, hence and comfort her;
But look thou stay not till the Watch be set[13],
For then thou canst not pass to Mantua,
Where thou shalt live till we can find a time 150
To blaze[14] your marriage, reconcile[15] your friends,
Beg pardon of the Prince, and call thee back
With twenty hundred thousand times more joy
Than thou went'st forth in lamentation.
Go before, Nurse, commend me to thy lady, 155
And bid her hasten all the house to bed,
Which heavy sorrow makes them apt unto[16].
Romeo is coming.

NURSE O Lord, I could have stayed here all the night
To hear good counsel. O, what learning is! 160
My lord, I'll tell my lady you will come.

ROMEO Do so, and bid my sweet prepare to chide.
[*Nurse offers to go in, and turns again.*]

NURSE Here, sir, a ring she bid me give you, sir.
Hie you, make haste, for it grows very late.

ROMEO How well my comfort is revived by this. 165
[*Exit Nurse*]

Friar Lawrence sends Romeo to Juliet, warning him to leave early for Mantua and await news. In Scene 4, Capulet tells Paris that because of Tybalt's death, he has not yet talked to Juliet about marriage.

剧情简介：劳润修士打发柔密欧去见茱丽叶，警告他尽早动身前往曼托瓦并在那里等消息。第4场，卡普莱告诉帕瑞，由于提巴尔刚死，他还没有跟茱丽叶谈她婚嫁的事。

Write about it 写作练习

Romeo: from misery to joy (in pairs)

Romeo leaves, expressing his deep desire to be with Juliet tonight ('a joy past joy'). But his mood has been very different for most of the scene. He feels full of anguish and despair until he finally sees hope in Friar Lawrence's plan. Some people think his emotions are too extreme and that he thinks only of himself, not Juliet.

- Look back through Scene 3 and identify where you think Romeo's feelings are genuine and where they are 'over the top'. On page 108 you created a 'mood graph' for Juliet. Now do the same for Romeo. Fill it out as you track his emotional state in this scene. Afterwards, put your Juliet and Romeo graphs together and compare how the two young lovers respond to the challenges they face.

1 **here stands all your state** 您的未来在此一举
2 **Sojourn** 逗留，暂住
3 **signify** 给您传信
4 **hap** = happening
5 **brief** 匆忙
6 **fall'n out** 发生
7 **move** 说动
8 **mewed up to her heaviness** 关进悲伤的牢笼里 (mew up是驯鹰术语)
9 **desperate tender** 大胆提出

1 Focus on Paris (in pairs)

In Baz Luhrmann's movie of the play, Paris was an ordinary, likeable character who appeared in a spacesuit at Capulet's party in Act 1 Scene 5.

a Talk together about your own views of Paris. How old do you think he is? How does he look? How different might he be from Romeo?

b Consider how you think he might behave in Scene 4. In your Director's Journal, write some notes of advice to an actor playing Paris, including how he should move and what tone of voice he should use.

Themes 主题分析

Fathers and daughters

Capulet is certain that Juliet will obey him ('I think she will be ruled / In all respects by me; nay more, I doubt it not'). Shakespeare often wrote about fathers who expected to dominate their daughters' lives – an attitude that would have been supported by an Elizabethan audience, which saw male power (particularly in the home) as very important.

- Do you think Shakespeare favours the father's point of view or the daughter's? Write down your thoughts, giving examples to support your opinion. Look out in later scenes for how Juliet openly challenges her father – and how Capulet reacts.

FRIAR LAWRENCE	Go hence, good night, and here stands all your state[1]:
	Either be gone before the Watch be set,
	Or by the break of day disguised from hence.
	Sojourn[2] in Mantua; I'll find out your man,
	And he shall signify[3] from time to time 170
	Every good hap[4] to you that chances here.
	Give me thy hand, 'tis late. Farewell, good night.
ROMEO	But that a joy past joy calls out on me,
	It were a grief, so brief[5] to part with thee:
	Farewell. 175

Exeunt

Act 3 Scene 4
Capulet's mansion

Enter old CAPULET, *his* WIFE, *and* PARIS.

CAPULET	Things have fall'n out[6], sir, so unluckily
	That we have had no time to move[7] our daughter.
	Look you, she loved her kinsman Tybalt dearly,
	And so did I. Well, we were born to die.
	'Tis very late, she'll not come down tonight. 5
	I promise you, but for your company,
	I would have been abed an hour ago.
PARIS	These times of woe afford no times to woo.
	Madam, good night, commend me to your daughter.
LADY CAPULET	I will, and know her mind early tomorrow; 10
	Tonight she's mewed up to her heaviness[8].
	[*Paris offers to go in, and Capulet calls him again.*]
CAPULET	Sir Paris, I will make a desperate tender[9]
	Of my child's love: I think she will be ruled
	In all respects by me; nay more, I doubt it not.

Capulet instructs his wife to tell Juliet that she is to be married to Paris. He decides the wedding will be in three days' time with only a few invited guests.

 剧情简介：卡普莱指示妻子告诉茱丽叶已经把她许配给帕瑞了。他决定婚礼三天后举行，只邀请少数几位宾客。

Write about it 写作练习
Husband and wife

Every production of the play must address the question of how Juliet's parents feel about each other. Do they love each other? Did they love each other when they married? What does Lady Capulet think of her husband in this scene?

a Write Lady Capulet's private thoughts, considering the following attitudes:
- she finds him tiresome and boring
- she is afraid of him
- she still loves him.

Remember that she appears to mock her husband's manhood in Act 1 Scene 1 (line 67) by suggesting that he needs a crutch rather than a sword. Also, some productions suggest that her extreme grief at Tybalt's death implies she was having an affair with the younger man.

b As a complementary piece, you might try to write as if you are Capulet. What does he really think of his wife?

1 Acquaint her 让她知道
2 my son （卡普莱已经把帕瑞视为自己的女婿了）
3 keep no great ado 不要大操大办
4 so late 这么近
5 held him carelessly 对他不尊重
6 revel much 大肆庆祝
7 against = for
8 Afore me 我的天啊
9 call … and by 很快就说早上好了

1 Time begins to run faster (in pairs)

a Read Scene 4 aloud, emphasising all the words relating to time. How many can you find (there are well over thirty of them)? Notice how these words add to the impression of fast-moving events.

b Read Capulet's lines 19–35 in a variety of different ways: frenzied (狂乱), hasty, ponderous (沉闷), agitated. Afterwards, talk together about which of these is the most effective in giving the audience a sense of the gathering momentum of events.

2 Dramatic irony (in pairs)

The scene is full of **dramatic irony** (戏剧反讽) – when the audience knows something that at least one of the characters on stage does not know, and when what is said contrasts with what happens elsewhere in the play. Even as Capulet plans Juliet's marriage, she is eagerly awaiting her husband Romeo in her bedroom.

- Identify and write down four or five examples of dramatic irony in this scene. Then suggest what it is that makes each example ironic (see also pp. 128, 132 and 150).

ROMEO AND JULIET ACT 3 SCENE 4
柔密欧与茱丽叶

	Wife, go you to her ere you go to bed,	15
	Acquaint her¹ here of my son² Paris' love,	
	And bid her – mark you me? – on Wednesday next –	
	But soft, what day is this?	
PARIS	Monday, my lord.	
CAPULET	Monday, ha, ha! Well, Wednesday is too soon,	
	A'Thursday let it be – a'Thursday, tell her,	20
	She shall be married to this noble earl.	
	Will you be ready? do you like this haste?	
	Well, keep no great ado³ – a friend or two,	
	For hark you, Tybalt being slain so late⁴,	
	It may be thought we held him carelessly⁵,	25
	Being our kinsman, if we revel much⁶:	
	Therefore we'll have some half a dozen friends,	
	And there an end. But what say you to Thursday?	
PARIS	My lord, I would that Thursday were tomorrow.	
CAPULET	Well, get you gone, a'Thursday be it then. –	30
	Go you to Juliet ere you go to bed,	
	Prepare her, wife, against⁷ this wedding day.	
	Farewell, my lord. Light to my chamber, ho!	
	Afore me⁸, it is so very late that we	
	May call it early by and by⁹. Good night.	35

Exeunt

After their wedding night together, Juliet tries to persuade Romeo that it is not yet dawn, not yet time for him to leave her. At first he says he must go, but then resolves to stay and face capture and death.

剧情简介：共度新婚之夜后，茱丽叶挽留柔密欧，说天未破晓，无须急着离开。柔密欧开始说一定要走，后来决心留下来，宁可被捕或被杀。

Stagecraft 导演技巧

Physical or not? (in small groups)

Most modern productions use the opportunity provided by this scene to suggest the physical passion and desire that exists between the two young lovers, often through imaginative use of costume, lighting or staging. For example, many have a bed on stage (whereas earlier productions did not).

- Read quickly up to line 59. Do you think the language is meant to highlight the physical intimacy between the young lovers, or is their exchange presented as more lyrical and poetic?

1 pomegranate 石榴
2 envious 怀恨在心（因为嫉妒夜晚）
3 severing 断绝；离别
4 Night's candles 夜晚的烛光（指星辰）
5 jocund 欢快，愉快
6 some … exhaled 是太阳喷吐的一颗流星（当时人们认为流星 [meteor] 是从地上升起的蒸汽被太阳吸引并点燃而形成）
7 tane = taken（被俘，被抓）
8 so … so 只要你愿意
9 reflex of Cynthia's brow 月神辛西娅脸庞反射的光（Cynthia 是希腊神话中的月亮女神）
10 vaulty heaven 天穹
11 care 欲望

▼ How would you stage this dialogue in order to enhance the mood you think is appropriate? Would you include a bed? Why, or why not?

1 How should the lines be spoken? (in pairs)

Take parts and try different ways of speaking lines 1–25 (for example, Juliet as loving, impatient, bossy or sleepy; Romeo as loving, afraid or secretly wanting to leave). Can you agree on how you think the lines should be delivered? In particular, how should lines 11 and 12 be spoken? Pick one or two favourite lines. Talk with your partner about why you enjoy them.

Act 3 Scene 5
Juliet's bedroom

Enter ROMEO *and* JULIET *aloft at the window.*

JULIET	Wilt thou be gone? It is not yet near day:
	It was the nightingale, and not the lark,
	That pierced the fearful hollow of thine ear;
	Nightly she sings on yond pomegranate[1] tree.
	Believe me, love, it was the nightingale. 5
ROMEO	It was the lark, the herald of the morn,
	No nightingale. Look, love, what envious[2] streaks
	Do lace the severing[3] clouds in yonder east:
	Night's candles[4] are burnt out, and jocund[5] day
	Stands tiptoe on the misty mountain tops. 10
	I must be gone and live, or stay and die.
JULIET	Yond light is not daylight, I know it, I:
	It is some meteor that the sun exhaled[6]
	To be to thee this night a torch-bearer,
	And light thee on thy way to Mantua. 15
	Therefore stay yet, thou need'st not to be gone.
ROMEO	Let me be tane[7], let me be put to death,
	I am content, so thou wilt have it so[8].
	I'll say yon grey is not the morning's eye,
	'Tis but the pale reflex of Cynthia's brow[9]; 20
	Nor that is not the lark whose notes do beat
	The vaulty heaven[10] so high above our heads.
	I have more care[11] to stay than will to go:
	Come, death, and welcome! Juliet wills it so.
	How is't, my soul? Let's talk, it is not day. 25

Juliet accepts that it is morning and time to part. The Nurse warns the lovers that Lady Capulet is coming. As Romeo leaves, Juliet's words are filled with foreboding.

 剧情简介：茱丽叶意识到天已大亮，该分手了。奶妈警告这对恋人卡普莱夫人要来了。柔密欧离开之时，茱丽叶的话里充满不祥预感。

1 'Some say the lark and loathèd toad changed eyes'

There was an old belief that skylarks and toads had exchanged eyes. This explained why toads' eyes were thought more beautiful than larks' eyes. Juliet wishes they had exchanged voices too, because the harsh voice of the toad is more suitable to the lovers' sad parting.

- If you were making a movie of the play and wanted to 'dub in' (配音，配乐) a sad or ominous sound as background here, what sound would it be? Share your suggestion with the class.

Stagecraft 导演技巧
'He goeth down'

As you continue reading you'll see that Juliet also 'goeth down' (stage direction, line 67).

- Work out how you would stage the scene to make these 'goeth down' movements by Romeo and Juliet as convincing as possible. Sketch a design for your stage set.

2 Visions of doom (in fours)

The final words that the lovers ever speak together are filled with fear about what lies ahead for them (lines 54–9). Both Juliet and Romeo imagine scenes involving their own deaths.

- Act out these six lines, two of you as Romeo, two as Juliet. One pair delivers the lines, the others present the vision of death that each of the characters 'sees'. Show your versions to the class. As you read to the end of the play, you will see how these dark forebodings unfold.

Write about it 写作练习
Last time together

Lines 1–59 are the last time Romeo and Juliet will see each other alive.

- Write out how you would stage this episode to bring out its poignancy (辛酸) and dramatic impact. Concentrate in particular on how you would manage the growing pressure that builds around the lovers' final parting.

---

1 sharps　刺耳音符
2 makes sweet division = makes division sweet （令分别甜蜜）
3 affray　惊吓（让两人不能拥抱在一起）
4 hunt's-up　猎人的晨歌
5 wary　谨慎，小心
6 much in years　变得很老
7 omit　错过
8 sweet discourses　甜言蜜语
9 ill-divining　占卜不祥
10 so low　在下面（茱丽叶从上往下看）
11 Dry sorrow　干涸的忧伤（伊丽莎白时代的人们认为每一声叹息都会消耗一滴血）

JULIET	It is, it is, hie hence, be gone, away!
	It is the lark that sings so out of tune,
	Straining harsh discords and unpleasing sharps[1].
	Some say the lark makes sweet division[2]:
	This doth not so, for she divideth us.	30
	Some say the lark and loathèd toad changed eyes;
	O now I would they had changed voices too,
	Since arm from arm that voice doth us affray[3],
	Hunting thee hence with hunt's-up[4] to the day.
	O now be gone, more light and light it grows.	35
ROMEO	More light and light, more dark and dark our woes!

Enter NURSE [*hastily*].

NURSE	Madam!
JULIET	Nurse?
NURSE	Your lady mother is coming to your chamber.
	The day is broke, be wary[5], look about. [*Exit*]	40
JULIET	Then, window, let day in, and let life out.
ROMEO	Farewell, farewell! one kiss, and I'll descend.

      [*He goeth down.*]

JULIET	Art thou gone so, love, lord, ay husband, friend?
	I must hear from thee every day in the hour,
	For in a minute there are many days.	45
	O, by this count I shall be much in years[6]
	Ere I again behold my Romeo!
ROMEO	[*From below*] Farewell!
	I will omit[7] no opportunity
	That may convey my greetings, love, to thee.	50
JULIET	O think'st thou we shall ever meet again?
ROMEO	I doubt it not, and all these woes shall serve
	For sweet discourses[8] in our times to come.
JULIET	O God, I have an ill-divining[9] soul!
	Methinks I see thee now, thou art so low[10],	55
	As one dead in the bottom of a tomb.
	Either my eyesight fails, or thou look'st pale.
ROMEO	And trust me, love, in my eye so do you:
	Dry sorrow[11] drinks our blood. Adieu, adieu! *Exit*

Lady Capulet mistakes Juliet's tears for Romeo as grief for Tybalt's death. Juliet's replies strengthen her mother's mistaken belief, and she threatens vengeance, promising to have Romeo poisoned in Mantua.

剧情简介：卡普莱夫人将茱丽叶为柔密欧流的泪误认为是因提巴尔的死而感到忧伤。茱丽叶的答话更让卡普莱夫人深信不疑。卡普莱夫人威胁报仇，答应她要在曼托瓦毒死柔密欧。

1 Fortune

Juliet turns fortune into a person in lines 60–4 (see pp. 214–15 for more on personification).

- Imagine you are designing a production of the play. The director tells you that he wants an image or a statue of Fortune (命运女神) to be on stage throughout the play. Make drawings of your suggestions for that statue. Talk with others about whether you think the director's request for such an ever-present image is a good idea.

◀ In medieval imagery, Fortune was depicted with a wheel, spinning it randomly.

2 Double meanings (in fours)

Lady Capulet thinks that Juliet is agreeing with her. But Juliet's replies to her mother are filled with double meaning, and she responds ambiguously each time. This is another example of dramatic irony (see p. 122), because the audience, like Juliet, knows what Lady Capulet does not. The activity below will help you emphasise this.

a One person reads Lady Capulet and one reads Juliet (lines 68–102); the other two are Juliet's alter ego (另一个自我). In their own words, they comment as many times as possible on what Juliet is really thinking as she speaks. Juliet reads slowly, a line or two at a time. For example:

> Juliet: Madam, I am not well.
> Alter ego: Because I've just parted from my husband and my heart is full of sorrow.
> Juliet: Yet let me weep for such a feeling loss.
> Alter ego: But let me weep for Romeo, who I love.

b Try the exercise several times, changing roles. Discuss what these double meanings tell you about Juliet's character, and how they add dramatic impact.

1	fickle	变化无常；不忠
2	unaccustomed cause	不同寻常的大事
3	procures	带来
4	And if	= Even if
5	have done	算了吧
6	friend	亲友
7	many miles asunder	相距万里；有天壤之别
8	venge	= avenge（报仇）
9	runagate	逃犯
10	dram	毒药

JULIET	O Fortune, Fortune, all men call thee fickle[1];
	If thou art fickle, what dost thou with him
	That is renowned for faith? Be fickle, Fortune:
	For then I hope thou wilt not keep him long,
	But send him back.

Enter Mother [LADY CAPULET *below*].

LADY CAPULET	Ho, daughter, are you up?
JULIET	Who is't that calls? It is my lady mother.
	Is she not down so late, or up so early?
	What unaccustomed cause[2] procures[3] her hither?

[*She goeth down from the window and enters below.*]

LADY CAPULET	Why how now, Juliet?
JULIET	Madam, I am not well.
LADY CAPULET	Evermore weeping for your cousin's death?
	What, wilt thou wash him from his grave with tears?
	And if[4] thou couldst, thou couldst not make him live;
	Therefore have done[5]. Some grief shows much of love,
	But much of grief shows still some want of wit.
JULIET	Yet let me weep for such a feeling loss.
LADY CAPULET	So shall you feel the loss, but not the friend[6]
	Which you weep for.
JULIET	Feeling so the loss,
	I cannot choose but ever weep the friend.
LADY CAPULET	Well, girl, thou weep'st not so much for his death
	As that the villain lives which slaughtered him.
JULIET	What villain, madam?
LADY CAPULET	That same villain Romeo.
JULIET	[*Aside*] Villain and he be many miles asunder[7]. –
	God pardon him, I do with all my heart:
	And yet no man like he doth grieve my heart.
LADY CAPULET	That is because the traitor murderer lives.
JULIET	Ay, madam, from the reach of these my hands.
	Would none but I might venge[8] my cousin's death!
LADY CAPULET	We will have vengeance for it, fear thou not:
	Then weep no more. I'll send to one in Mantua,
	Where that same banished runagate[9] doth live,
	Shall give him such an unaccustomed dram[10]
	That he shall soon keep Tybalt company;
	And then I hope thou wilt be satisfied.

Juliet continues to mislead her mother. Lady Capulet tells her she must marry Paris on Thursday. Juliet, appalled, refuses to do so. Capulet comes in and mistakes Juliet's tears for sorrow for Tybalt.

剧情简介：茱丽叶继续误导母亲。卡普莱夫人告诉她星期四要嫁给帕瑞，她震惊不已，坚决不从。卡普莱进来，看到茱丽叶流泪，以为她在为提巴尔伤心。

Themes 主题分析

Fathers and daughters (in small groups)

What does this arranged marriage suggest to you about male-female relationships in Verona?

- If you are female, what would you do if you were suddenly told that your father had arranged a marriage for you to a man you barely know? If you are male, do you think fathers should decide whom their daughters should marry? Record your answers to share with the class.

1. **temper** 调配（茱丽叶的另一层意思是：亲自配药，让毒性减弱，使柔密欧安然入睡；参见下文）
2. **abhors** 惊恐；憎恨
3. **wreak** 施加，回报
4. **heaviness** 悲伤
5. **It rains downright** 大雨倾盆（指茱丽叶痛哭流泪）
6. **conduit** 人形喷泉（口中喷水）

Stagecraft 导演技巧

Capulet: from comforting to furious father

As you read what Capulet says in this scene, you will find that the tone and style of his language change. He begins (lines 126–38) by offering comfort and support to Juliet. Then, as he learns of Juliet's refusal to marry Paris, his language changes and in lines 141–5, he speaks of her in the third person ('she', 'her'). This signals that he is distancing himself from his daughter and in his speeches that follow he explodes in fury, heaping all his rage on Juliet. In one production, Capulet hurled (猛掷) a glass of wine in his daughter's face; in others he is seen to slap Juliet.

- Can either of these interpretations be justified? What staging ideas do you have for showing Capulet's gathering rage? Try some out!

Romeo and Juliet Act 3 Scene 5
柔密欧与茱丽叶

JULIET   Indeed I never shall be satisfied
With Romeo, till I behold him – dead –
Is my poor heart, so for a kinsman vexed.
Madam, if you could find out but a man
To bear a poison, I would temper[1] it,
That Romeo should upon receipt thereof
Soon sleep in quiet. O how my heart abhors[2]
To hear him named and cannot come to him,
To wreak[3] the love I bore my cousin
Upon his body that hath slaughtered him!

LADY CAPULET   Find thou the means, and I'll find such a man.
But now I'll tell thee joyful tidings, girl.

JULIET   And joy comes well in such a needy time.
What are they, beseech your ladyship?

LADY CAPULET   Well, well, thou hast a careful father, child,
One who, to put thee from thy heaviness[4],
Hath sorted out a sudden day of joy,
That thou expects not, nor I looked not for.

JULIET   Madam, in happy time, what day is that?

LADY CAPULET   Marry, my child, early next Thursday morn,
The gallant, young, and noble gentleman,
The County Paris, at Saint Peter's Church,
Shall happily make thee there a joyful bride.

JULIET   Now by Saint Peter's Church and Peter too,
He shall not make me there a joyful bride.
I wonder at this haste, that I must wed
Ere he that should be husband comes to woo.
I pray you tell my lord and father, madam,
I will not marry yet, and when I do, I swear
It shall be Romeo, whom you know I hate,
Rather than Paris. These are news indeed!

LADY CAPULET   Here comes your father, tell him so yourself;
And see how he will take it at your hands.

Enter CAPULET *and Nurse.*

CAPULET   When the sun sets, the earth doth drizzle dew,
But for the sunset of my brother's son
It rains downright[5].
How now, a conduit[6], girl? What, still in tears?

95

100

105

110

115

120

125

Capulet elaborately compares Juliet's tears to a shipwrecking storm. But he then flies into a towering rage on hearing of Juliet's refusal to marry Paris. He threatens and insults her.

 剧情简介：卡普莱把茱丽叶的泪水精巧地比作让船倾覆的暴风雨，但听到茱丽叶不想嫁给帕瑞后勃然大怒，他不断吓唬、羞辱她。

Themes 主题分析

Fathers and daughters: Capulet's rage (in large groups)

This is an activity for the hall or drama studio, but it can also be adapted for the classroom.

- One person is Juliet; all the others are Lord Capulet. Juliet sits still in the middle of a circle, with the others all round her. Those reading Capulet will speak everything in lines 149–57, 160–8 and 176–95. They walk around Juliet and hurl their language at her. Each Capulet speaks just a phrase or a line or two before the next Capulet carries on. For example: first Capulet, 'How how, how how, chopt-logic?'; second Capulet, 'What is this?'; third Capulet, ' "Proud" and "I thank you", and "I thank you not" ', and so on (it becomes far worse!).
- Juliet replies to every Capulet with her lines 158–9 ('Good father, I beseech you on my knees, / Hear me with patience but to speak a word').
- Work through the activity several times, with a different Juliet each time. Remember that it's a difficult thing for Juliet to endure because she's on the receiving end of a terrifying tongue-lashing (严词斥责) by her father. So don't force anyone into playing Juliet; only use volunteers!
- When you've tried this activity a number of times, talk together about the language. What is it like to undergo this verbal abuse? How does it feel to be delivering it? What does it tell you about Capulet's character? And what does it add to your understanding of the play's exploration of the theme of relationships between parents and their children?

1. counterfeits 仿造
2. bark 船
3. overset 倾覆
4. decree 决定
5. take me with you 解释给我听（我不明白你的意思）
6. proud 感到荣耀
7. wrought 劝说
8. bride = bridegroom （新郎）
9. chopt-logic 牛头不对马嘴
10. mistress minion you 您这心肝宝贝小姐
11. fettle your fine joints 准备好您的小身子骨（讽刺语气，这本是养马用语）
12. hurdle 木架（古时将叛徒绑在木架上，拖在地上拉去游街行刑）
13. green-sickness carrion 得了黄萎病的臭肉（黄萎病的症状特点是面色苍白光亮；参见第52页注解3）
14. tallow-face 蜡白脸色
15. My fingers itch 我的手指头发痒（想打人）
16. hilding 贱人（骂人话）

1 Does Lady Capulet mean it? (in pairs)

'I would the fool were married to her grave', says Lady Capulet (line 140). Do you think she really means it?

- Take turns to speak her nine words aloud in a variety of ways until you have what you think is the most convincing version. Then talk together about the impact these words might have on Juliet. Look out for how this becomes another example of dramatic irony as the play unfolds and the audience sees what finally happens to Juliet.

Romeo and Juliet Act 3 Scene 5
柔密欧与茱丽叶

	Evermore show'ring? In one little body	130
	Thou counterfeits[1] a bark[2], a sea, a wind:	
	For still thy eyes, which I may call the sea,	
	Do ebb and flow with tears; the bark thy body is,	
	Sailing in this salt flood; the winds, thy sighs,	
	Who, raging with thy tears and they with them,	135
	Without a sudden calm, will overset[3]	
	Thy tempest-tossèd body. How now, wife,	
	Have you delivered to her our decree[4]?	
LADY CAPULET	Ay, sir, but she will none, she gives you thanks.	
	I would the fool were married to her grave.	140
CAPULET	Soft, take me with you[5], take me with you, wife.	
	How, will she none? doth she not give us thanks?	
	Is she not proud[6]? doth she not count her blest,	
	Unworthy as she is, that we have wrought[7]	
	So worthy a gentleman to be her bride[8]?	145
JULIET	Not proud you have, but thankful that you have:	
	Proud can I never be of what I hate,	
	But thankful even for hate that is meant love.	
CAPULET	How how, how how, chopt-logic[9]? What is this?	
	'Proud', and 'I thank you', and 'I thank you not',	150
	And yet 'not proud', mistress minion you[10]?	
	Thank me no thankings, nor proud me no prouds,	
	But fettle your fine joints[11] 'gainst Thursday next,	
	To go with Paris to Saint Peter's Church,	
	Or I will drag thee on a hurdle[12] thither.	155
	Out, you green-sickness carrion[13]! out, you baggage!	
	You tallow-face[14]!	
LADY CAPULET	Fie, fie, what, are you mad?	
JULIET	Good father, I beseech you on my knees,	
	Hear me with patience but to speak a word.	
	[*She kneels down.*]	
CAPULET	Hang thee, young baggage, disobedient wretch!	160
	I tell thee what: get thee to church a'Thursday,	
	Or never after look me in the face.	
	Speak not, reply not, do not answer me!	
	My fingers itch[15]. Wife, we scarce thought us blest	
	That God had lent us but this only child,	165
	But now I see this one is one too much,	
	And that we have a curse in having her.	
	Out on her, hilding[16]!	

Capulet, further enraged by the Nurse's defence of Juliet, continues to storm at Juliet, threatening to disown her if she will not obey him and marry Paris. Lady Capulet refuses to help her daughter.

 剧情简介：看见奶妈护着茱丽叶，卡普莱心中的怒火越烧越旺，继续大骂茱丽叶，威胁说如果不听从他的安排嫁给帕瑞，他就不认她这个女儿。卡普莱夫人拒不为女儿说情。

Write about it 写作练习

The power of fathers

> *But and you will not wed, I'll pardon you* (line 187)
> *And you be mine, I'll give you to my friend* (line 191)

'If you don't wed Paris, get out!' is what Capulet says, using 'pardon' (forgive) ironically. He then stresses his absolute possession of Juliet: she is like an object he can give away to anyone he pleases.

a Carry out some research into what power fathers had over their daughters in Shakespeare's time. Write up your findings. How closely do Capulet's attitudes match what you have discovered?

b Write a paragraph in which you explore how you think a modern audience would respond to Capulet's (and his wife's) treatment of Juliet in this scene.

1 The Capulets' conversation (in pairs)

a In line 198, Juliet pleads: 'O sweet my mother, cast me not away!' Why do you think Lady Capulet replies as she does in lines 202–3?

b Imagine that Lady Capulet catches up with her husband shortly after leaving Juliet. Have her explain to him exactly what she feels about Juliet's behaviour. How will he reply and what else do they say to each other? Improvise their conversation.

Language in the play 剧中语言

Imagery: Juliet's ominous prediction

Again Juliet uses an image that links marriage and death, when she says: 'make the bridal bed / In that dim monument where Tybalt lies.'

- Produce a drawing to illustrate Juliet's dark and troubling prophecy (预言) in lines 200–1.

---

1 rate 责骂
2 smatter 唠叨，闲扯
3 God-i-goden! 再见吧！(相当于生气时说Good evening)
4 gravity 高见
5 o'er a gossip's bowl 啜着老娘儿们的酒碗
6 God's bread 上帝的面包（骂人话）
7 still = always（本剧多次出现）
8 parentage 出身
9 demesnes 家产
10 ligned 血统
11 parts 品质
12 puling 哭哭啼啼
13 mammet 玩偶，木偶
14 in her fortune's tender 命运眷顾她的时候
15 Graze （像牛羊一样）觅食
16 advise 认真想想
17 be forsworn 食言

ROMEO AND JULIET ACT 3 SCENE 5
柔密欧与茱丽叶

NURSE	God in heaven bless her!	
	You are to blame, my lord, to rate[1] her so.	
CAPULET	And why, my Lady Wisdom? Hold your tongue,	170
	Good Prudence, smatter[2] with your gossips, go.	
NURSE	I speak no treason.	
CAPULET	O God-i-goden![3]	
NURSE	May not one speak?	
CAPULET	Peace, you mumbling fool!	
	Utter your gravity[4] o'er a gossip's bowl[5],	
	For here we need it not.	
LADY CAPULET	You are too hot.	175
CAPULET	God's bread[6], it makes me mad! Day, night, work, play,	
	Alone, in company, still[7] my care hath been	
	To have her matched; and having now provided	
	A gentleman of noble parentage[8],	
	Of fair demesnes[9], youthful and nobly ligned[10],	180
	Stuffed, as they say, with honourable parts[11],	
	Proportioned as one's thought would wish a man,	
	And then to have a wretched puling[12] fool,	
	A whining mammet[13], in her fortune's tender[14],	
	To answer 'I'll not wed, I cannot love;	185
	I am too young, I pray you pardon me.'	
	But and you will not wed, I'll pardon you:	
	Graze[15] where you will, you shall not house with me.	
	Look to't, think on't, I do not use to jest.	
	Thursday is near, lay hand on heart, advise[16]:	190
	And you be mine, I'll give you to my friend;	
	And you be not, hang, beg, starve, die in the streets,	
	For by my soul, I'll ne'er acknowledge thee,	
	Nor what is mine shall never do thee good.	
	Trust to't, bethink you, I'll not be forsworn[17]. *Exit*	195
JULIET	Is there no pity sitting in the clouds	
	That sees into the bottom of my grief?	
	O sweet my mother, cast me not away!	
	Delay this marriage for a month, a week,	
	Or if you do not, make the bridal bed	200
	In that dim monument where Tybalt lies.	
LADY CAPULET	Talk not to me, for I'll not speak a word.	
	Do as thou wilt, for I have done with thee. *Exit*	

Juliet seeks comfort from the Nurse, who urges her to marry Paris. Feeling betrayed, Juliet sends the Nurse away, vowing never to trust her again. Juliet resolves to seek Friar Lawrence's aid.

剧情简介：茱丽叶想从奶妈那里寻求慰藉，她却劝茱丽叶嫁给帕瑞。茱丽叶感到奶妈背叛了她，把她撵走，发誓不再信任她。茱丽叶决定去向劳润修士求助。

Write about it 写作练习

The Nurse confesses

Towards the end of this scene, Juliet says that she is going to see Friar Lawrence to 'make confession' (if Juliet frankly confesses her sins to the Friar in private then he will be able to pardon her for the things she has done wrong).

- Imagine that the Nurse also goes to a religious man to make her own confession. What would she say? What has she done so far that might weigh heavily on her mind and might bother her so much that she needs to talk about it? Script her confessional speech.

1 The Nurse's betrayal (whole class)

Some critics see the Nurse's suggestion that Juliet should marry Paris as the ultimate betrayal of their relationship – a complete rejection of the loyalty and trust between them.

- Put the Nurse on trial. Question her about her motives and work out whether she really has Juliet's best interests at heart. Afterwards, give your verdict on whether the Nurse is guilty of betrayal or not.

Characters 人物分析

Juliet: dealing with disasters

Juliet feels trapped. Her father has threatened her, her mother has abandoned her and she feels the Nurse has proved a false friend. She also feels that her religion adds to her desolation (凄凉). In lines 205–8, she recognises that only by Romeo's death can she sincerely take a faithful (religious) vow to marry Paris. Her final line as she leaves to visit the Friar (line 242) is full of foreboding.

- Review Juliet's experiences in this scene and consider carefully how she deals with the wide range of tests and challenges thrown at her. What aspects of her character do you think emerge most strongly? Create a 'word wall' of adjectives that describe her. Then link them to evidence and quotations from the scene.

1. **stratagems** 计谋
2. **all the world to nothing** 用全世界打赌
3. **challenge you** （在婚礼仪式上）质疑你（没有资格结婚）
4. **by stealth** 偷偷摸摸
5. **dishclout** = dishcloth （抹布）
6. **green** （绿色的眼睛在当时备受青睐）
7. **Beshrew my very heart** 我说句没良心的话（beshrew是语气较弱的骂人话，表示诅咒）
8. **absolved** 宽恕
9. **Ancient damnation!** 该死的老东西！（ancient: 年龄大; damnation: 遭诅咒的人，要下地狱的人）
10. **wish me thus forsworn** 令我背弃誓言
11. **dispraise** 贬损，诋毁
12. **bosom** 心胸
13. **twain** 两个（分开，表示不再同心同德）

JULIET	O God! – O Nurse, how shall this be prevented?	
	My husband is on earth, my faith in heaven;	205
	How shall that faith return again to earth,	
	Unless that husband send it me from heaven	
	By leaving earth? Comfort me, counsel me.	
	Alack, alack, that heaven should practise stratagems[1]	
	Upon so soft a subject as myself!	210
	What say'st thou? hast thou not a word of joy?	
	Some comfort, Nurse.	
NURSE	Faith, here it is:	
	Romeo is banished, and all the world to nothing[2]	
	That he dares ne'er come back to challenge you[3];	
	Or if he do, it needs must be by stealth[4].	215
	Then since the case so stands as now it doth,	
	I think it best you married with the County.	
	O, he's a lovely gentleman!	
	Romeo's a dishclout[5] to him. An eagle, madam,	
	Hath not so green[6], so quick, so fair an eye	220
	As Paris hath. Beshrew my very heart[7],	
	I think you are happy in this second match,	
	For it excels your first, or if it did not,	
	Your first is dead, or 'twere as good he were	
	As living here and you no use of him.	225
JULIET	Speak'st thou from thy heart?	
NURSE	And from my soul too, else beshrew them both.	
JULIET	Amen.	
NURSE	What?	
JULIET	Well, thou hast comforted me marvellous much.	230
	Go in, and tell my lady I am gone,	
	Having displeased my father, to Lawrence' cell,	
	To make confession and to be absolved[8].	
NURSE	Marry, I will, and this is wisely done. [*Exit*]	
JULIET	[*She looks after Nurse.*] Ancient damnation![9] O most wicked fiend!	235
	Is it more sin to wish me thus forsworn[10],	
	Or to dispraise[11] my lord with that same tongue	
	Which she hath praised him with above compare	
	So many thousand times? Go, counsellor,	
	Thou and my bosom[12] henceforth shall be twain[13].	240
	I'll to the Friar to know his remedy;	
	If all else fail, myself have power to die. *Exit*	

ROMEO AND JULIET
柔密欧与茱丽叶

Looking back at Act 3 第3幕回顾
Activities for groups or individuals

1 Shakespeare's stagecraft: contrasts

One reason why Shakespeare's plays work so well on stage is because he ensured that every scene contrasts in some way with the scene that precedes or follows it. These **juxtapositions** (并置，这里有"对照"的意思) (contrasts) are often ironic. For example, Act 3 Scene 1 ends with Mercutio and Tybalt killed and Romeo banished on pain of death. But Scene 2 opens with Juliet in an ecstatic (欣喜) mood, longing for Romeo to come to her. The audience knows – but she is unaware of – the disasters that have occurred. This dramatic irony adds to the emotional impact of the play on the audience as they watch a joyful Juliet, knowing her happiness will shortly be shattered.

- Work through Act 3 and write a paragraph (like the explanation given above) of how each scene contrasts with the one that precedes it. You could focus your enquiries on aspects such as setting, exploration of theme/character, mood and the unfolding story.

2 Characters' motives

List each character that appears in this act. Write a single sentence for each that begins 'What I want most is …'. How much agreement is there in the class on each character's major motive?

3 Discussing banishment

- Is there a modern equivalent of the punishment of banishment?
- Is banishment really worse than death, as Romeo imagines?
- Why doesn't Juliet simply decide to join Romeo in Mantua?

4 Soundbites

Soundbites are very short clips of what someone has said, broadcast on television or radio.

- Make up soundbites for each scene. They should be pithy (精练) and attention-grabbing, like headlines.

5 Why did Mercutio have to die?

Mercutio dies before the play even reaches its halfway point. Many reasons have been suggested for why Shakespeare kills him off so early in the play, including the idea that he was developing into such an attractive character that his continuing presence would adversely affect the presentation of the main protagonist (主人公) Romeo, with whom Shakespeare frequently compares and contrasts him.

a Use this suggestion as a starting point for investigating the possible reasons behind the decision to have Mercutio die. Consider Mercutio's character, his role in the play, how he reflects its key themes and his part in the developing tragedy. Supplement your enquiries by looking at the information in the 'Characters' section on page 208 and by referring back to your Character file on Mercutio.

b Write an essay on Mercutio's character and his 'early' death. You could answer the question 'Why did Mercutio have to die?'

6 Guess the incident … or the line

Select an incident or line from Act 3 and prepare a short mime (哑剧) or a tableau. Tell the class which scene your incident or line comes from, then show your mime or tableau. If other people can guess the incident or line correctly, that's a compliment to their perception – and to your ability in performance!

7 Young or grown up?

In Act 3, the relationship between Romeo and Juliet quickly develops: they move from young lovers to husband and wife. Besides that, they each have a host of problems heaped on them from outside their relationship.

- Trace the lovers' journey through Act 3, then prepare an oral presentation comparing how Romeo and Juliet each deal with what is thrown at them. Which of them copes better with the tests and challenges?

Discuss the contrasting moods created by these two images, both taken from Act 3 Scene 5.

Paris tells Friar Lawrence that Capulet, believing Juliet is grieving for Tybalt, wishes to have her married soon. Capulet thinks an early marriage will ease her sorrow.

  剧情简介：帕瑞对劳润修士说，卡普莱相信茱丽叶因为提巴尔的死而悲伤，希望把她尽快嫁出去。卡普莱认为早些嫁人能抚平她的伤痛。

Characters 人物分析

Paris: Lord Capulet's choice

Paris is related to Prince Escales and therefore has a high status in Verona. He's a very desirable son-in-law: if he marries Juliet, the standing of the Capulet family will rise, giving them more social prestige than the Montagues.

a Consider the variety of tones Paris might adopt towards Friar Lawrence. For example, he might view the Friar as socially inferior, and therefore resent having to explain the reason for a hasty marriage. Think of other possible attitudes he might adopt.

b On page 120 you were asked for your initial ideas about Paris's appearance and mannerisms (言谈举止). Refine your thinking by designing a range of costumes for him in a modern-dress production that reflect his high social standing.

1 My father   我岳父
2 nothing slow to slack   不愿磨磨蹭蹭拖延
3 Uneven is the course   麻烦了，这件事（字面意思是 "不直了，这条航道"）
4 Immoderately   不节制，没完没了
5 counts   认为
6 sway   影响力
7 inundation   泛滥
8 Which too much minded = Which is too much minded （Which 指Tybalt's death; mind的意思是 "在意"）
9 society   伴侣
10 That's a certain text   那是定论了

Themes 主题分析

Chance versus choice

As the play nears its tragic climax, there is an increasing sense that the two lovers' destinies are beyond their own control.

- Find a line from Juliet in the script opposite that hints at that idea. Return to the Evidence Grid you began on page 20. Note down this and all other references to fate, either in what the characters say or what happens to them, as this act unfolds. Explain clearly why you have selected and included your evidence.

1 Paris and Juliet talk to each other (in pairs)

Juliet is in a difficult position. She knows (as does the Friar) what Paris does not: that she is already married to Romeo. So her responses to Paris are full of meanings that Paris does not understand.

- Take parts as Paris and Juliet, and read aloud lines 18–43 (leaving out Friar Lawrence's lines). Experiment with different ways of speaking your character's lines. For example, Paris might speak tenderly and courteously, then bossily, treating her like a possession (e.g. 'Thy face is mine', line 35). Also explore different ways in which Juliet might deliver her lines. Talk together about your different styles of speaking.

Act 4 Scene 1
Friar Lawrence's cell

Enter FRIAR LAWRENCE *and* COUNTY PARIS.

FRIAR LAWRENCE	On Thursday, sir? the time is very short.	
PARIS	My father[1] Capulet will have it so,	
	And I am nothing slow to slack[2] his haste.	
FRIAR LAWRENCE	You say you do not know the lady's mind?	
	Uneven is the course[3], I like it not.	5
PARIS	Immoderately[4] she weeps for Tybalt's death,	
	And therefore have I little talked of love,	
	For Venus smiles not in a house of tears.	
	Now, sir, her father counts[5] it dangerous	
	That she do give her sorrow so much sway[6];	10
	And in his wisdom hastes our marriage	
	To stop the inundation[7] of her tears,	
	Which too much minded[8] by herself alone	
	May be put from her by society[9].	
	Now do you know the reason of this haste.	15
FRIAR LAWRENCE	[*Aside*] I would I knew not why it should be slowed. –	
	Look, sir, here comes the lady toward my cell.	

Enter JULIET.

PARIS	Happily met, my lady and my wife!	
JULIET	That may be, sir, when I may be a wife.	
PARIS	That 'may be' must be, love, on Thursday next.	20
JULIET	What must be shall be.	
FRIAR LAWRENCE	That's a certain text[10].	

Juliet's replies to Paris are filled with double meaning. After Paris leaves, Juliet asks Friar Lawrence for help, threatening to kill herself if she is forced to marry Paris.

 剧情简介：茱丽叶回复帕瑞的话都是双层意思。帕瑞走后，茱丽叶向劳润修士求助，说如果逼她嫁给帕瑞，她就自杀。

Stagecraft 导演技巧
'keep this holy kiss' (by yourself)

Step into role as director and advise an actor playing Paris just how he should kiss Juliet at line 43. How does she receive the kiss?

Write about it 写作练习
Celebrity interview

Imagine that you work for a celebrity gossip magazine. You're lucky enough to get an interview with the soon-to-be married Paris. Write up your feature, based on how you think he would respond to questions about his marriage, his future bride and his lifestyle.

1 Juliet and the knife (in pairs)

a In the script opposite, Juliet speaks of 'this knife'. But what kind of knife is it? Where does she get it and what does she do with it as she delivers lines 50–65? Make some suggestions about how you could give this prop (道具) real dramatic impact.

b In the production pictured below, the knife was being used by the Friar to chop herbs. What do you think the director had in mind by staging it this way? Discuss this in your pairs.

1 of more price　更有价值
2 abused　毁容
3 spite　毁坏
4 that report　那样讲
5 spake = spoke
6 to my face　当着我的面
7 evening mass　晚弥撒（天主教宗教仪式）
8 pensive　忧伤
9 shield　禁止
10 rouse ye　把你叫醒
11 cure　救治
12 It … wits　给我的压力超出我的心理承受范围（compass 意思是"范围"）
13 prorogue　拖延，耽搁
14 resolution　决心，决定
15 presently = immediately（立刻）
16 label　印章（代指婚约）
17 deed　婚约

ROMEO AND JULIET ACT 4 SCENE 1
柔密欧与茱丽叶

PARIS	Come you to make confession to this father?
JULIET	To answer that, I should confess to you.
PARIS	Do not deny to him that you love me.
JULIET	I will confess to you that I love him.
PARIS	So will ye, I am sure, that you love me.
JULIET	If I do so, it will be of more price[1],
	Being spoke behind your back, than to your face.
PARIS	Poor soul, thy face is much abused[2] with tears.
JULIET	The tears have got small victory by that,
	For it was bad enough before their spite[3].
PARIS	Thou wrong'st it more than tears with that report[4].
JULIET	That is no slander, sir, which is a truth,
	And what I spake[5], I spake it to my face[6].
PARIS	Thy face is mine, and thou hast slandered it.
JULIET	It may be so, for it is not mine own.
	Are you at leisure, holy father, now,
	Or shall I come to you at evening mass[7]?
FRIAR LAWRENCE	My leisure serves me, pensive[8] daughter, now.
	My lord, we must entreat the time alone.
PARIS	God shield[9] I should disturb devotion!
	Juliet, on Thursday early will I rouse ye[10];
	Till then adieu, and keep this holy kiss. *Exit*
JULIET	O shut the door, and when thou hast done so,
	Come weep with me, past hope, past cure[11], past help!
FRIAR LAWRENCE	O Juliet, I already know thy grief,
	It strains me past the compass of my wits[12].
	I hear thou must, and nothing may prorogue[13] it,
	On Thursday next be married to this County.
JULIET	Tell me not, Friar, that thou hearest of this,
	Unless thou tell me how I may prevent it.
	If in thy wisdom thou canst give no help,
	Do thou but call my resolution[14] wise,
	And with this knife I'll help it presently[15].
	God joined my heart and Romeo's, thou our hands,
	And ere this hand, by thee to Romeo's sealed,
	Shall be the label[16] to another deed[17],
	Or my true heart with treacherous revolt
	Turn to another, this shall slay them both:

25

30

35

40

45

50

55

Juliet pleads for the Friar's advice, and again threatens to kill herself. Friar Lawrence begins to devise a plan to prevent Juliet's marriage to Paris. Juliet declares that she will do anything to escape the wedding.

剧情简介：茱丽叶恳请劳润修士出主意，再次威胁要自杀。劳润修士开始设计阻止茱丽叶嫁给帕瑞，茱丽叶说为了逃婚什么都愿意做。

1 'rather than marry Paris'

Shakespeare enjoyed compiling lists, piling up item on item and so enabling the character to give different emphasis to each to increase dramatic effect.

- Lines 77–86 list six things Juliet says she would do rather than marry Paris. Work out a mime to show each of the six actions.

Characters 人物分析

Juliet's fearlessness? (in pairs)

Juliet's character continues to develop in this scene. You have already begun to chart her growing maturity in the face of severe difficulties. Now, consider her words in lines 87–8:

And I will do it without fear or doubt,
To live an unstained wife to my sweet love.

- Take turns to read these lines, experimenting with ways of saying them. Is Juliet feeling genuinely courageous here? Or do you think she is putting on a brave face? Which individual words have the greatest impact on your thinking?

Write about it 写作练习

Juliet reacts to the Friar's plan

Juliet listens to Friar Lawrence's long explanation of his plan (lines 89–120), but she does not speak.

- Look at the image below. How do you think Juliet reacts as she hears him outline his scheme? Imagine that you are Juliet. Write down your thoughts as each of his ideas takes hold.

1	present counsel	现场指教
	(present = immediate)	
2	extremes	让人绝望的处境
3	umpire	裁判
4	arbitrating	仲裁
5	commission	权威
6	issue	结局
7	long = slow	(本行后一个long意思是"盼望")
8	Hold	等等，慢来
9	spy	看见，窥见
10	execution	实施，手段
11	chide away this shame	避免受此羞辱
12	cop'st with	遭遇
13	battlements	城垛
14	thievish ways	盗贼猖獗的街道
15	lurk	隐藏
16	charnel-house	藏尸所
17	reeky shanks	恶臭的小腿骨
18	chapless skulls	没有下颌骨的骷髅
19	shroud	裹尸布
20	look that thou lie alone	确保你一个人睡

>   Therefore, out of thy long-experienced time,
>   Give me some present counsel[1], or, behold,
>   'Twixt my extremes[2] and me this bloody knife
>   Shall play the umpire[3], arbitrating[4] that
>   Which the commission[5] of thy years and art
>   Could to no issue[6] of true honour bring.
>   Be not so long[7] to speak, I long to die,
>   If what thou speak'st speak not of remedy.
>
> FRIAR LAWRENCE   Hold[8], daughter, I do spy[9] a kind of hope,
>   Which craves as desperate an execution[10]
>   As that is desperate which we would prevent.
>   If, rather than to marry County Paris,
>   Thou hast the strength of will to slay thyself,
>   Then is it likely thou wilt undertake
>   A thing like death to chide away this shame[11],
>   That cop'st with[12] Death himself to scape from it;
>   And if thou dar'st, I'll give thee remedy.
>
> JULIET   O bid me leap, rather than marry Paris,
>   From off the battlements[13] of any tower,
>   Or walk in thievish ways[14], or bid me lurk[15]
>   Where serpents are; chain me with roaring bears,
>   Or hide me nightly in a charnel-house[16],
>   O'ercovered quite with dead men's rattling bones,
>   With reeky shanks[17] and yellow chapless skulls[18];
>   Or bid me go into a new-made grave,
>   And hide me with a dead man in his shroud[19] –
>   Things that to hear them told have made me tremble –
>   And I will do it without fear or doubt,
>   To live an unstained wife to my sweet love.
>
> FRIAR LAWRENCE   Hold then, go home, be merry, give consent
>   To marry Paris. Wednesday is tomorrow;
>   Tomorrow night look that thou lie alone[20],
>   Let not the Nurse lie with thee in thy chamber.

Friar Lawrence explains his plan. He will give Juliet a potion to make her seem dead. She will be placed in the Capulet vault and Romeo will be with her when she awakens to take her to Mantua.

 剧情简介：劳润修士解释了他的计划：他会给茱丽叶一剂药，让她假死过去，之后她会被安置于卡普莱家族的墓室，醒来时柔密欧会跟她在一起，带她一起逃往曼托瓦。

1 Is the Friar's plan sensible? (in pairs)

Friar Lawrence sees that Juliet's willingness to kill herself means that she will endure any danger rather than marry Paris. So he invents a dangerous and gruesome (可怕) plan to reunite her with Romeo.

a One person reads the Friar's plan (lines 89–120) in sections, one small part at a time, like this: 'Hold then', 'go home', 'be merry', … 'Take thou this vial', 'being then in bed', 'And this distilling liquor drink thou off', and so on. As each small section is spoken aloud, the other person sketches the action the Friar has just described. Swap roles, then compare your sketches. In what ways are the two versions similar? In what ways are they different?

b Talk together about what you think of the Friar's scheme. One of you argues strongly for its merits, the other against its risks. Decide, on balance, whether you think Juliet should agree to it.

Characters 人物分析

What are the Friar's motives? (in fours)

From all your knowledge of the Friar so far, what are your opinions of this character?

- Explore why he works out such a complicated and risky plan. What are his motives? Juliet trusts him – do you think she is wise to take the risk? Collect your ideas in a spider diagram, adding useful quotations. Continue to review the Friar's behaviour as the play heads towards its conclusion.

Language in the play 剧中语言

More images of death … and of haste (in pairs)

As the tragic momentum develops, Shakespeare loads this scene with images of death (there are well over a dozen explicit mentions, as well as others that are more implicit) and of speed or haste.

- Each of you focuses on words connected with either death or haste, and locates as many examples as possible of your chosen 'language chain' in this scene.
- Afterwards, write a paragraph or two, analysing some of the more effective examples you have picked out and exploring what dramatic impact they have on the scene. Share your responses.

1 vial 小瓶
2 this … off = drink off this distilled liquor（喝光这提炼出的液体）
3 When … humour = Then presently a cold and drowsy humour shall run through all thy veins（drowsy humour：令人昏昏欲睡的潮气）
4 surcease 停止跳动
5 wanny ashes 苍白的死灰
6 eyes' windows fall 眼睛的百叶窗落下（这里的windows指意大利盛行的可放下来遮阳的百叶窗，喻指眼睑）
7 Like … life = Like Death shutting up the daylight of life（其中Death指死神，life指生命）
8 supple government 灵活控制
9 stiff and stark 僵硬死板（这两个同义词经常连用）
10 uncovered on the bier 不加覆盖，放在殓板上
11 vault 地下（穹顶）墓室
12 kindred 家族
13 against 针对，预备
14 drift 意图；计划
15 inconstant toy 变化无常的念头，突发的奇想
16 Abate 降低，减弱
17 Hold 拿住
18 prosperous 成功

ROMEO AND JULIET ACT 4 SCENE 1
柔密欧与茱丽叶

          Take thou this vial¹, being then in bed,
          And this distilling liquor drink thou off²,
          When presently through all thy veins shall run   95
          A cold and drowsy humour³; for no pulse
          Shall keep his native progress, but surcease⁴;
          No warmth, no breath shall testify thou livest;
          The roses in thy lips and cheeks shall fade
          To wanny ashes⁵, thy eyes' windows⁶ fall,   100
          Like Death when he shuts up the day of life⁷;
          Each part, deprived of supple government⁸,
          Shall stiff and stark⁹ and cold appear like death,
          And in this borrowed likeness of shrunk death
          Thou shalt continue two and forty hours,   105
          And then awake as from a pleasant sleep.
          Now when the bridegroom in the morning comes
          To rouse thee from thy bed, there are thou dead.
          Then as the manner of our country is,
          In thy best robes, uncovered on the bier¹⁰,   110
          Thou shall be borne to that same ancient vault¹¹
          Where all the kindred¹² of the Capulets lie.
          In the mean time, against¹³ thou shalt awake,
          Shall Romeo by my letters know our drift¹⁴,
          And hither shall he come, and he and I   115
          Will watch thy waking, and that very night
          Shall Romeo bear thee hence to Mantua.
          And this shall free thee from this present shame,
          If no inconstant toy¹⁵, nor womanish fear,
          Abate¹⁶ thy valour in the acting it.   120

JULIET   Give me, give me! O tell not me of fear.

FRIAR LAWRENCE   Hold¹⁷, get you gone, be strong and prosperous¹⁸
          In this resolve; I'll send a friar with speed
          To Mantua, with my letters to thy lord.

JULIET   Love give me strength, and strength shall help afford.   125
          Farewell, dear father.

                                        Exeunt

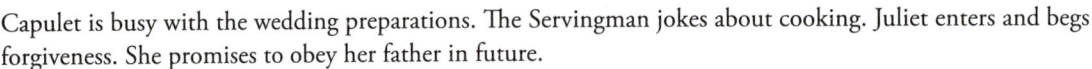

Capulet is busy with the wedding preparations. The Servingman jokes about cooking. Juliet enters and begs forgiveness. She promises to obey her father in future.

剧情简介：卡普莱忙着准备婚礼。仆人讲关于厨子做饭的笑话。茱丽叶上，请求父亲原谅，保证今后听话。

Write about it 写作练习

Capulet – what picture emerges? (in pairs, then by yourself)

Lord Capulet's moods swing wildly from mild-mannered and pleasant (Act 1 Scenes 2 and 5) to violent and angry (Act 3 Scene 5). Now Capulet is planning a grand wedding feast. He seems to have forgotten his earlier intention to have 'no great ado' (Act 3 Scene 4, line 23). Remind yourself of how Capulet is presented in the earlier scenes and then explore his characterisation in this scene.

- Begin by looking at the type of relationship he has with his servants at the start of the scene. Then consider his attitude towards Juliet. Try speaking line 15 in as many different ways as you can. Talk together about how you think it should be spoken on stage. What more does it tell you about Capulet's character?
- Juliet begs forgiveness at line 21; however, Capulet's first words are not to her, but to a servant. He orders that the wedding be brought forward to tomorrow (from Thursday to Wednesday: 'tomorrow morning'). Do you think that Capulet's two lines 22–3 suggest he is less interested in Juliet than in ensuring a prestigious marriage in his family?
- What does the closing exchange with his wife show about his changing attitude towards Juliet?

Use all your discussions and enquiries to help write a detailed study of how Capulet is presented in this scene. Remember to support your analytical comments with evidence from the text.

1 writ = written down
2 cunning 手艺好的
3 none ill 没有一个差的
4 try 检验，测试
5 lick their fingers 舔自己的手指头（出自谚语 "He is an ill cook that cannot lick his own finger."）
6 unfurnished 没准备好
7 this time 这一次（指这次婚礼）
8 forsooth 没错，的确
9 peevish 无脑
10 harlotry 蠢货，贱人，小蹄子
11 it = she
12 gadding 闲逛
13 behests 命令
14 enjoined 嘱咐
15 fall prostrate 五体投地
16 Henceforward … you 从今往后我一切听您吩咐

Stagecraft 导演技巧

Direct an episode

Look at the part of the scene between Juliet's entrance and her exit (at line 36). Imagine that you are directing this short episode.

- In your Director's Journal, write detailed notes for the three actors playing the Nurse, Juliet and Capulet. Explain how they should perform their lines, where they should be positioned and how they should move and react at each important line or phrase. In particular, think carefully about how Juliet enters, how she should kneel before her father and how he responds. What about her exit with the Nurse? How would you stage it?

Act 4 Scene 2
Capulet's mansion

Enter Father CAPULET, *Mother* [LADY CAPULET], NURSE, *and* SERVINGMEN, *two or three*.

CAPULET So many guests invite as here are writ[1].

[*Exit Servingman*]

Sirrah, go hire me twenty cunning[2] cooks.

SERVINGMAN You shall have none ill[3], sir, for I'll try[4] if they can lick their fingers[5].

CAPULET How canst thou try them so?

SERVINGMAN Marry, sir, 'tis an ill cook that cannot lick his own fingers; therefore he that cannot lick his fingers goes not with me.

CAPULET Go, be gone.

[*Exit Servingman*]

We shall be much unfurnished[6] for this time[7].
What, is my daughter gone to Friar Lawrence?

NURSE Ay forsooth[8].

CAPULET Well, he may chance to do some good on her.
A peevish[9] self-willed harlotry[10] it[11] is.

Enter JULIET.

NURSE See where she comes from shrift with merry look.

CAPULET How now, my headstrong, where have you been gadding[12]?

JULIET Where I have learnt me to repent the sin
Of disobedient opposition
To you and your behests[13], and am enjoined[14]
By holy Lawrence to fall prostrate[15] here
To beg your pardon.

[*She kneels down.*]

Pardon, I beseech you!
Henceforward I am ever ruled by you[16].

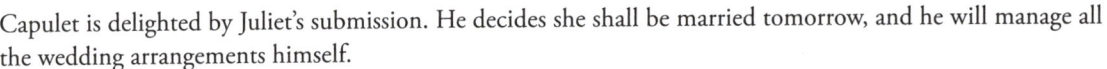

Capulet is delighted by Juliet's submission. He decides she shall be married tomorrow, and he will manage all the wedding arrangements himself.

剧情简介：看到茱丽叶顺服，卡普莱满心欢喜，决定明天就把她嫁出去，还要亲自张罗婚礼的所有安排。

1 True, false or double meaning? (in small groups)

a Look at everything Juliet says between lines 16 and 34. Judge whether you think each thing she says is 'true', 'false' or 'double meaning'. One person speaks Juliet's words. The others say 'true' or 'false' or 'double meaning' for each small section.

b Talk together about what you think of Juliet's behaviour here. Does it alter your feelings about her in any way?

2 More dramatic irony (in pairs)

There are many examples of dramatic irony (see p. 122) in the script opposite. Write down as many as you can find. Then compare your list with those of other pairs.

▼ 'Since this same wayward girl is so reclaimed.' Capulet believes that Juliet has come round to the idea of marrying Paris. How would you stage the 'reconciliation' (和解) between Juliet and her father?

1	this knot knit up	把这个婚结好（knot本身的意思是"绳子结"）
2	becomèd	适当，恰当
3	reverend	尊敬的（对神职人员的敬称）
4	much bound to him	对他充满感激
5	closet	卧室，闺房
6	needful ornaments	必要的穿戴
7	furnish me	装扮我
8	short in our provision	出现供应短缺
9	Tush	唷（表轻蔑或申斥）
10	stir about	到处张罗
11	deck up	打扮
12	let me alone	让我一个人来
13	huswife = housewife	
14	wayward	任性，执拗
15	reclaimed	悔过自新，回心转意

ROMEO AND JULIET ACT 4 SCENE 2
柔密欧与茱丽叶

CAPULET   Send for the County, go tell him of this.
             I'll have this knot knit up¹ tomorrow morning.
JULIET   I met the youthful lord at Lawrence' cell,
             And gave him what becomèd² love I might,   25
             Not stepping o'er the bounds of modesty.
CAPULET   Why, I am glad on't, this is well, stand up.
             This is as't should be. Let me see the County;
             Ay, marry, go, I say, and fetch him hither.
             Now afore God, this reverend³ holy Friar,   30
             All our whole city is much bound to him⁴.
JULIET   Nurse, will you go with me into my closet⁵,
             To help me sort such needful ornaments⁶
             As you think fit to furnish me⁷ tomorrow?
LADY CAPULET No, not till Thursday, there is time enough.   35
CAPULET   Go, Nurse, go with her, we'll to church tomorrow.
                                                     Exeunt [Juliet and Nurse]
LADY CAPULET We shall be short in our provision⁸,
             'Tis now near night.
CAPULET   Tush⁹, I will stir about¹⁰,
             And all things shall be well, I warrant thee, wife:
             Go thou to Juliet, help to deck up¹¹ her;   40
             I'll not to bed tonight; let me alone¹²,
             I'll play the huswife¹³ for this once. What ho!
             They are all forth. Well, I will walk myself
             To County Paris, to prepare up him
             Against tomorrow. My heart is wondrous light,   45
             Since this same wayward¹⁴ girl is so reclaimed¹⁵.
                                                                    Exeunt

Juliet sends her Nurse and mother away. Alone, she fights her fears, plucking up courage to drink the 'poison'. If it does not work she will kill herself with a dagger rather than be married.

 剧情简介：茱丽叶把奶妈和母亲支开。她独自一人，她克服恐惧，鼓足勇气准备喝下"毒剂"。如果药不管用，她宁可拿短剑自尽也不愿意出嫁。

1 Juliet's double meanings (in pairs)

Juliet deliberately deceives her mother and the Nurse. In lines 1–12, she once again uses language rich in double meanings and dramatic irony. This short activity explores what is in her mind.

- One person speaks everything Juliet says up to line 12, pausing after each short section. In each pause, your partner says aloud what Juliet is really thinking. Talk together about how this adds to your understanding of Juliet's character, and of her feelings about her mother and the Nurse.

1 attires   衣服
2 orisons   祷告
3 smile upon my state   保佑我，降福于我
4 cross   乖戾，固执
5 culled   挑选
6 behoveful   适宜，适合
7 state   社会地位，身份
8 thrills   冷战，寒战

▼ Choose a quotation from Scene 3 to caption this photograph.

Stagecraft 导演技巧

Juliet's soliloquy (by yourself)

Read through to the end of Scene 3. Write notes for an actor playing Juliet, advising her how to deliver her soliloquy in lines 15–58. Suggest actions, expressions, tone of voice and pauses. Note that the stage direction 'within the curtains' after line 58 was written for the Elizabethan theatre, which had a curtained alcove (凹室) at the back of the stage.

Act 4 Scene 3
Juliet's bedroom

Enter JULIET *and* NURSE.

JULIET   Ay, those attires[1] are best, but, gentle Nurse,
I pray thee leave me to myself tonight:
For I have need of many orisons[2]
To move the heavens to smile upon my state[3],
Which, well thou knowest, is cross[4] and full of sin.   5

Enter Mother [LADY CAPULET].

LADY CAPULET   What, are you busy, ho? need you my help?
JULIET   No, madam, we have culled[5] such necessaries
As are behoveful[6] for our state[7] tomorrow.
So please you, let me now be left alone,
And let the Nurse this night sit up with you,   10
For I am sure you have your hands full all,
In this so sudden business.
LADY CAPULET   Good night.
Get thee to bed and rest, for thou hast need.

Exeunt [*Lady Capulet and Nurse*]

JULIET   Farewell! God knows when we shall meet again.
I have a faint cold fear thrills[8] through my veins   15
That almost freezes up the heat of life:
I'll call them back again to comfort me.
Nurse! – What should she do here?
My dismal scene I needs must act alone.
Come, vial.   20
What if this mixture do not work at all?
Shall I be married then tomorrow morning?
No, no, this shall forbid it; lie thou there.

[*Laying down her dagger.*]

Juliet is filled with fearful thoughts. Is the Friar honest? Will she awake in the tomb before Romeo comes? Will she go mad with dread? She drinks the potion.

 剧情简介：茱丽叶生出很多可怕的念头：修士的话可信吗？万一她在墓穴中醒来时柔密欧没到怎么办？她会不会因恐惧而发疯？她饮下了药剂。

1 What is Juliet thinking and feeling?

Try the following activities to express Juliet's thoughts and feelings as she contemplates drinking the Friar's secret potion.

a **Echo the ominous words (in pairs)** Take lines 30–57. One person reads the lines. The other echoes every word to do with fear or death. You will find that Shakespeare loads the speech with such words to express Juliet's fears.

b **Whispering (in small groups)** Put your heads as close together as possible. Speak lines 15–58 around the group as a whispered, fearful conversation, with each person speaking a short section, then handing on.

c **Transforming genre (in pairs)** Together, work through Juliet's speech, carefully turning the lines of Shakespeare's original verse into modern English prose. In your first version, try to make your writing as literal as you can, avoiding flowery language and heightened expression. Then, in a second draft, aim at producing a rewrite that draws on the style of a modern ghost or horror story. Fill it with atmospheric words and images. Imagine, for example, that Juliet sits down one cold, dark evening in a secluded (僻静) place. She is alone. The wind whistles eerily (奇异地) outside. She begins her story …

2 Conscience alley: Juliet (in large groups)

- After a whole group reading of Juliet's lines 15–58, one person in the group plays Juliet, holding in their mind Juliet's thoughts at the end of her soliloquy before she drinks the Friar's potion. The others in the group form two lines, facing each other but separated by an 'alley' (a narrow corridor) down which Juliet must walk slowly.

- As Juliet does this, all those on the left-hand side of her try to find reasons to persuade her not to drink the Friar's potion; those on her right try to persuade her that this is her best course of action. Juliet remains silent until she reaches the end of the 'alley'.

- Afterwards, Juliet should share with the group what it is like having to make such a momentous decision in the face of these different pressures and uncertainties.

1 Subtly 诡诈地
2 ministered = administered （施用药物）
3 still been tried 总是被证明
4 redeem 解救
5 stifled 窒息
6 healthsome 有益健康
7 strangled 窒息，闷死
8 like = likely
9 conceit 想象，想法
10 receptacle 收容所
11 green in earth 新近入土
12 fest'ring in his shroud 腐烂在裹尸布中
13 mandrakes 曼陀罗草（其根为人形，可制药，古时人们认为它长在绞刑架下，吸人血，被拔出时会尖叫）
14 living mortals 活人
15 distraught 被吓疯
16 Environèd 被包围
17 joints 骨头
18 dash out 击碎
19 spit 刺穿

ROMEO AND JULIET ACT 4 SCENE 3
柔密欧与茱丽叶

What if it be a poison which the Friar
Subtly¹ hath ministered² to have me dead, 25
Lest in this marriage he should be dishonoured,
Because he married me before to Romeo?
I fear it is, and yet methinks it should not,
For he hath still been tried³ a holy man.
How if, when I am laid into the tomb, 30
I wake before the time that Romeo
Come to redeem⁴ me? There's a fearful point!
Shall I not then be stifled⁵ in the vault,
To whose foul mouth no healthsome⁶ air breathes in,
And there die strangled⁷ ere my Romeo comes? 35
Or if I live, is it not very like⁸
The horrible conceit⁹ of death and night,
Together with the terror of the place –
As in a vault, an ancient receptacle¹⁰,
Where for this many hundred years the bones 40
Of all my buried ancestors are packed,
Where bloody Tybalt, yet but green in earth¹¹,
Lies fest'ring in his shroud¹², where, as they say,
At some hours in the night spirits resort –
Alack, alack, is it not like that I, 45
So early waking – what with loathsome smells,
And shrieks like mandrakes'¹³ torn out of the earth,
That living mortals¹⁴ hearing them run mad –
O, if I wake, shall I not be distraught¹⁵,
Environèd¹⁶ with all these hideous fears, 50
And madly play with my forefathers' joints¹⁷,
And pluck the mangled Tybalt from his shroud,
And in this rage, with some great kinsman's bone,
As with a club, dash out¹⁸ my desp'rate brains?
O look! methinks I see my cousin's ghost 55
Seeking out Romeo that did spit¹⁹ his body
Upon a rapier's point. Stay, Tybalt, stay!
Romeo, Romeo, Romeo! Here's drink – I drink to thee.
  [*She falls upon her bed, within the curtains.*]

It is early morning and the wedding preparations are well under way. Lady Capulet hints that Capulet has been an unfaithful husband in the past.

剧情简介：大清早，婚礼的准备工作很顺利。卡普莱夫人暗示丈夫卡普莱过去曾对她不忠。

1 Textual puzzles

a No one is quite sure whether Angelica is the Nurse's name or Lady Capulet's. In one production, Angelica was a young serving-woman with whom Capulet was obviously having an affair. Talk together about who you think Capulet is addressing in line 5. It may be helpful to know that for Shakespeare and his contemporaries, Angelica probably meant 'beautiful princess'.

b Some people think that it should be Lady Capulet, rather than the Nurse, who speaks lines 6–8. This edition gives the lines to the Nurse, and so implies that she can be very familiar with her master when she wishes. Who do you think is most likely to speak the lines?

Write about it 写作练习
Juliet explains to her parents (in pairs)

Throughout the play, Shakespeare has taken the opportunity to suggest the type of relationship Juliet's parents have with each other. Here, in lines 11–12, he adds to the picture: Lady Capulet seems to suggest that her husband has chased after other women, but that she will now keep a close eye on him. In response, Capulet accuses her of being jealous. In light of this, what impact do you think living with her parents has had on Juliet? Remember – if all goes well with the Friar's plan she will be with Romeo and may never see her parents again.

- Imagine that she leaves behind a letter for her parents to find sometime in the future. In it she explains her course of action, but also talks about relationships at home and the part they have played in her momentous decision. Write Juliet's letter.

Language in the play 剧中语言
Watching for puns

Notice how all three characters play on the word 'watch' (lines 7–12). Can you work out the various meanings of their puns?

1 dates 椰枣
2 quinces 木梨（学名榲桲，果实是梨形，色金黄，味酸甜，略涩，可制果酱）
3 pastry 糕点间
4 second cock hath crowed 鸡叫已经第二遍了（凌晨三点）
5 curfew bell 宵禁钟（提醒人们夜间熄火睡觉的钟）
6 cot-quean 家务男
7 watching 不合眼，不睡觉
8 whit 一点点
9 mouse-hunt 偷腥的夜猫子（指与其他女人有染）
10 jealous hood 醋坛子（hood 指女人）
11 spits 烤肉扦子

Act 4 Scene 4
A room in Capulet's mansion

Enter lady of the house LADY CAPULET *and* NURSE *with herbs.*

LADY CAPULET Hold, take these keys and fetch more spices, Nurse.
NURSE They call for dates[1] and quinces[2] in the pastry[3].

Enter old CAPULET.

CAPULET Come, stir, stir, stir! the second cock hath crowed[4],
The curfew bell[5] hath rung, 'tis three a'clock.
Look to the baked meats, good Angelica,   5
Spare not for cost.
NURSE Go, you cot-quean[6], go,
Get you to bed. Faith, you'll be sick tomorrow
For this night's watching[7].
CAPULET No, not a whit[8]. What, I have watched ere now
All night for lesser cause, and ne'er been sick.   10
LADY CAPULET Ay, you have been a mouse-hunt[9] in your time,
But I will watch you from such watching now.
Exeunt Lady [Capulet] and Nurse
CAPULET A jealous hood[10], a jealous hood!

Enter three or four [SERVINGMEN] *with spits*[11] *and logs and baskets.*

Now, fellow,
What is there?
FIRST SERVINGMAN Things for the cook, sir, but I know not what.   15

Capulet fusses busily with the wedding arrangements. He tells the Nurse to wake Juliet. The next scene opens with the Nurse attempting to rouse Juliet.

剧情简介：卡普莱咋咋呼呼操持着婚礼的各项准备工作。他让奶妈去叫醒茱丽叶。下一场开始，奶妈试图唤醒茱丽叶。

Write about it 写作练习

A servant's viewpoint

On page 156 you were invited to write about some aspects of Juliet's home life from her point of view. The servants in Capulet's household will also have their opinions about the Capulet family and what it is like to work for them. They will almost certainly see day-to-day events differently from their masters.

- Take on (研判) the persona (人设) of one of the unnamed servants in this scene. Use all the evidence you have read in the play so far about what it is like to live and work inside the Capulet mansion, then script a short piece of dialogue in which your invented character talks to a friend (perhaps a servant for another family) about life with the Capulets. Describe some of the tensions surrounding the dramatic preparations for the wedding.

1. I have a head   我有脑子
2. Mass = By the Mass（语气温和的骂人话，可以解释为"臭小子"）
3. whoreson   龟儿子，王八蛋（语气较温和）
4. loggerhead   榆木脑袋
5. straight   马上
6. trim her up   帮她打扮好
7. Fast = Fast asleep
8. slug-a-bed   床上的懒虫
9. pennyworths   几分钱的觉
10. set up his rest   下定决心（本义是"押上剩下所有的钱"）
11. rest but little   得不到什么休息

Stagecraft 导演技巧

Make the scene flow (in pairs)

Scenes 3, 4 and 5 are set in Capulet's mansion (in Juliet's bedroom and another room). How could you ensure that the stage action flows smoothly throughout these scenes?

- Work out how that 'flow' might be achieved in these three scenes. Design a stage set and accompany it with a description of how it enables the action to move swiftly from one place to another without delay for elaborate scene-shifting. (On Shakespeare's stage, Juliet almost certainly lay in an alcove concealed by a curtain at the back of the stage.)

1 Dramatic construction

With its bustle, humour and much talk of 'haste', Scene 4 sharply contrasts with the mood of Scenes 3 and 5. This technique of contrasting scenes is typical of Shakespeare's stagecraft. The playwright knew that he could increase dramatic effect by means of such juxtapositions (see p. 138).

- Give two or three reasons why you think Shakespeare places Scene 4 between the serious ones that precede and follow it in this act.

CAPULET	Make haste, make haste.

[*Exit First Servingman*]

Sirrah, fetch drier logs.
Call Peter, he will show thee where they are.

SECOND SERVINGMAN   I have a head[1], sir, that will find out logs,
And never trouble Peter for the matter.

CAPULET   Mass[2], and well said, a merry whoreson[3], ha!   20
Thou shalt be loggerhead[4].

[*Exeunt Second Servingman and any others*]

Good faith, 'tis day.
The County will be here with music straight[5],
For so he said he would.

(*Play music* [*within*].)

I hear him near.
Nurse! Wife! What ho! What, Nurse, I say!

Enter Nurse.

Go waken Juliet, go and trim her up[6],   25
I'll go and chat with Paris. Hie, make haste,
Make haste, the bridegroom he is come already,
Make haste, I say.   [*Exit*]

Act 4 Scene 5
Juliet's bedroom

NURSE   Mistress, what mistress! Juliet! Fast[7], I warrant her, she.
Why, lamb! why, lady! fie, you slug-a-bed[8]!
Why, love, I say! madam! sweet heart! why, bride!
What, not a word? You take your pennyworths[9] now;
Sleep for a week, for the next night I warrant   5
The County Paris hath set up his rest[10]
That you shall rest but little[11]. God forgive me!

The Nurse, thinking Juliet to be dead, raises the house with her cries. Lady Capulet and her husband express their grief. Paris, unaware, enters to take Juliet to church.

剧情简介：奶妈以为茱丽叶死了，惊叫着把家人全叫了过来。卡普莱夫妇悲痛不已。帕瑞还一无所知，来接茱丽叶去教堂。

1 The Nurse's changing mood (in pairs)

The Nurse begins the scene trying to wake Juliet. Her language in lines 4–11 contains playfully sexual double meanings about Juliet's wedding night. But the Nurse's mood changes as she comes to believe that Juliet is dead. Her language now is full of alarmed, brief exclamations and cries.

- With a partner, read lines 1–16 to each other, trying out different ways of saying each line. Can you agree on a version you prefer? Work out the actions and movements you would use to accompany the Nurse's words. Decide whether your version includes a 'sudden' or 'gradual' realisation by the Nurse of Juliet's death. When you have produced your definitive version, write up a short commentary on lines 1–16, explaining your ideas and choices.

1 take you　收服您
2 fright you up　吓 / 压得您心颤
　　（fright与freight"载重"谐音，暗指帕瑞压在茱丽叶身上）
3 down again　又躺下
4 lamentable　可悲
5 deceased　过世了
6 settled　凝固

Characters 人物分析

Lady Capulet's anguish (in pairs)

Lady Capulet's feelings towards her daughter have varied dramatically throughout the play. When Juliet refused to marry Paris, her mother showed no sympathy or affection. But now, thinking Juliet is dead, she seems broken-hearted. As you read on, you will find she becomes even more grief-stricken.

- Imagine that Lady Capulet seeks support from a counsellor whose role it is, in the first instance, to encourage her to talk honestly and in detail about her problems. One person takes the role of counsellor and scripts a dozen or so questions that might help Lady Capulet to open up about her relationship with her daughter. The other person plays Lady Capulet and answers those questions. You could record your interview and play it back to the class for reaction and comment.

Write about it 写作练习

Friar Lawrence's private thoughts

Friar Lawrence arrives with Paris and the musicians. He alone knows that Juliet is not dead.

- Use the format of an interior monologue to write what he is probably thinking as he enters. Include a comment on why he poses his question at line 33, since he already knows the answer to it!

Marry and amen! How sound is she asleep!
I needs must wake her. Madam, madam, madam!
Ay, let the County take you[1] in your bed, 10
He'll fright you up[2], i'faith. Will it not be?
            [*Draws back the curtains.*]
What, dressed, and in your clothes, and down again[3]?
I must needs wake you. Lady, lady, lady!
Alas, alas! Help, help! my lady's dead!
O weraday that ever I was born! 15
Some aqua-vitae, ho! My lord! My lady!

            [*Enter Mother,* LADY CAPULET.]

LADY CAPULET   What noise is here?
NURSE   O lamentable[4] day!
LADY CAPULET   What is the matter?
NURSE   Look, look! O heavy day!
LADY CAPULET   O me, O me, my child, my only life!
            Revive, look up, or I will die with thee. 20
            Help, help! Call help.

            Enter Father [CAPULET].

CAPULET   For shame, bring Juliet forth, her lord is come.
NURSE   She's dead, deceased[5], she's dead, alack the day!
LADY CAPULET   Alack the day, she's dead, she's dead, she's dead!
CAPULET   Hah, let me see her. Out alas, she's cold, 25
            Her blood is settled[6], and her joints are stiff:
            Life and these lips have long been separated;
            Death lies on her like an untimely frost
            Upon the sweetest flower of all the field.
NURSE   O lamentable day!
LADY CAPULET   O woeful time! 30
CAPULET   Death that hath tane her hence to make me wail
            Ties up my tongue and will not let me speak.

            Enter FRIAR [LAWRENCE] *and the* COUNTY [PARIS *with the*
                    MUSICIANS].

FRIAR LAWRENCE   Come, is the bride ready to go to church?

The Capulets, the Nurse and Paris mourn for Juliet. The Friar attempts to offer consolation, saying that Juliet is now in a better state because she is in heaven.

剧情简介： 卡普莱夫妇、奶妈和帕瑞都为茱丽叶感到哀痛。修士试着抚慰大家，说茱丽叶已经去了更好的地方，因为她已升天。

1 Mourning for Juliet (in fours)

a Each person takes a part: Capulet, Paris, Lady Capulet, the Nurse. Read aloud lines 35–64. First, have a go at reading all parts simultaneously so that you create a 'chorus' of grief. Then change parts and read again, this time in the natural order of the lines in the play. Change again until everyone has read all four parts. You could perhaps organise this reading by standing around an imaginary figure of the 'dead' Juliet. Afterwards, talk together about the different ways in which the four characters express their grief.

b Critics of the play have said that this mourning is selfish, artificial and self-indulgent – even absurd (and in some productions this episode is cut). Other critics defend the language, saying it is sincere and typical of the characters and the occasion (it was also a familiar convention in the tragic plays of the time). What are your views? Work together to write a statement about each character, explaining whether you think that the way in which they mourn matches their personality.

2 What should the audience feel? (in pairs)

If you were directing the play, what effect on an audience would you hope to achieve in your staging of this scene of mourning? After all, the audience knows that Juliet is alive, not dead.

- With a partner, discuss possible options and decide on your favourite idea. Explain it to other pairs.

Language in the play 剧中语言

'In lasting labour of his pilgrimage!' (in pairs)

In lines 44–5, Lady Capulet personifies time, turning it into a pilgrim working tirelessly every day. But the major personification throughout this mourning scene is that of Death.

- How many examples of personification can you find in this scene? Add them to your Language file (see p. 44).
- In each case, write a sentence explaining how the personification heightens the dramatic impact of the image.
- Choose one and make a sketch of the image it suggests to you.

---

1 deflowerèd 被破了花苞
2 thought long 等得不耐烦
3 Accursed 受到诅咒
4 lasting 永恒
5 solace 安慰，抚慰
6 catched = caught（夺去，抢走）
7 Beguiled 受欺骗
8 detestable 可憎，可恶
9 solemnity 庆典（这里指婚庆）
10 Confusion's cure 走出不幸的法子
11 confusions 不管不顾的哭闹
12 Your part in her 你们拥有的她那部分（指茱丽叶的肉体）
13 heaven keeps his part 上天将保存自己那部分（指茱丽叶的灵魂）

CAPULET   Ready to go, but never to return. –
                  O son, the night before thy wedding day
                  Hath Death lain with thy wife. There she lies,
                  Flower as she was, deflowerèd[1] by him.
                  Death is my son-in-law, Death is my heir,
                  My daughter he hath wedded. I will die,
                  And leave him all; life, living, all is Death's.

PARIS   Have I thought long[2] to see this morning's face,
                  And doth it give me such a sight as this?

LADY CAPULET   Accursed[3], unhappy, wretched, hateful day!
                  Most miserable hour that e'er time saw
                  In lasting[4] labour of his pilgrimage!
                  But one, poor one, one poor and loving child,
                  But one thing to rejoice and solace[5] in,
                  And cruel Death hath catched[6] it from my sight!

NURSE   O woe! O woeful, woeful, woeful day!
                  Most lamentable day, most woeful day
                  That ever, ever, I did yet behold!
                  O day, O day, O day, O hateful day!
                  Never was seen so black a day as this.
                  O woeful day, O woeful day!

PARIS   Beguiled[7], divorcèd, wrongèd, spited, slain!
                  Most detestable[8] Death, by thee beguiled,
                  By cruel, cruel thee quite overthrown!
                  O love! O life! not life, but love in death!

CAPULET   Despised, distressèd, hated, martyred, killed!
                  Uncomfortable time, why cam'st thou now
                  To murder, murder our solemnity[9]?
                  O child, O child! my soul, and not my child!
                  Dead art thou. Alack, my child is dead,
                  And with my child my joys are burièd.

FRIAR LAWRENCE   Peace ho, for shame! Confusion's cure[10] lives not
                  In these confusions[11]. Heaven and yourself
                  Had part in this fair maid, now heaven hath all,
                  And all the better is it for the maid:
                  Your part in her[12] you could not keep from death,
                  But heaven keeps his part[13] in eternal life.

Friar Lawrence rebukes the family for their grief. They should stop crying because Juliet is now in heaven. He tells them to prepare her funeral. Everyone leaves except Peter and the musicians.

剧情简介：劳润修士训斥茱丽叶的家人为她悲痛欲绝，说他们应该止住哭啼，因为茱丽叶已经升天。他让他们为她准备葬礼。大家都下场，台上仅剩下皮特和众乐师。

1 More of the Friar's secret thoughts (in pairs)

The Friar knows that Juliet is not dead, but he talks to the family as though she were.

- One person reads aloud Friar Lawrence's lines 65–83. Pause frequently. In each pause, the other person says aloud what the Friar is really thinking at that moment.

Language in the play 剧中语言
'black funeral' – make the antitheses physical

You will need an empty space for this activity. It will help you identify the antitheses in Capulet's speech.

- Capulet's lines 84–90 have a rhythm all of their own. Walk around the room reading the lines aloud. Every time you come to a 'turning' word such as 'turn', 'to' or 'serve', change direction in your walking.
- Invent different ways of physically expressing the movement of Capulet's speech (e.g. sitting down but turning your hand or body from side to side as the language 'turns'). Is there a 'natural' way in which these lines might be spoken – that is, where the speech is spoken without the formal, rhetorical style it seems to require? You will find another activity based on Capulet's lines 84–90 and "Juliet's funeral procession" on page 168.

1 **her promotion** 让她有个好出路
2 **rosemary** 迷迭香（用于葬礼或婚礼的纪念）
3 **Yet … merriment** 天性的眼泪是理性的嬉笑
4 **that we ordainèd festival** = that we ordained for a festival（我们为一场喜庆安排的）
5 **office** 功能，目的
6 **cheer** 餐饮
7 **dirges** 挽歌
8 **low'r** 生气蹙眉，面色阴沉
9 **ill** （你们犯下的）罪恶
10 **Move** 惹怒
11 **put up our pipes** 收起我们的箫笛
12 **the case may be amended** 这个盒子是可以修的（此处的 case与上一行的case [情况] 双关）
13 **dump** 哀乐，悲歌（因此merry dump用的是矛盾修辞法；参见第215页）

Themes 主题分析
Chance versus choice

In lines 94–5, Friar Lawrence suggests that the 'heavens' are already punishing the Capulet parents (with Juliet's 'death') and should not be provoked any further. Of course, he knows that Juliet is still alive.

- What reasons can you suggest for Shakespeare giving the Friar these two lines at this point in the play? Add your ideas to the spider diagram that you began on page 146. Explain carefully the decisions you reach.

Romeo and Juliet Act 4 Scene 5
柔密欧与茱丽叶

	The most you sought was her promotion[1],
	For 'twas your heaven she should be advanced,
	And weep ye now, seeing she is advanced
	Above the clouds, as high as heaven itself?
	O, in this love, you love your child so ill

          The most you sought was her promotion[1],
For 'twas your heaven she should be advanced,
And weep ye now, seeing she is advanced
Above the clouds, as high as heaven itself?
O, in this love, you love your child so ill   75
That you run mad, seeing that she is well.
She's not well married that lives married long,
But she's best married that dies married young.
Dry up your tears, and stick your rosemary[2]
On this fair corse, and as the custom is,   80
And in her best array, bear her to church;
For though fond nature bids us all lament,
Yet nature's tears are reason's merriment[3].

CAPULET   All things that we ordainèd festival[4],
Turn from their office[5] to black funeral: 85
Our instruments to melancholy bells,
Our wedding cheer[6] to a sad burial feast;
Our solemn hymns to sullen dirges[7] change;
Our bridal flowers serve for a buried corse;
And all things change them to the contrary.   90

FRIAR LAWRENCE   Sir, go you in, and, madam, go with him,
And go, Sir Paris. Every one prepare
To follow this fair corse unto her grave.
The heavens do low'r[8] upon you for some ill[9];
Move[10] them no more by crossing their high will.   95

        [*They all, but the Nurse and the Musicians, go forth,*
              casting rosemary on her, and shutting the curtains]

FIRST MUSICIAN   Faith, we may put up our pipes[11] and be gone.

NURSE   Honest good fellows, ah put up, put up,
For well you know this is a pitiful case.   [*Exit*]

FIRST MUSICIAN   Ay, by my troth, the case may be amended[12].

              Enter PETER.

PETER   Musicians, O musicians, 'Heart's ease', 'Heart's ease'! O,   100
and you will have me live, play 'Heart's ease'.

FIRST MUSICIAN   Why 'Heart's ease'?

PETER   O musicians, because my heart itself plays 'My heart is full'.
O play me some merry dump[13] to comfort me.

Peter talks with the musicians. He variously insults, threatens and mocks them. They do not care for his humour.

剧情简介：皮特和乐师们找话说；他变着样地羞辱、吓唬、取笑他们。乐师们则对他的幽默无动于衷。

Stagecraft 导演技巧
Playing the musicians (in fours)

a Each person takes a part (Peter and the musicians). Read through lines 100–38. Work out how you would stage them.

b The musicians' episode changes the mood of the scene. It descends into **bathos*** (anti-climax). So what is the purpose of bringing them on? Discuss this in your groups.

c Sometimes lines 100–38 are cut from performances. Talk together about whether you would cut the musicians and Peter from your production. Two argue for leaving out this part of the play. Two argue for keeping it in. Share your verdict and reasons with the rest of the class.

Themes 主题分析
Disputes at all levels?

Between lines 100 and 138, Peter and the musicians spar with language just like the Montague and Capulet servants at the start of the play. Although they don't actually come to blows, there are several insulting comments and threats of violence.

- Look back to the start of Act 1 Scene 1 and compare it with this episode. What do you think those scenes show about the behaviour and attitudes that exist in the lower levels of society in Verona? Write a couple of paragraphs to summarise your findings. Include a comment on the fact that both scenes show male-only behaviour.

1 Get musical (in pairs)

Choose one of the following activities.

a Set Peter's three lines 120–2 ('When griping griefs the heart doth wound … her silver sound') to your own music.

b In lines 100–4, you will find the titles of two popular songs of Shakespeare's day: 'Heart's ease' and 'My heart is full'. Their words are now lost. Make up a song using one or both titles. You could, of course, incorporate some elements of the story of *Romeo and Juliet* into your song.

1 soundly 彻底；大声
2 gleek 辱骂（换作今天，皮特肯定会打出V字手势 [手背向外，表示侮辱、蔑视]）
3 minstrel （参见第92页注解4）
4 serving-creature 狗奴才
5 pate 脑袋
6 carry no crotchets 唱不出奇声怪调来（crotchet 指音乐中的"四分音符"，也有"奇怪想法"的意思）
7 I'll re you, I'll fa you 我可以在你们脑袋上敲出re音和fa音
8 note 谱曲（与上一行的note [听见] 双关）
9 dry-beat （参见第94页注解3）
10 griping 痛苦
11 doleful dumps 寂寞忧愁
12 Catling / Rebeck / Soundpost 肠弦、三弦琴、音柱（皮特故意用乐师手里乐器的部件称呼他们，是对他们的蔑视）
13 Prates! 胡说八道！
14 sound 演奏，演唱
15 cry you mercy 请您原谅
16 for sounding 通过演奏或演唱（来挣钱）
17 pestilent 讨人厌
18 tarry for 等候
19 stay dinner 推迟开饭

* **bathos** 突降法，一种修辞手法，指美好、庄重的内容突然变得平庸可笑。这种效果常常不是言者有意所为。

MUSICIANS   Not a dump we, 'tis no time to play now.
PETER   You will not then?
FIRST MUSICIAN   No.
PETER   I will then give it you soundly[1].
FIRST MUSICIAN   What will you give us?
PETER   No money, on my faith, but the gleek[2]; I will give you the minstrel[3].
FIRST MUSICIAN   Then will I give you the serving-creature[4].
PETER   Then will I lay the serving-creature's dagger on your pate[5]. I will carry no crotchets[6], I'll re you, I'll fa you[7]. Do you note me?
FIRST MUSICIAN   And you re us and fa us, you note[8] us.
SECOND MUSICIAN   Pray you put up your dagger, and put out your wit.
PETER   Then have at you with my wit! I will dry-beat[9] you with an iron wit, and put up my iron dagger. Answer me like men:
   'When griping[10] griefs the heart doth wound,
      And doleful dumps[11] the mind oppress,
   Then music with her silver sound –'
Why 'silver sound'? why 'music with her silver sound'? What say you, Simon Catling[12]?
FIRST MUSICIAN   Marry, sir, because silver hath a sweet sound.
PETER   Prates![13] What say you, Hugh Rebeck[12]?
SECOND MUSICIAN   I say 'silver sound' because musicians sound[14] for silver.
PETER   Prates too! What say you, James Soundpost[12]?
THIRD MUSICIAN   Faith, I know not what to say.
PETER   O, I cry you mercy[15], you are the singer; I will say for you: It is 'music with her silver sound' because musicians have no gold for sounding[16].
   'Then music with her silver sound
      With speedy help doth lend redress.'   *Exit*
FIRST MUSICIAN   What a pestilent[17] knave is this same!
SECOND MUSICIAN   Hang him, Jack! Come, we'll in here, tarry for[18] the mourners, and stay dinner[19].

Exeunt

ROMEO AND JULIET
柔密欧与茱丽叶

Looking back at Act 4 第4幕回顾
Activities for groups or individuals

1 Juliet's funeral procession (送葬)

> Every one prepare
> To follow this fair corse unto her grave.
> Act 4 Scene 5, lines 92–3

In the eighteenth and nineteenth centuries, theatre productions often added a scene to show the funeral of Juliet. The playbill (戏单) opposite advertises a production at Drury Lane in 1756, mentioning the funeral procession as a highlight of the production.

- In groups of eight to twelve, work out how you could stage Juliet's funeral. Use Capulet's lines 84–90 from Scene 5. Make your presentation as dramatically striking as possible. You could speak or sing or chant the words. Each group member can choose to be a character and use some of that person's mourning language (lines 34–64 in Scene 5) in the funeral march.
- Try to find some music to accompany your group's actions, such as 'The Dead March' from Handel's *Saul*, or Fauré's *Requiem*.

2 Focus on Juliet – Romeo's absence

Romeo does not appear in Act 4. Shakespeare keeps the dramatic focus tightly on Juliet throughout. Even in 'death' in Scene 5, she remains the centre of other characters' attention. Not only that, she becomes an increasingly isolated figure – by the end of the act she is hiding things from the Nurse for the first time in the play.

- Consider all the scenes in turn, then write a paragraph on each one, identifying how Juliet is central to it, reflecting on her isolation and explaining how this adds to the dramatic impact of the scene. Focus on how tension is increased, and how the pressure relentlessly builds on Juliet and the decisions and choices she must make.

3 Keeping Romeo in mind?

Although Romeo does not appear on stage in Act 4, some productions use staging devices to remind the audience of his 'presence' in the background of the play. For example, there might be an image or prop visible throughout the act that clearly links with Romeo.

- Do you think this is a good idea or not? Argue your case in a written paragraph.

4 A scene full of artificiality (做作)?

Scene 5 is often a problem in performance. It contains over-the-top (过火) mourning for Juliet (which some critics find ridiculous), the 'acting' of the Friar (who, like the audience, knows that Juliet is not dead) and the inappropriate fooling around of the musicians. What do you think Shakespeare set out to do in this scene? Why close Act 4 in ways that seem at odds with the gathering forces of tragedy?

- Step into role as Shakespeare. Try to explain to your company of actors what you have in mind. Give his rationale (道理) – either in written or spoken form.

5 Dramatic irony

There are many striking examples of dramatic irony in Act 4 (see p. 122). For example, Paris knows nothing about the truth of Juliet's situation as he speaks with her. Lord Capulet believes that his daughter actually agrees to marry Paris. Lady Capulet and the Nurse do not understand why Juliet wants to be alone the night before the marriage. All the characters who mourn the 'dead' Juliet are misled by Juliet's pretence. Only the Friar knows the truth – and he deliberately deceives the others.

- Work through the examples given above. In each case, explain fully and in detail how the dramatic irony operates and consider how it might be used to add to the act's power and intensity. Write up your ideas.

Looking back at Act 4

AT THE
Theatre Royal in Drury-Lane,

This present *Tuesday*, being the 16th of *November*, 1756
Will be presented a PLAY, call'd
ROMEO and JULIET.
Romeo by Mr. GARRICK,

Escalus by Mr. BRANSBY,
Capulet by Mr. BERRY,
Paris by Mr. JEFFERSON,
Benvolio by Mr. USHER,
Mountague by Mr. BURTON,
Tibalt by Mr. BLAKES,
Fryar *Lawrence* by Mr. HAVARD,
Mercutio by Mr. WOODWARD,
Lady *Capulet* by Mrs. PRITCHARD,
Nurse by Mrs. MACKLIN,
Juliet by Miss PRITCHARD.

With the ADDITIONAL SCENE Representing
The Funeral PROCESSION
To the MONUMENT of the CAPULETS.

The VOCAL PARTS by
Mr. *Beard*, Mr. *Champness* and *Others*.
In Act I. a *Masquerade* Dance proper to the Play.
To which will be added a FARCE, call'd
The ANATOMIST.

Monf. *Le Medecin* by Mr. BLAKES,
Crispin by Mr. YATES,
Beatrice by Mrs. BENNET.

Boxes 5s.   Pit 3s.   First Gallery 2s.   Upper Gallery 1s.
Places for the Boxes to be had of Mr. VARNEY, at the Stage-
door of the *Theatre*.
† *No Persons to be admitted behind the Scenes, nor any Money to be returned
after the Curtain is drawn up.*   Vivat REX.

To-morrow, the MOURNING BRIDE. *Osmyn* by Mr. MOSSOP,
(Being the First Time of his appearing in that Character.)

Romeo, in Mantua, talks joyfully of his strange dream: he dreamt that he died, but Juliet revived him with kisses. Then Balthasar brings him dreadful news.

 剧情简介：柔密欧身在曼托瓦，满怀喜悦地讲述自己做的怪梦：他梦见自己死了，但是茱丽叶的香吻让他复活。接下来巴尔特扎给他带来了骇人的消息。

1 Romeo's dream: another premonition? (in pairs)

This is the second ominous premonition that Romeo speaks about. His earlier one (at the end of Act 1 Scene 4) was full of dark thoughts about the future. Here (lines 6–9) his dream seems to reassure him: Juliet brings a dead Romeo back to life with her kisses.

a Between you, write a quick summary in modern English of the content of Romeo's first 'vision' and this one. Try to come up with at least three reasons why you think Shakespeare begins the final act with these lines from Romeo and write the reasons below your summary.

b When you have read through to the end of the play, discuss how closely Romeo's dreams reflect the way things actually turn out.

Write about it 写作练习

Balthasar's predicament (by yourself)

Imagine you are Balthasar, speeding from Verona to Mantua to inform Romeo about Juliet's death. What are your thoughts as you ride? How are you going to break the shocking news to Romeo?

- Think of different ways you might tell Romeo what has happened, and try to assess the risks of each one. Just what is the best way to tackle this awful job? Write down your thoughts as a kind of dialogue with yourself.

Stagecraft 导演技巧

Change the scene to Mantua

The previous scene is set in Juliet's bedroom in Verona. Act 5 begins in Mantua, twenty-five miles away. Work out how you would carry out the scene change swiftly and effectively. In Baz Luhrmann's movie version, for example, Mantua is a rundown trailer park (旅行拖车停车场) in the desert.

- Come up with an idea for the scene change that would work well in the theatre. Follow up by thinking how you might show it in a film version.
- Consider what Romeo would be doing as he speaks his first eleven lines and how you would stage Balthasar's entry to give it dramatic impact.
- Sharpen your strongest ideas from above. You have a maximum of ten seconds to share them with the rest of your class!

1 If … sleep　如果我可以相信美梦能成真
2 *presage*　预示
3 *bosom's lord*　胸中之主（指心脏）
4 *unaccustomed spirit*　不寻常的心情
5 how … possessed　爱情本身得到享受会多么甜蜜
6 but love's shadows　仅仅爱情的幻影就
7 *booted*　穿着马靴
8 *immortal part*　不朽的部分（即灵魂）
9 *presently took post*　一刻不停骑上驿马
10 *office*　责任

Act 5 Scene 1
A street in Mantua

Enter ROMEO.

ROMEO
If I may trust the flattering truth of sleep[1],
My dreams presage[2] some joyful news at hand.
My bosom's lord[3] sits lightly in his throne,
And all this day an unaccustomed spirit[4]
Lifts me above the ground with cheerful thoughts. 5
I dreamt my lady came and found me dead
(Strange dream that gives a dead man leave to think!),
And breathed such life with kisses in my lips
That I revived and was an emperor.
Ah me, how sweet is love itself possessed[5], 10
When but love's shadows[6] are so rich in joy!

Enter Romeo's man [BALTHASAR, *booted*[7]].

News from Verona! How now, Balthasar?
Dost thou not bring me letters from the Friar?
How doth my lady? Is my father well?
How doth my Juliet? That I ask again, 15
For nothing can be ill if she be well.

BALTHASAR
Then she is well and nothing can be ill:
Her body sleeps in Capels' monument,
And her immortal part[8] with angels lives.
I saw her laid low in her kindred's vault, 20
And presently took post[9] to tell it you.
O pardon me for bringing these ill news,
Since you did leave it for my office[10], sir.

There is no word from the Friar. Romeo dismisses Balthasar to hire horses. He resolves to kill himself that night in the tomb with Juliet. But how? The apothecary who sells poisons comes into his mind.

剧情简介：修士那里没有消息。柔密欧打发巴尔特扎去租马，他决定当晚去茱丽叶的墓地自尽。可是如何自杀呢？他想到有个卖毒药的药剂师。

Themes 主题分析

'then I defy you, stars!'

The sense that fate determines human lives recurs frequently as an idea throughout the play. Just like Romeo's dream (lines 6–9), the mentioning of 'stars' links this scene back to Act 1 Scene 4.

- Turn to your Evidence Grid on 'Chance versus Choice'. Update it by adding the ideas mentioned above. Remember to explain why you think each of these details is important.

Characters 人物分析

Is Romeo brave, foolish or something else?
(in small groups)

> *Well, Juliet, I will lie with thee tonight.*

Romeo makes up his mind to kill himself that night in the Capulets' monument, but is he fully in control of his feelings? Balthasar points out that Romeo's 'looks are pale and wild' (line 28).

- Put Romeo in the hot-seat and question him about his motives. Ask him whether this is a brave decision. How else might it be seen? Is he being too impetuous? What alternatives might he have? Take turns in the role of Romeo while others in the group fire questions at him.

1 e'en = even
2 hence 去那里
3 import 显示，暗示
4 misadventure 灾祸
5 see for means 看看有什么办法
6 apothecary 药剂师
7 tattered weeds 破烂衣服
8 overwhelming brows 突出的额头
9 Culling of simples 采集单味草药
10 meagre 消瘦
11 beggarly account 可怜巴巴的几个
12 Remnants of packthread 打包的绳头线尾
13 cakes of roses 玫瑰花瓣压成的饼（能散发香气）
14 penury 赤贫
15 Whose sale is present death 销售此物者立即处死
16 caitiff 悲惨
17 forerun 预示

1 Draw the Apothecary's shop (in fours)

a Lines 42–8 give a detailed description of the inside of the Apothecary's shop. Whilst one member of the group reads, the others listen closely without looking at the text. Then the three listeners work together to create from memory an imaginative drawing that includes as many of Shakespeare's details as they can remember. Have a go at labelling your drawing with Shakespeare's own words.

b Suggest reasons why such a precise description might have been included at this point in the play. This task will help you prepare for Activity 5 on page 200.

ROMEO	Is it e'en[1] so? then I defy you, stars!	
	Thou knowest my lodging, get me ink and paper,	25
	And hire post-horses; I will hence[2] tonight.	
BALTHASAR	I do beseech you, sir, have patience:	
	Your looks are pale and wild, and do import[3]	
	Some misadventure[4].	
ROMEO	Tush, thou art deceived.	
	Leave me, and do the thing I bid thee do.	30
	Hast thou no letters to me from the Friar?	
BALTHASAR	No, my good lord.	
ROMEO	No matter, get thee gone,	
	And hire those horses; I'll be with thee straight.	

Exit [Balthasar]

Well, Juliet, I will lie with thee tonight.
Let's see for means[5]. O mischief, thou art swift   35
To enter in the thoughts of desperate men!
I do remember an apothecary[6],
And hereabouts 'a dwells, which late I noted
In tattered weeds[7], with overwhelming brows[8],
Culling of simples[9]; meagre[10] were his looks,   40
Sharp misery had worn him to the bones;
And in his needy shop a tortoise hung,
An alligator stuffed, and other skins
Of ill shaped fishes, and about his shelves
A beggarly account[11] of empty boxes,   45
Green earthen pots, bladders, and musty seeds,
Remnants of packthread[12], and old cakes of roses[13]
Were thinly scattered, to make up a show.
Noting this penury[14], to myself I said,
'And if a man did need a poison now,   50
Whose sale is present death[15] in Mantua,
Here lives a caitiff[16] wretch would sell it him.'
O this same thought did but forerun[17] my need,
And this same needy man must sell it me.
As I remember, this should be the house.   55
Being holiday, the beggar's shop is shut.
What ho, apothecary!

The penniless Apothecary sells poison to Romeo even though he knows the penalty for doing so is death. Romeo leaves for Verona and Juliet's tomb, determined to drink the poison there.

剧情简介：身无分文的药剂师虽然知道把毒药卖给柔密欧会面临死刑的惩罚，还是把药卖给了他。柔密欧前往维罗纳茱丽叶的坟墓，决心在那里服毒自尽。

1 The Apothecary

- Shakespeare gives a powerful and striking description of the Apothecary in lines 39–41 and 69–71. Use these details and your own imagination to design the costume and appearance of the Apothecary in a production of your own.
- Consider what kind of voice and mannerisms your Apothecary would have, and the type of dramatic impact you would want him to create. How might you show his connection with some of the key themes and issues in the play?
- Put all your ideas together as a character 'montage' (蒙太奇): draw or find a suitable image to represent your Apothecary and then assemble all your ideas around the central figure.

1 ducats 达克（旧时一种金币）
2 a dram 一剂，一服
3 soon-speeding gear 速效毒药
4 life-weary 厌世
5 trunk 身体
6 any he 任何人
7 utters 售卖
8 Need and oppression 难以承受的贫穷
9 dispatch 杀死
10 get thyself in flesh 让自己长胖点儿
11 cordial 良药

▼ How effective do you think this representation of the Apothecary might be in a stage production? Write a paragraph giving your response.

2 Act out Romeo's meeting with the Apothecary (in pairs)

First read through lines 57–86, with each partner taking a role. Then talk about how you might stage the action. Think carefully about the character of the Apothecary you created in the activity above, as well as Romeo's feelings and emotions at this moment. How effectively can you show the characters' contrasting states of mind in your presentation?

[*Enter* APOTHECARY.]

APOTHECARY   Who calls so loud?

ROMEO   Come hither, man. I see that thou art poor.
Hold, there is forty ducats[1]; let me have
A dram[2] of poison, such soon-speeding gear[3]   60
As will disperse itself through all the veins,
That the life-weary[4] taker may fall dead,
And that the trunk[5] may be discharged of breath
As violently as hasty powder fired
Doth hurry from the fatal cannon's womb.   65

APOTHECARY   Such mortal drugs I have, but Mantua's law
Is death to any he[6] that utters[7] them.

ROMEO   Art thou so bare and full of wretchedness,
And fearest to die? Famine is in thy cheeks,
Need and oppression[8] starveth in thy eyes,   70
Contempt and beggary hangs upon thy back;
The world is not thy friend, nor the world's law,
The world affords no law to make thee rich;
Then be not poor, but break it and take this.

APOTHECARY   My poverty, but not my will, consents.   75

ROMEO   I pay thy poverty and not thy will.

APOTHECARY   Put this in any liquid thing you will
And drink it off, and if you had the strength
Of twenty men, it would dispatch[9] you straight.

ROMEO   There is thy gold, worse poison to men's souls,   80
Doing more murder in this loathsome world,
Than these poor compounds that thou mayst not sell.
I sell thee poison, thou hast sold me none.
Farewell, buy food, and get thyself in flesh[10].

                                  [*Exit Apothecary*]

Come, cordial[11] and not poison, go with me   85
To Juliet's grave, for there must I use thee.   *Exit*

Friar John tells how an unlucky mischance prevented him delivering Friar Lawrence's letter to Romeo. Friar Lawrence determines to break into Capulet's monument to be with Juliet when she awakes.

剧情简介：约翰修士说发生了一件倒霉事，使得他没能顺利地把劳润修士的信交给柔密欧。劳润修士决定闯入卡普莱家的墓室，以便在茱丽叶醒来时陪着她。

Themes 主题分析

'Unhappy fortune!'

Friar John explains that he was looking for another Franciscan friar to accompany him to Mantua in order to deliver Friar Lawrence's letter to Romeo. He found his brother friar visiting some sick people. There disaster struck: the 'searchers' called!

The 'searchers' were health officers of the town, appointed to prevent the spread of disease by examining dead bodies to establish the cause of death. They thought that the Franciscans were in a house where plague raged, so they refused to allow them to travel ('Sealed up the doors'). Once again, the plans of humans are thwarted by the intervention of forces beyond mortal control.

- Add these details to your Evidence Grid.

1 Friar John's delay

Work on one or more of the following activities to explore the dramatic impact of Friar John not reaching Mantua in time to deliver Friar Lawrence's letter to Romeo.

a **Echo!** (in pairs) Read lines 5–12 aloud, but add 'Unhappy fortune!' after every punctuation mark.

b **Improvise!** (in groups of five or six) Two of the group take the roles of Friar John and his fellow monk. The others are the 'searchers' who will not let them leave the infected house. Improvise what took place as the searchers refuse to listen to the Friars' pleas to be allowed to travel to Mantua.

c **Act out the scene** (in pairs) Take the roles of Friar Lawrence and Friar John. Act the scene to bring out Friar Lawrence's increasing agitation and his growing awareness that urgent action is needed.

Write about it 写作练习

The Friar's undelivered letter (by yourself)

Step into role as Friar Lawrence and write his letter to Romeo. The letter explains the desperate plan he has devised for Juliet's fake death (see Act 4 Scene 1, lines 89–117).

1 if his mind be writ 如果他写信了（而不是捎口信）
2 barefoot brother 赤脚兄弟（方济各会修士均赤脚修行）
3 order （宗教团体的）派，社
4 associate 陪伴（依方济各派教规，修道士不得单独外出，同门须结伴而行）
5 pestilence 瘟疫
6 stayed 耽搁
7 bare 带给
8 nice （参见第98页注解6）
9 full of charge 极为重要
10 dear import 意义重大
11 crow 撬棍
12 beshrew 责怪
13 accidents 事件

Act 5 Scene 2
Friar Lawrence's cell

Enter FRIAR JOHN.

FRIAR JOHN   Holy Franciscan Friar, brother, ho!

Enter [FRIAR] LAWRENCE.

FRIAR LAWRENCE   This same should be the voice of Friar John.
Welcome from Mantua. What says Romeo?
Or if his mind be writ[1], give me his letter.

FRIAR JOHN   Going to find a barefoot brother[2] out, 5
One of our order[3], to associate[4] me,
Here in this city visiting the sick,
And finding him, the searchers of the town,
Suspecting that we both were in a house
Where the infectious pestilence[5] did reign, 10
Sealed up the doors, and would not let us forth,
So that my speed to Mantua there was stayed[6].

FRIAR LAWRENCE   Who bare[7] my letter then to Romeo?

FRIAR JOHN   I could not send it – here it is again –
Nor get a messenger to bring it thee, 15
So fearful were they of infection.

FRIAR LAWRENCE   Unhappy fortune! By my brotherhood,
The letter was not nice[8] but full of charge[9],
Of dear import[10], and the neglecting it
May do much danger. Friar John, go hence, 20
Get me an iron crow[11] and bring it straight
Unto my cell.

FRIAR JOHN   Brother, I'll go and bring it thee.   *Exit*

FRIAR LAWRENCE   Now must I to the monument alone,
Within this three hours will fair Juliet wake. 25
She will beshrew[12] me much that Romeo
Hath had no notice of these accidents[13];
But I will write again to Mantua,
And keep her at my cell till Romeo come,
Poor living corse, closed in a dead man's tomb!   *Exit*   30

Paris visits Juliet's tomb to lay flowers and mourn. He is anxious not to be observed, so orders his Page to keep watch. The Page whistles to warn him someone is coming.

剧情简介：帕瑞来到茱丽叶的墓地献花哀悼她。他非常怕被别人发现，因此命他的小厮放风。小厮吹口哨警示有人来了。

Stagecraft 导演技巧

Night and churchyards (in small groups)

a Shakespeare uses words to conjure up (唤起) time, place and atmosphere. For example, in line 3 Paris refers to 'yew trees', which are often found in churchyards and are associated with death and mourning. Sharing the lines between you, speak everything in the script opposite. Emphasise each word and phrase that helps to create the impression of night-time and the graveyard setting (e.g. your first emphasised word would be 'torch').

b Make a list of each of the words you emphasised. After each word, add your own comment about how it creates an atmosphere of time ('night'), or place ('churchyard').

c Think about staging this scene for a modern theatre audience. As each 'episode' of this scene (the longest one in the play) unfolds, discuss how you would light it to create specific dramatic effects that match the mood of that part of the scene. Between you, decide on the most dramatic part of the scene and produce a sketch to show how you would light it.

d Consider how you might use sound effects or music to enhance the mood at the start of this scene. Focus on the first fifty-three lines (until Paris confronts Romeo in the tomb). Work out a suitable 'soundscape' that would complement the action. Try recording it and, as you play it to other groups, explain the reasons behind your choices.

1 stand aloof   站远点儿
2 put it out   熄灭火把
3 for I would not 因为我不想
4 yew trees   紫杉树
5 lay thee all along 平躺下
6 Being loose   松软
7 stand   逗留
8 adventure   豁出去
9 strews   撒满
10 Sweet flower   (指茱丽叶)
11 canopy   华盖
12 sweet water   芬芳的甘露
13 dew   洒水
14 wanting   短缺
15 distilled by   从……中提取
16 obsequies   追悼
17 cross   妨碍，干扰
18 Muffle   遮挡

Language in the play 剧中语言

Paris mourns for Juliet – does he mean it?

- Focus on Paris's lines 12–17. Do you find them artificial and formal, or do they seem to come from the heart? Does the fact that they rhyme affect your response?
- Now re-read Paris's six lines in Act 4 Scene 5. Are there any similarities? Write a paragraph exploring and comparing how Paris expresses his grief for Juliet in the way he speaks in the two scenes.

Act 5 Scene 3
A churchyard, outside the tomb of the Capulets

Enter PARIS *and his* PAGE [*with flowers and sweet water and a torch*].

PARIS   Give me thy torch, boy. Hence, and stand aloof[1].
Yet put it out[2], for I would not[3] be seen.
Under yond yew trees[4] lay thee all along[5],
Holding thy ear close to the hollow ground,
So shall no foot upon the churchyard tread,   5
Being loose[6], unfirm with digging up of graves,
But thou shalt hear it. Whistle then to me
As signal that thou hear'st something approach.
Give me those flowers. Do as I bid thee, go.

PAGE   [*Aside*] I am almost afraid to stand[7] alone   10
Here in the churchyard, yet I will adventure[8].   [*Retires*]

[*Paris strews[9] the tomb with flowers.*]

PARIS   Sweet flower[10], with flowers thy bridal bed I strew –
O woe, thy canopy[11] is dust and stones! –
Which with sweet water[12] nightly I will dew[13],
Or wanting[14] that, with tears distilled by[15] moans.   15
The obsequies[16] that I for thee will keep
Nightly shall be to strew thy grave and weep.
              Whistle Boy.
The boy gives warning, something doth approach.
What cursèd foot wanders this way tonight,
To cross[17] my obsequies and true love's rite?   20
What, with a torch? Muffle[18] me, night, a while.   [*Retires*]

Romeo, determined to force open the tomb, dismisses Balthasar on pain of death. Balthasar resolves to stay and watch. As Romeo begins to force entry, Paris steps forward to challenge him.

 剧情简介：柔密欧决心强行打开墓室，他打发巴尔特扎走开，不走就杀了他。巴尔特扎决心留下来观望。柔密欧刚要闯入墓室，就遇见了帕瑞前来挑战。

Characters 人物分析

Different sides to Romeo? (in pairs)

a Stand facing your partner. As one person reads short sections of Romeo's lines 22–42, the other mimes each action and echoes each word of command or words that are threatening.

b Divide the lines into four sections: lines 22–7, 28–32, 33–9 and 41–2. Talk together about how each section reveals a different aspect of Romeo's feelings and personality.

c Why do you think Romeo lies to Balthasar in lines 28–32? Remember, there is no 'right' answer to this. Write up your conclusions after exploring possible explanations.

d In lines 33–9, Romeo uses the hyperbolic (extravagant, 'over the top') language of **Revenge Tragedy** (a type of play in which the main character is a 'revenger', which was popular in the 1590s when Shakespeare was writing *Romeo and Juliet*). Romeo's threat ('tear thee joint by joint') and his imagery ('More fierce and more inexorable far / Than empty tigers or the roaring sea') are certainly very powerful and dramatic. But are they suited to a man stricken with grief and the sense of loss? Does he really mean what he says? Talk together about why you think Romeo speaks to Balthasar in this way.

1 *mattock* 鹤嘴锄
2 *wrenching iron* 撬棍
3 *all aloof* 远远地
4 *my course* 我要做的事
5 *In dear employment* 派大用场
6 *jealous* 猜疑
7 *pry* 刺探
8 *intents* 意图
9 *inexorable* 冷酷无情
10 *maw* 胃
11 *Gorged* 吞噬，狼吞虎咽
12 *dearest morsel of the earth* 最珍贵的一抔土（指茱丽叶）
13 *haughty* 傲慢，自大
14 *do some villainous shame* 干一件邪恶可耻之事
15 *apprehend* 逮捕

Stagecraft 导演技巧

Problems with the set

At line 48, Romeo begins to open the tomb. The problem for set designers is that Scene 3 takes place both outside and inside the Capulet monument. The lines in the script opposite present two further challenges:

- All the events are being watched by Paris's Page and Balthasar – so where are they?
- How and where will the fight be staged?

Today (as in Shakespeare's time) most designers solve the problems by non-realistic staging. Such stagings ask the audience to use its imagination and to suspend disbelief (that is, to willingly accept non-realistic stagings and events). Keep all these puzzles in mind and have a go at sketching a design for the set.

ROMEO AND JULIET ACT 5 SCENE 3
柔密欧与茱丽叶

Enter ROMEO *and* [BALTHASAR *with a torch, a mattock[1], and a crow of iron*].

ROMEO	Give me that mattock and the wrenching iron[2].
	Hold, take this letter; early in the morning
	See thou deliver it to my lord and father.
	Give me the light. Upon thy life I charge thee, 25
	What e'er thou hear'st or seest, stand all aloof[3],
	And do not interrupt me in my course[4].
	Why I descend into this bed of death
	Is partly to behold my lady's face,
	But chiefly to take thence from her dead finger 30
	A precious ring, a ring that I must use
	In dear employment[5]; therefore hence, be gone.
	But if thou, jealous[6], dost return to pry[7]
	In what I farther shall intend to do,
	By heaven, I will tear thee joint by joint, 35
	And strew this hungry churchyard with thy limbs.
	The time and my intents[8] are savage-wild,
	More fierce and more inexorable[9] far
	Than empty tigers or the roaring sea.
BALTHASAR	I will be gone, sir, and not trouble ye. 40
ROMEO	So shalt thou show me friendship. Take thou that,
	[*Gives a purse.*]
	Live and be prosperous, and farewell, good fellow.
BALTHASAR	[*Aside*] For all this same, I'll hide me hereabout,
	His looks I fear, and his intents I doubt. [*Retires*]
ROMEO	Thou detestable maw[10], thou womb of death, 45
	Gorged[11] with the dearest morsel of the earth[12],
	Thus I enforce thy rotten jaws to open,
	And in despite I'll cram thee with more food.
	[*Romeo begins to open the tomb.*]
PARIS	This is that banished haughty[13] Montague,
	That murdered my love's cousin, with which grief 50
	It is supposèd the fair creature died,
	And here is come to do some villainous shame[14]
	To the dead bodies. I will apprehend[15] him.
	[*Steps forth.*]

181

Paris tries to arrest Romeo, but is slain by him. Romeo, dismayed to find whom he has killed, resolves to grant Paris's dying wish, and lays his body beside Juliet's.

 剧情简介：帕瑞试图逮捕柔密欧，反而被他杀死。柔密欧惊愕地发现自己杀死了帕瑞，决定满足他的临终遗愿，将他的尸体置于茱丽叶身边。

Write about it 写作练习

Two opposing narratives? (in pairs)

In lines 43–4, Balthasar expresses concern about what Romeo is up to and hides himself to watch what happens. Paris's Page has already concealed himself (line 11). Both these characters witness the angry exchanges between Romeo and Paris and the deadly fight that follows.

- One of you is Balthasar, the other the Page. Write your accounts of what you observe from your hiding place. Remember that your different loyalties might lead to some bias in your writing. Afterwards, compare your two accounts of the event.

1 'sour misfortune's book!'

Who else in the play do you think would join Romeo and Paris in a book of people troubled by unhappy misfortune and accident?

- Turn to the character list on page 1. Copy the names of any characters who you think might fall into this category. Alongside each character, write a couple of sentences describing their particular misfortunes.

Characters 人物分析

Romeo's final moments

In your Director's Journal, write notes to the actor playing Romeo on how to deliver his long final soliloquy.

- Although he has killed Paris, Romeo doesn't recognise his opponent until line 75. How would you advise the actor to speak that line?
- Romeo creates four striking personifications of death. How should these be delivered?
- Identify the different sections of the speech and suggest actions, expressions, and so on, for each. One way of dividing up the speech is: lines 74–87; lines 88–91 (end at 'light'ning'); lines 91–6; lines 97–101 (end at 'cousin'); lines 101–5; lines 106–12 (end at 'flesh'); lines 112–18; lines 119–20.
- When you have written your notes, give them to a partner and let them test out your ideas in a dramatic reading of Romeo's death speech.

1 **unhallowed toil** 亵渎死者的勾当
2 **affright** 惊吓
3 **armed against myself** 准备自尽
4 **conjuration** 恳求
5 **felon** 罪犯
6 **Watch** 巡夜（莎士比亚时代没有今天这样的警察，而是由市民在夜里执勤巡夜，维护治安）
7 **peruse** 仔细看
8 **betossèd** 心乱如麻
9 **triumphant** 富丽堂皇
10 **lantern** 灯笼阁（常见于教堂房顶，四周是玻璃窗，用来采光）
11 **feasting presence** （王宫中招待宾客的）宴会厅
12 **dead man** （指柔密欧）
13 **interred** 埋葬

	Stop thy unhallowed toil[1], vile Montague!	
	Can vengeance be pursued further than death?	55
	Condemnèd villain, I do apprehend thee.	
	Obey and go with me, for thou must die.	
ROMEO	I must indeed, and therefore came I hither.	
	Good gentle youth, tempt not a desp'rate man,	
	Fly hence and leave me. Think upon these gone,	60
	Let them affright[2] thee. I beseech thee, youth,	
	Put not another sin upon my head,	
	By urging me to fury: O be gone!	
	By heaven, I love thee better than myself,	
	For I come hither armed against myself[3].	65
	Stay not, be gone; live, and hereafter say,	
	A madman's mercy bid thee run away.	
PARIS	I do defy thy conjuration[4],	
	And apprehend thee for a felon[5] here.	
ROMEO	Wilt thou provoke me? then have at thee, boy!	70
	[*They fight.*]	
PAGE	O Lord, they fight! I will go call the Watch[6].	[*Exit*]
PARIS	O, I am slain! [*Falls.*] If thou be merciful,	
	Open the tomb, lay me with Juliet. [*Dies.*]	
ROMEO	In faith, I will. Let me peruse[7] this face.	
	Mercutio's kinsman, noble County Paris!	75
	What said my man, when my betossèd[8] soul	
	Did not attend him as we rode? I think	
	He told me Paris should have married Juliet.	
	Said he not so? or did I dream it so?	
	Or am I mad, hearing him talk of Juliet,	80
	To think it was so? O give me thy hand,	
	One writ with me in sour misfortune's book!	
	I'll bury thee in a triumphant[9] grave.	
	A grave? O no, a lantern[10], slaughtered youth;	
	For here lies Juliet, and her beauty makes	85
	This vault a feasting presence[11] full of light.	
	Death, lie thou there, by a dead man[12] interred[13].	
	[*Laying Paris in the tomb.*]	

> Romeo gazes on Juliet and admires her beauty. He asks Tybalt for forgiveness, and imagines that Death wants Juliet as a lover. To prevent that, and determined to join her in death, he drinks the poison.
>
> **剧情简介**：柔密欧凝视着茱丽叶，沉醉于其美丽的容颜。他请求提巴尔原谅自己，还想象死神想霸占茱丽叶为情人。为了阻止此事，他决心一死与茱丽叶相会，于是饮下毒药。

Stagecraft 导演技巧

The funeral vault

a In Baz Luhrmann's movie, Juliet lay in magnificent state in a cathedral, bathed in the light of thousands of burning candles (see the picture below). Imagine that you are filming this episode. How would you convey the contrast between the radiant light associated with Juliet and the darkness of the funeral vault? Write up your ideas ready for a meeting with the production designer.

b Romeo's last words possess a terrible irony. Unlike the audience, he does not know that Juliet lives. In some productions he sees Juliet showing signs of life just before he dies. This increases the irony of Romeo's last moments, as he realises the tragic waste of his life. What do you think of such staging? Produce one argument in favour and one against.

1. keepers 狱卒
2. light'ning 回光返照
3. ensign 旗
4. sunder his = sunder his youth 割断他的青春（即杀死他）
5. unsubstantial 无形，虚无
6. abhorrèd 面目可憎
7. paramour 情人
8. set up my everlasting rest 搭建我永远安息之所
9. yoke 轭，束缚
10. inauspicious 不祥，不吉利
11. dateless bargain 没有期限的契约
12. engrossing 拥有一切，吞噬一切（前文的seal和bargain都与柔密欧想象"与死神签署永恒的契约"呼应）
13. conduct 导引（这里指毒药；注意conduct、guide、pilot和bark都在强调柔密欧把悲剧人生比作海上航行，以灾难收尾）
14. unsavoury 令人厌恶
15. seasick weary bark 经受不住惊涛骇浪的船

Themes 主题分析

Death, love, light versus darkness, fate, shipwreck

Romeo's final speech carries echoes of many of the thematic concerns of the play.

- Trace each of the themes listed above as you work through Romeo's speech. Write out explanations of how these key thematic ideas are expressed through the imagery that Romeo uses. Which do you think is most powerfully expressed?

ROMEO AND JULIET ACT 5 SCENE 3
柔密欧与茱丽叶

How oft when men are at the point of death
Have they been merry, which their keepers[1] call
A light'ning before death! O how may I   90
Call this a light'ning[2]? O my love, my wife,
Death, that hath sucked the honey of thy breath,
Hath had no power yet upon thy beauty:
Thou art not conquered, beauty's ensign[3] yet
Is crimson in thy lips and in thy cheeks,   95
And Death's pale flag is not advancèd there.
Tybalt, liest thou there in thy bloody sheet?
O, what more favour can I do to thee
Than with that hand that cut thy youth in twain
To sunder his[4] that was thine enemy?   100
Forgive me, cousin. Ah, dear Juliet,
Why art thou yet so fair? Shall I believe
That unsubstantial[5] Death is amorous,
And that the lean abhorrèd[6] monster keeps
Thee here in dark to be his paramour[7]?   105
For fear of that, I still will stay with thee,
And never from this palace of dim night
Depart again. Here, here will I remain
With worms that are thy chambermaids; O here
Will I set up my everlasting rest[8],   110
And shake the yoke[9] of inauspicious[10] stars
From this world-wearied flesh. Eyes, look your last!
Arms, take your last embrace! and, lips, O you
The doors of breath, seal with a righteous kiss
A dateless bargain[11] to engrossing[12] Death!   115
Come, bitter conduct[13], come, unsavoury[14] guide!
Thou desperate pilot, now at once run on
The dashing rocks thy seasick weary bark[15]!
Here's to my love! [*Drinks*.] O true apothecary!
Thy drugs are quick. Thus with a kiss I die. [*Dies*.]   120

185

Balthasar tells Friar Lawrence that Romeo is in the tomb. Entering the vault, the Friar finds the dead Romeo and Paris. Juliet begins to awaken.

 剧情简介：巴尔特扎告诉劳润修士柔密欧在墓地。他走进墓室，发现已经断气的柔密欧和帕瑞。这时茱丽叶开始苏醒。

1 Urgency and fear in the Friar's words (in pairs)

Take each line the Friar says in the script opposite, but say aloud only words and phrases that create an atmosphere of urgency and fear. Then gather together the words you have selected and display them on a poster. You may find it helpful to know that if someone 'stumbled' (绊倒), it would be considered by Elizabethans to be a bad omen (if you 'stumbled', things would begin to go wrong). Compare your poster with other groups' and reflect on the similarities and differences of the words you have chosen.

Write about it 写作练习

Friar Lawrence surveys the wreckage of his plan

Between the Friar's arrival at line 121 and his entrance to the tomb at line 140, he begins to fear that all his planning has gone horribly wrong.

- Imagine that you are the Friar. What thoughts flood into your mind as you find Paris and Romeo dead amongst the blood and weapons? And how do you react to Juliet suddenly stirring?
- Write up your thoughts as an interior monologue, in which you begin to weigh up the dreadful consequences of the actions you have set in motion.

1 *Enter* FRIAR （注意场景转至墓室之外；参见第180页）
2 *Bliss be upon you!* 上帝赐福于您！
3 vainly 徒劳无用
4 grubs 蛆虫
5 discern 辨认，识别
6 knows … hence 不知道我没离开这里
7 menace 威胁，恐吓
8 unthrifty 不幸
9 sepulchre 坟墓
10 masterless and gory swords 无主的血淋淋的剑
11 discoloured 变了颜色（即沾满血污）
12 steeped 沉浸于
13 unkind 反常，不自然
14 lamentable chance 悲伤的意外

Enter FRIAR[1] [LAWRENCE] *with lantern, crow, and spade.*

FRIAR LAWRENCE   Saint Francis be my speed! how oft tonight
Have my old feet stumbled at graves! Who's there?

BALTHASAR   Here's one, a friend, and one that knows you well.

FRIAR LAWRENCE   Bliss be upon you![2] Tell me, good my friend,
What torch is yond that vainly[3] lends his light   125
To grubs[4] and eyeless skulls? As I discern[5],
It burneth in the Capels' monument.

BALTHASAR   It doth so, holy sir, and there's my master,
One that you love.

FRIAR LAWRENCE   Who is it?

BALTHASAR   Romeo.

FRIAR LAWRENCE   How long hath he been there?

BALTHASAR   Full half an hour.   130

FRIAR LAWRENCE   Go with me to the vault.

BALTHASAR   I dare not, sir.
My master knows not but I am gone hence[6],
And fearfully did menance[7] me with death
If I did stay to look on his intents.

FRIAR LAWRENCE   Stay then, I'll go alone. Fear comes upon me.   135
O, much I fear some ill unthrifty[8] thing.

BALTHASAR   As I did sleep under this yew tree here,
I dreamt my master and another fought,
And that my master slew him.   [*Retires*]

FRIAR LAWRENCE   Romeo!
[*Friar stoops and looks on the blood and weapons.*]
Alack, alack, what blood is this which stains   140
The stony entrance of this sepulchre[9]?
What mean these masterless and gory swords[10]
To lie discoloured[11] by this place of peace?
                    [*Enters the tomb.*]
Romeo! O, pale! Who else? What, Paris too?
And steeped[12] in blood? Ah, what an unkind[13] hour   145
Is guilty of this lamentable chance[14]!
                    [*Juliet rises.*]
The lady stirs.

Friar Lawrence, fearful of discovery, leaves the tomb, begging Juliet to go with him. She refuses, and stabs herself because she prefers to join Romeo in death. The Watch enter.

 剧情简介：劳润修士害怕被人发现，于是离开墓室。他离开时央求茱丽叶跟他一起走。茱丽叶拒绝，持剑自尽，因为她甘愿死后与柔密欧在一起。巡夜上。

Characters 人物分析

What is Friar Lawrence thinking? (in small groups)

Friar Lawrence tries to take Juliet away, to hide her in a convent (女修道院). But when she refuses, he simply abandons her. His action increases the sense of Juliet's isolation; ultimately, she must act her final scene completely alone.

a   Is Friar Lawrence's action cruel and self-centred? To help you decide, read lines 151–9 to each other, each person speaking a sentence then handing on. Repeat several times, with a different person beginning each reading.

b   What do these lines tell you about the Friar at this moment? What is his state of mind? What are his motives and his feelings for Juliet?

1	comfortable	令人安心
2	contagion	传染病
3	unnatural sleep	不自然的睡眠（即吃了药的睡眠状态）
4	thwarted our intents	挫败了我们的计划
5	in thy bosom	躺在你怀中
6	timeless	过早
7	churl	吝啬鬼
8	Haply	也许
9	restorative	滋补药
10	sheath	剑鞘
11	attach	逮捕

Stagecraft 导演技巧

Juliet's final moments (in pairs)

Shakespeare gives Juliet a much shorter 'death speech' than he gives Romeo. Despite this, her words and actions are incredibly powerful as the tragedy reaches its dramatic climax. As the Friar leaves Juliet on her own and she hears the Captain of the Watch approaching, she refuses to leave the tomb, kisses Romeo and stabs herself with Romeo's dagger.

• First decide what you make of her final actions in the play (for example, is she courageous in seeking death?). Then produce a commentary to explain how you would have her enact her last moments in the play to greatest dramatic effect.

1 Alike in death? (in pairs)

Contrast Juliet's final words with Romeo's. Complete a Venn diagram (文氏图，用以表示集合或类别) that shows the overlap between what the two characters say and think as they approach their deaths.

JULIET	O comfortable[1] Friar, where is my lord?	
	I do remember well where I should be;	
	And there I am. Where is my Romeo?	150

[*Noise within.*]

FRIAR LAWRENCE I hear some noise, lady. Come from that nest
Of death, contagion[2], and unnatural sleep[3].
A greater power than we can contradict
Hath thwarted our intents[4]. Come, come away.
Thy husband in thy bosom[5] there lies dead;   155
And Paris too. Come, I'll dispose of thee
Among a sisterhood of holy nuns.
Stay not to question, for the Watch is coming.
Come go, good Juliet, I dare no longer stay.   *Exit*

JULIET Go get thee hence, for I will not away.   160
What's here? a cup closed in my true love's hand?
Poison I see hath been his timeless[6] end.
O churl[7], drunk all, and left no friendly drop
To help me after? I will kiss thy lips,
Haply[8] some poison yet doth hang on them,   165
To make me die with a restorative[9].
Thy lips are warm.

CAPTAIN OF THE WATCH [*Within*] Lead, boy, which way?

JULIET Yea, noise? Then I'll be brief. O happy dagger,
    [*Taking Romeo's dagger.*]
This is thy sheath[10];
    [*Stabs herself.*]
        there rust, and let me die.   170
    [*Falls on Romeo's body and dies.*]

Enter [Paris's] Boy and WATCH.

PAGE This is the place, there where the torch doth burn.
CAPTAIN OF THE WATCH The ground is bloody, search about the churchyard.
Go, some of you, whoe'er you find attach[11].
    [*Exeunt some of the Watch*]
    [*The Captain enters the tomb and returns.*]
Pitiful sight! here lies the County slain,
And Juliet bleeding, warm, and newly dead,   175
Who here hath lain this two days burièd.

Balthasar and the Friar are arrested by the Watch. The Prince and the Capulets enter, disturbed by the commotion and shouting. The Captain tells what he knows.

剧情简介：巴尔特扎和修士被巡夜逮捕。亲王和卡普莱夫妇受到骚动和喧哗的打扰也来了。队长讲述了他了解的情况。

1 Should the play end here? (in pairs)
In the nineteenth century, productions often ended with the death of Juliet.

- As you read through to the end of the play, make a list of all the things that happen and all those that are spoken about by the surviving characters. Afterwards, one of you argues for the merits of ending the play at Juliet's death, the other argues against that view.

2 The Prince arrives
Look back at the two other occasions when Prince Escales has appeared (Act 1 Scene 1, line 72 and Act 3 Scene 1, line 132).

- How does his entrance mark a change in mood? How does he speak? Write a paragraph discussing what his three appearances have in common and exploring the effect they have on the action of each scene.

1 **ground** 地面（下一行的 ground 指动机、理由；双关）
2 **woes** 惨死的人（下一行的 woes 指惨案、惨状；双关）
3 **circumstance** 细节信息
4 **descry** 探明，理解
5 **Hold him in safety** 看管好他
6 **Stay** 拘留
7 **is so early up** 发生得这么早
8 **startles** 爆发巨响

▲ A tableau of death. How would you arrange the bodies in the tomb?

Go tell the Prince, run to the Capulets,
Raise up the Montagues; some others search.
                    [*Exeunt others of the Watch*]
We see the ground[1] whereon these woes[2] do lie,
But the true ground[1] of all these piteous woes[2]   180
We cannot without circumstance[3] descry[4].

Enter [one of the Watch with] Romeo's man [Balthasar].

SECOND WATCHMAN   Here's Romeo's man, we found him in the churchyard.
CAPTAIN OF THE WATCH   Hold him in safety[5] till the Prince come hither.

Enter Friar [Lawrence] and another Watchman.

THIRD WATCHMAN   Here is a friar that trembles, sighs, and weeps.
We took this mattock and this spade from him,   185
As he was coming from this churchyard's side.
CAPTAIN OF THE WATCH   A great suspicion. Stay[6] the friar too.

Enter the PRINCE *[with others].*

PRINCE   What misadventure is so early up[7],
That calls our person from our morning rest?

*Enter Capels [*CAPULET, LADY CAPULET*].*

CAPULET   What should it be that is so shrieked abroad?   190
LADY CAPULET   O, the people in the street cry 'Romeo',
Some 'Juliet', and some 'Paris', and all run
With open outcry toward our monument.
PRINCE   What fear is this which startles[8] in your ears?
CAPTAIN OF THE WATCH   Sovereign, here lies the County Paris slain,   195
And Romeo dead, and Juliet, dead before,
Warm and new killed.
PRINCE   Search, seek, and know how this foul murder comes.
CAPTAIN OF THE WATCH   Here is a friar, and slaughtered Romeo's man,
With instruments upon them, fit to open   200
These dead men's tombs.

The Capulets and Montague enter the tomb to view their dead children. The Prince promises to investigate, and to punish wrongdoers with death. At the Prince's command, Friar Lawrence begins to explain.

 剧情简介：卡普莱夫妇和芒特鸠来到墓室看他们死去的孩子。亲王承诺要彻查，处死凶犯。劳润修士服从亲王的命令，开始解释事情的原委。

Stagecraft 导演技巧

There are now many characters brought together. Romeo, Juliet, Paris and Tybalt are all dead and their bodies lie on stage. But a director also has to deal with the presence of the Captain, Paris's Page, members of the Watch, Balthasar, Friar Lawrence, the Prince, Capulet, Lady Capulet and Montague inside the tomb.

a Return to the sketch of the set that you drew on page 180. On it, indicate where you would position (or 'block') the characters for the long speech from the Friar that begins at line 229.

b In turn, work through the list of characters above. For each of them, write a few lines answering the following questions:
- What would this character be doing as they listen?
- Why is this character easy or challenging to deal with?

Write about it 写作练习

Lady Montague's death

Montague's announcement that his wife is dead adds an extra layer of poignancy to the play. But that death happens off stage and Romeo's mother has had only a very small part in the play. Montague tells that 'Grief of my son's exile hath stopped her breath' (line 211). Apart from that, we know little about her final moments of life.

- On page 10, you were invited to expand her voice; now try to do so again. Write the story of her death. Use either first or third person narrative.

1 An insensitive Prince? (in pairs)

The Prince's three lines (lines 208–9 and 213) seem very unsympathetic towards Montague's feelings.

- Explore different ways of saying and staging Prince Escales's lines. Try making him compassionate towards Montague. For example, might he offer a consoling hand? Then make him hard and unfeeling. Which approach do you think works more powerfully in this episode? Discuss your responses and then show your preferred version to other students.

1 hath mistane = has mistaken （插错了地方）
2 his house 它的鞘
3 liege 君主，殿下
4 conspires 密谋，图谋
5 thou untaught 你这个没教养的（芒特鸠训斥死去的柔密欧）
6 press ... grave 抢在你父亲之前入土
7 Seal ... outrage 暂停激昂悲恸
8 ambiguities 疑点，不明之处
9 spring 起因（与后面的head同义）
10 true descent 真相
11 general 总判官
12 death （罪犯的）死刑
13 be slave to 臣服于
14 parties of suspicion 嫌犯
15 greatest 最主要
16 direful 可怕
17 impeach and purge 控告和认定无辜
18 my short date of breath 我短暂的余生

	[Capulet and Lady Capulet enter the tomb.]	
CAPULET	O heavens! O wife, look how our daughter bleeds!	
	This dagger hath mistane[1], for lo his house[2]	
	Is empty on the back of Montague,	
	And it mis-sheathèd in my daughter's bosom!	205
LADY CAPULET	O me, this sight of death is as a bell	
	That warns my old age to a sepulchre.	
	[They return from the tomb.]	

Enter MONTAGUE.

PRINCE	Come, Montague, for thou art early up	
	To see thy son and heir now early down.	
MONTAGUE	Alas, my liege[3], my wife is dead tonight;	210
	Grief of my son's exile hath stopped her breath.	
	What further woe conspires[4] against mine age?	
PRINCE	Look and thou shalt see.	
	[Montague enters the tomb and returns.]	
MONTAGUE	O thou untaught[5]! what manners is in this,	
	To press before thy father to a grave[6]?	215
PRINCE	Seal up the mouth of outrage[7] for a while,	
	Till we can clear these ambiguities[8],	
	And know their spring[9], their head, their true descent[10],	
	And then will I be general[11] of your woes,	
	And lead you even to death[12]. Mean time forbear,	220
	And let mischance be slave to[13] patience.	
	Bring forth the parties of suspicion[14].	
FRIAR LAWRENCE	I am the greatest[15], able to do least,	
	Yet most suspected, as the time and place	
	Doth make against me, of this direful[16] murder;	225
	And here I stand both to impeach and purge[17]	
	Myself condemnèd and myself excused.	
PRINCE	Then say at once what thou dost know in this.	
FRIAR LAWRENCE	I will be brief, for my short date of breath[18]	
	Is not so long as is a tedious tale.	230
	Romeo, there dead, was husband to that Juliet,	
	And she, there dead, that Romeo's faithful wife:	

Friar Lawrence tells his story to the Prince: the marriage, the killing of Tybalt, Romeo's banishment, Capulet's attempt to force Juliet to marry Paris, the Friar's desperate plan … and much more.

剧情简介：劳润修士向亲王讲述事情的来龙去脉：从结婚到提巴尔被杀，从柔密欧被放逐到卡普莱逼茱丽叶嫁给帕瑞，再到修士孤注一掷实施计划……如此这般，这般如此。

1 Friar Lawrence's explanation of events

Friar Lawrence's story (lines 229–66) provides a valuable summary of events, even though it leaves out his reasons for acting as he did (to unite the families). The language is different from that of most of the play. It is direct and easy to follow. There are no puns or wordplay and little imagery. Sometimes this long explanation (which the Friar describes as 'brief'!) is cut in productions of the play. The activities below will help your understanding of the story (and the action of the play).

a **Point out who is involved (in eights)** Each person takes a part (Friar, Romeo, Juliet, Tybalt, Paris, Friar John, the Nurse, Capulet). Stand in a circle. The Friar slowly reads the lines. Everyone points to whoever is mentioned, for example to the Friar on 'I'; to Romeo and Juliet on 'them' and 'their', and so on.

b **Breaking news!** Imagine that the television station for which you work has just found out about the dreadful events unfolding in the Capulet monument. You manage to get inside to hear the Friar giving his account of what has happened. You are given a two-minute slot on the latest bulletin (新闻简报). Use the Friar's speech as the basis for your report – but remember that you will need to make your version of events as dramatic and engaging as possible in order to 'hook' your watching audience. Have a go at writing your feature and then record it. You could add a short section in which your presentation is introduced by the main newsreader.

2 Advice to the Friar (in pairs)

As director, you have to make decisions about how the Friar will deliver his long speech.

- Discuss with each other the impressions you wish to create both of the Friar's character (remember, he has tried to run away from the vault, leaving Juliet alone, and has been caught by the Watch) and the mood at this point in the play. For example, when he offers to sacrifice his life if found guilty, what tone does he adopt? What kind of response would you seek to generate amongst the audience?
- Write up your thoughts and ideas in your Director's Journal.

---

1 pined 渴望
2 siege 围攻
3 Betrothed 与……订婚
4 tutored 学会
5 wrought … death 让她看上去像死了一般
6 dire 可怕，悲惨
7 prefixèd hour 预定的时间
8 closely 秘密地
9 untimely 在错误时间
10 true 忠诚
11 bear 忍受
12 did violence on herself 自杀身亡
13 privy 秘密参与者
14 Miscarried 出错
15 rigour 严格，严厉

Romeo and Juliet Act 5 Scene 3
柔密欧与茱丽叶

I married them, and their stol'n marriage day
Was Tybalt's doomsday, whose untimely death
Banished the new-made bridegroom from this city,   235
For whom, and not for Tybalt, Juliet pined[1].
You, to remove that siege[2] of grief from her,
Betrothed[3] and would have married her perforce
To County Paris. Then comes she to me,
And with wild looks bid me devise some mean   240
To rid her from this second marriage,
Or in my cell there would she kill herself.
Then gave I her (so tutored[4] by my art)
A sleeping potion, which so took effect
As I intended, for it wrought on her   245
The form of death[5]. Mean time I writ to Romeo
That he should hither come as this dire[6] night
To help to take her from her borrowed grave,
Being the time the potion's force should cease.
But he which bore my letter, Friar John,   250
Was stayed by accident, and yesternight
Returned my letter back. Then all alone,
At the prefixèd hour[7] of her waking,
Came I to take her from her kindred's vault,
Meaning to keep her closely[8] at my cell,   255
Till I conveniently could send to Romeo.
But when I came, some minute ere the time
Of her awakening, here untimely[9] lay
The noble Paris and true[10] Romeo dead.
She wakes, and I entreated her come forth   260
And bear[11] this work of heaven with patience.
But then a noise did scare me from the tomb,
And she too desperate would not go with me,
But as it seems, did violence on herself[12].
All this I know, and to the marriage   265
Her nurse is privy[13]; and if ought in this
Miscarried[14] by my fault, let my old life
Be sacrificed, some hour before his time,
Unto the rigour[15] of severest law.

Balthasar and Paris's Page tell what they know. The Prince reads Romeo's letter, then calls Capulet and Montague to look on the deadly results of their quarrels.

 剧情简介：巴尔特扎和帕瑞的小厮也讲了他们了解的事情。亲王读了柔密欧写的信，唤卡普莱和芒特鸠看看他们相互敌对种下的夺命恶果。

1 Three other viewpoints (in small groups)

The stories of Balthasar and the Page, and the Prince's report of Romeo's letter are, like the Friar's account, plain narrative, simply expressed.

a In what tone of voice do Balthasar and the Page speak? Fearfully, afraid of punishment? Or in some other way? Read each aloud, experimenting with different styles until you find the ones that work best.

b Take the stories of Balthasar (lines 272–7), the Page (lines 281–5) and the Prince (lines 286–90). In each case, talk together about whether you think it adds to the play or could be safely cut from a stage production. Make your recommendations to the director (who could be a member of another group in role), explaining your decisions. The director might disagree!

1	still	= always
2	in post	赶快（= post-haste：尽快）
3	what ... place?	您的主人为何来此？
4	make good	证实
5	therewithal	随身带来
6	scourge	惩罚
7	kill your joys	杀死你们的孩子；毁灭你们的幸福
8	for winking at your discords	对你们的不和视而不见
9	a brace of kinsmen	一对族人（指莫丘休和帕瑞）

Write about it 写作练习

Romeo's letter (by yourself)

What is in Romeo's letter to his father? The Prince reads a brief outline (lines 286–90).

- Write the full contents of the letter. Try to express Romeo's state of mind at the moment he wrote it, shortly after hearing of Juliet's death.

Themes 主题分析

'heaven finds means to kill your joys with love!'

a Do you agree that 'heaven' has killed Romeo and Juliet? Look back at the Evidence Grid you have compiled to record the references to chance and choice, fate and destiny, throughout the play, and reflect on how important a part they have played in the unfolding of tragic events.

b Work on a five-minute presentation to deliver to your class, focusing just on the lives of Romeo and Juliet. Explore all the interventions of fate and their impact on what happens to the two young lovers. Link your presentation clearly to the evidence you have gathered.

PRINCE	We still[1] have known thee for a holy man.	270
	Where's Romeo's man? what can he say to this?	
BALTHASAR	I brought my master news of Juliet's death,	
	And then in post[2] he came from Mantua	
	To this same place, to this same monument.	
	This letter he early bid me give his father,	275
	And threatened me with death, going in the vault,	
	If I departed not and left him there.	
PRINCE	Give me the letter, I will look on it.	
	Where is the County's page that raised the Watch?	
	Sirrah, what made your master in this place?[3]	280
PAGE	He came with flowers to strew his lady's grave,	
	And bid me stand aloof, and so I did.	
	Anon comes one with light to ope the tomb,	
	And by and by my master drew on him,	
	And then I ran away to call the Watch.	285
PRINCE	This letter doth make good[4] the Friar's words,	
	Their course of love, the tidings of her death;	
	And here he writes that he did buy a poison	
	Of a poor pothecary, and therewithal[5]	
	Came to this vault to die, and lie with Juliet.	290
	Where be these enemies? Capulet, Montague?	
	See what a scourge[6] is laid upon your hate,	
	That heaven finds means to kill your joys[7] with love!	
	And I for winking at your discords[8] too	
	Have lost a brace of kinsmen[9]. All are punished.	295

Capulet and Montague make up their quarrel. They promise to set up a golden statue of Juliet and Romeo. The Prince closes the play, promising pardon for some and punishment for others.

 剧情简介：卡普莱和芒特鸠了结争斗，双方和解，他们答应为茱丽叶和柔密欧打造金塑像。亲王宣布剧终，承诺有人获得原谅，而有人得到惩罚。

1 Is the feud really ended? (in pairs)

Do you think that a promised golden statue really marks the end of the bitter feud? Experiment with Montague's and Capulet's lines 296–304. Try speaking and acting the lines in ways that show the quarrel will continue. For example, is Montague trying to 'outbid' (出价高于) Capulet, and does Capulet respond by showing he is as wealthy as Montague?

1 *jointure* 聘礼（卡普莱向芒特鸠要的聘礼只是一个握手，表示双方和解）
2 *at such rate be set* 用如此高的价钱来立
3 *Poor sacrifices* 可怜的牺牲品
4 *glooming peace* 阴云笼罩下的和平
5 *Exeunt omnes* 所有人退场

Stagecraft 导演技巧

The final image (in small groups)

Talk about the last image you wish the audience to see (refer back to the pictures on p. xii in the photo gallery). Will it be an empty stage? If so, work out how you will get everyone off, including the bodies. Or do you want the audience to see a final tableau?

- Rehearse and then show the class your image of the final moment of the play before the lights fade.

▲ How might the last moments of the play be staged for greatest impact?

2 Pardoned and punished (whole class)

Although some argue that fate or destiny play a huge part in the tragic outcome of the play, it is also true that various characters have a significant impact on events. Who do you think is responsible for the tragedy?

- Arrange a trial of some of the major figures who you consider might be accused of having a part in the deaths. Appoint a judge, prosecuting and defending counsels. Both sides will be able to call witnesses if they wish. This activity will take time to prepare, so appoint a 'trial day' and do the necessary preparations.

ROMEO AND JULIET ACT 5 SCENE 3
柔密欧与茱丽叶

CAPULET   O brother Montague, give me thy hand.
               This is my daughter's jointure¹, for no more
               Can I demand.
MONTAGUE   But I can give thee more,
               For I will raise her statue in pure gold,
               That whiles Verona by that name is known,   300
               There shall no figure at such rate be set²
               As that of true and faithful Juliet.
CAPULET   As rich shall Romeo's by his lady's lie,
               Poor sacrifices³ of our enmity!
PRINCE   A glooming peace⁴ this morning with it brings,   305
               The sun for sorrow will not show his head.
               Go hence to have more talk of these sad things;
               Some shall be pardoned, and some punishèd:
               For never was a story of more woe
               Than this of Juliet and her Romeo.   310

                                          [*Exeunt omnes*⁵]

ROMEO AND JULIET
柔密欧与茱丽叶

Looking back at the play 本剧回顾
Activities for groups or individuals

1 Show the whole play

Take the Prologue's fourteen lines (on p. 3) and the Prince's last six lines in the play (305–10). As one student reads aloud all the lines, the others act them out. You'll find that you have produced a version of the whole play!

2 Capulet's dream – the ghosts return

In groups, make up a short play entitled 'Capulet's Dream' (or 'Nightmare'). It brings back all those who have died in the play. You might have each ghost explaining why they died, and how they now feel about the feuding families.

3 Obituaries (讣告)

You have been commissioned to write the obituaries of Romeo Montague and Juliet Capulet for the *Verona Herald*. With a partner, talk about what might be included in an obituary, then settle down to write.

4 Friar Lawrence writes his memoirs (回忆录)

'It's ten years now since the deaths of Romeo and Juliet …'. What does the Friar think, looking back over this stretch of time? He has had to face up to a cruel irony: he married Romeo and Juliet, hoping that their marriage would end the feud between the Montagues and Capulets. But it was only their deaths that caused Montague and Capulet to shake hands. The Friar also has to cope with his abandonment of Juliet in the tomb. What does he now think of that?

- Imagine yourself as Friar Lawrence and write your memoirs.

5 The balance of life and death

Shakespeare takes several opportunities to remind his audience of its mortality. Mercutio's dying curse refers to the 'plague'. 'Infectious pestilence' stops Friar John from delivering Lawrence's letter. Juliet imagines being buried in a 'charnel-house'. Death is personified numerous times. But there are also references in the play to medicine and healing – for example, the Friar's preoccupation with herbs and the Apothecary's appearance in Act 5.

- Research Elizabethan attitudes towards life and death. What did they think about death and dying? And how did they view the importance of medicine? Prepare a mini-presentation.

6 Juliet's emotional journey

In the course of the play, Juliet matures from innocent young girl to tragic heroine. She experiences the brief happiness of unconditional love, violent rejection by her parents, betrayal by her Nurse and an agony of fear aroused by Friar Lawrence's dangerous plan. But she finds the courage to endure the horrors of the Capulet tomb. In the end, she determines to kill herself rather than live without Romeo.

- Write an extended essay that traces Juliet's emotional journey. Is it accurate to say that Juliet is emotionally mature by the end of the play?

7 In the medium of film

You have to work on a trailer (预告片) for a new movie adaptation of *Romeo and Juliet*. Your editor has asked you to select five key scenes or moments from the play and to include one other episode that Shakespeare doesn't cover.

- Storyboard the key scenes and write the voiceover for the trailer. Remember that it has to be engaging and dramatic, with a really strong 'hook' for the audience. And you can't give away the whole story – there must be some elements of suspense or mystery. You could then try to create the trailer through live tableaux or mimes, or perhaps by actually filming it!

8 The dartboard (镖靶) of blame

Draw an image of a dartboard on a large sheet of paper. Arrange the characters on it in terms of who you think is most to blame for the tragedy. The character nearest the bullseye (靶心) should be the one you think is most responsible.

201

Romeo and Juliet
柔密欧与茱丽叶

The story of *Romeo and Juliet*
《柔密欧与茱丽叶》故事介绍

Is *Romeo and Juliet* true?

There is no simple answer to that question. It all depends on what you mean by 'true'. In thirteenth-century Italy there certainly were two Italian families, the Montecchi and the Capelletti, locked in political struggle. But the Montecchi lived in Verona, and the Capelletti lived in Cremona, sixty miles away. No one knows whether the families had children called Romeo and Juliet.

However, the story of two young lovers from opposing families was very popular in Italy and France. Myths and folktales about them existed for hundreds of years before Shakespeare. He based his play on a poem published two years before he was born: *The Tragicall Historye of Romeus and Juliet* (1562) by Arthur Brooke. That poem was an English translation of a French translation of an Italian version! Below is an extract from a section of Brooke's poem. You can see how Shakespeare used this source material as the starting point for the beginning of Act 4 Scene 3.

> Unto her chamber doth the pensive wight repair
> And in her hand a percher light the Nurse bears up the stair.
> In Juliet's chamber was her wonted use to lie,
> Wherefore her mistress dreading that she should her
>   work descry
> As soon as she began her pallet to unfold
> Thinking to lie that night, where she was wont to lie of old,
> Doth gently pray her seek her lodging somewhere else.

◆ Re-read the extract above. What differences can you find between Shakespeare's version and the original? Look back at the script to make comparisons and compile a list of the changes Shakespeare makes.

◆ Find a copy of Brooke's poem (e.g. in the New Cambridge Shakespeare edition of the play). Compare it with *Romeo and Juliet*. What kind of similarities and differences do you find?

Although you can argue that it is probably not true historically, *Romeo and Juliet* still remains 'true' in other ways. Because it has proved so enduring, and because people still find the story fascinating, it has a truth in human experience. In every age, young people have fallen in love against their parents' wishes. Where families or societies are in conflict, trouble always lies in store for a boy and a girl from opposing camps who wish to marry. Poets, playwrights and novelists have been irresistibly drawn to write about the troubles and torments of such young lovers.

To help you deepen your understanding of the tragic story of *Romeo and Juliet*, try one or more of the following activities.

'Forbidden love' – your own version

◆ Research other examples of young lovers experiencing huge difficulties because of a clash between their families, cultures or societies.

◆ Afterwards, try writing your own version of what happens. You could base your story on a real situation or relationship you have researched, or you could invent or adapt your own. Give your story a title that reflects the lovers' predicament.

The bare bones of the script

◆ Have a go at retelling the story of the play in just one sentence, or rewrite the play as a mini-saga (微型传奇故事) in exactly fifty words.

◆ Imagine you are the same newspaper sub-editor who wrote the headlines for Act 2 (see Activity 1 on p. 88). Now that the whole story has unfolded, write brief, memorable headlines for each of the five acts in the play. Of course, they may include puns or clever wordplay to gain attention and interest, but they must also be accurate.

Longer versions

◆ In a group of five, each takes responsibility for retelling the story of an individual act, then puts the narrative together. Display your version on the classroom wall and compare it with that of other groups. What have they included that you have missed out? Argue your case.

◆ Try writing a sentence about Act 1 Scene 1, then pass your paper to another student who should pick up the narrative. Keep working around the group, adding a sentence about each scene, until you reach the end of the play.

◆ Use the scene summaries in modern English at the top of each left-hand page to help you recreate a full-length retelling of the action of the play.

◆ Review the photo gallery at the start of this edition, which gives a version of the play in pictures and captions. What pictures have been missed out? Suggest three other images you would include, giving reasons for your choices.

Change the genre

◆ In small groups, discuss what *Romeo and Juliet* might be like if the script was transformed into a quite different genre:
- a cliffhanger (悬念片): a serial in five episodes with each one ending at a moment of climax or suspense
- a morality story for young children
- a fairy story
- a television production cut to two hours (run the production meeting, deciding which episodes and incidents to keep).

From another perspective

Shakespeare focuses pretty closely on events seen through either Romeo's or Juliet's eyes. Other characters might, therefore, have a completely different view of what happens during the action of the play.

◆ Take on the persona of one of those other characters and write up the events of the play from your point of view. Perhaps working as a larger group, you could each select a different character and then put your stories together as a myriad of (大量) contrasting (and conflicting?) viewpoints. How would Tybalt's story weigh against Mercutio's or Benvolio's, for example? How closely would Lord and Lady Capulet's narratives match?

Fifteen-minute theatre

◆ Split into five groups, with each group taking one act of the play. Produce a three-minute version of your chosen act, using only the words from the script.

◆ When you are ready, put each of the five acts together in turn to create a fifteen-minute version of the whole play.

Sculpture park

◆ The class divides into two groups. As one group looks away, the other half of the class – working in pairs – freezes into 'sculptures' that represent some of the key moments of the play. When the first group of students turns round, they see various statues depicting moments from the play set out before them. Their task is to identify as many of the sculptures as possible.

Produce a timeline for the play

Shakespeare allocates only four days to the action of the play. It begins on Sunday morning and ends as dawn is about to break on the following Thursday.

◆ Look carefully at the signals given in each scene about the timing of the action, then produce a timeline for the play. Afterwards, discuss why you think Shakespeare focuses so specifically on the issue of time in the play.

Romeo and Juliet
柔密欧与茱丽叶

Characters 人物分析

In earlier centuries, people writing about characters tended to do so as if they were living human beings with real personalities. More recently, critics have argued that playwrights such as Shakespeare were not concerned with creating psychologically consistent 'people', but rather with dramatic 'constructs', embodying certain dramatic functions and set in a social and political world with particular values, attitudes and beliefs. Keep these different viewpoints in mind as you explore Shakespeare's characterisation.

Juliet

In thinking about how Juliet is presented in the play, first study the two images opposite. Which image best reflects how *you* see Juliet, and why? Then consider the comments below that come from directors and performance critics.

> Juliet is first seen mutinously (桀骜不驯地) playing with a toy whip as her marriage prospects are discussed. But … what is striking is her bold teasing sexuality in the balcony scene and her constant awareness of 'love-devouring death'.
> Critic Michael Billington, 2010

> There's a tenderness and sincerity in the lovers' meetings, but Shakespeare gives Juliet language that shows she is aware of the physical aspects of love.
> Director Alasdair Ramsay, 2001

> [She is] totally the product of a rich, aspirational upper-class … gorgeous and uncluttered (整洁).
> Director Peter Gill, 2004

> [Juliet is] alert to the transformation from social conformity to rebellion, as well as from girlhood to womanhood.
> Review of RSC performance, 2004

> [Although] Juliet flourished under the effects of a new-found sexuality there also lingered within her a childish terror and naivety.
> Review of RSC performance, 1995

◆ Talk with a partner about which of these quotations you think most accurately defines the essence of Juliet's character, and why.

When she first appears, Juliet seems very shy. She is only thirteen, and as the Nurse and her mother talk about her age, she can come across as innocent and docile (温顺). Sometimes she is played as almost tongue-tied – reluctant to take part in adult conversation. She appears to respect her mother's authority. But this thirteen-year-old girl, seemingly so quiet and modest, matures rapidly after first encountering Romeo. They have only just met when she allows him to kiss her, and when she appears on the balcony, she is full of longing for him. Throughout the 'balcony' scene she takes the lead, speaking twice as many lines as Romeo. Juliet even proposes their marriage and arranges (through the Nurse) the nuptials for the very next day.

CHARACTERS

Juliet's swift journey towards independence is evident when she defies her father's demand that she marry Count Paris. Visiting Friar Lawrence, she displays remarkable courage, first in her determination to kill herself rather than marry Paris, then in willingly accepting the Friar's dangerous plan. She returns home and deceives her father, but becomes isolated when the Nurse lets her down, advising her to marry Paris. But even in her isolation, she bravely carries out the Friar's plan and drinks the 'poison' that will make her appear to be dead. She displays resolution and fearlessness when, unwilling to live without Romeo, she kills herself.

◆ Explore the commentary above, then flick back through the play to find the 'Characters' boxes about Juliet (pp. 26, 60, 136 and 144). How do your enquiries there qualify your evaluation of Juliet? Produce a final character study of Juliet. Include quotations and evidence to back up any points you make.

Romeo

Hannah Miller, the casting co-ordinator for the Royal Shakespeare Company (RSC), describes what she was looking for in Romeo for the 2004 production:

> A sensitive, good natured, loyal young man, Romeo could be a few years older than Juliet. He is part of the Montague gang, a group of educated, restless young men – though Romeo is certainly not a troublemaker at heart. He is teased for his romanticism and has a history of falling head over heels in love (沉溺于爱河中). He is, however, blown away when the real thing hits him and he becomes irrational and impetuous. He is truly on an emotional rollercoaster once Juliet is in his life and he becomes increasingly reckless.

Below, actors and critics discuss Romeo's character.

> *There is a brooding (幽怨), withdrawn quality ... as if Romeo only comes fully to life in the presence of Juliet; YET ... there are sudden sparks of humour as when [he] does a wild, exultant (欢欣鼓舞) dance at the realisation that the balconied Juliet is smitten (突然爱上).*
> Critic Michael Billington, 2010

> *I wanted to tell the story of a disaffected youth at odds with his predicament, his environment and himself, and full of the 'nobody-understands-me' ire (愤怒) of adolescence ... Romeo is always upstaged (被抢风头) by Juliet.*
> Actor David Tennant, 2003

> *Streetwise Romeo [is] full of energy, rashness and vigour, swaggering (趾高气扬) in at the start of the play ... and mellowing (变平和) into devotion to Juliet.*
> Actor David Tennant, 2003

> *Romeo is very passionate but does have a tendency to moan ... When he enters, Romeo is a woebegone (愁眉苦脸), melancholic figure: poetic and indulgent, a lover. He thinks he's rather gorgeous and he revels in his misery.*
> Actor Matthew Rhys, 2004

> *[This is] a petulant (暴躁), awkward Romeo of childlike extremes, fidgeting (坐立不安) with awkward delight when speaking with Juliet, and reacting to his banishment with an almighty tantrum (使性子).*
> Review of RSC performance, 1995

◆ Discuss these viewpoints with a partner and keep in mind what you think are the key ideas as you read the commentary that follows.

Romeo and Juliet
柔密欧与茱丽叶

In his first appearance, Romeo declares his love for Rosaline (whom he does not name). This makes him seem a stock character of traditional drama: the melancholy young lover who is rejected by an unattainable (高不可攀) woman. But when he meets Juliet, there is a progressive deepening of his character (even though evidence of his immaturity and early style of speaking are sometimes found later in the play). The first sign that he will develop into a tragic figure is just before he enters Capulet's mansion for the party. He fearfully broods on the future (Act 1 Scene 4, lines 106–7):

> my mind misgives
> Some consequence yet hanging in the stars

Although Romeo grows in maturity, he is hasty and impetuous. His moods change quickly. He falls in love at first sight, marries Juliet the next day, and revenges Mercutio's death by slaying Tybalt. His language is sometimes hyperbolic and exaggerated ('that vast shore washed with the farthest sea'). In Friar Lawrence's cell, he becomes emotionally childlike and distraught (心烦意乱). He seems to lose all self-control in his hysterical outbursts and actions.

In Mantua, learning of Juliet's death, his impulsiveness is again evident in his passionate words 'then I defy you, stars!' He instantly resolves to kill himself in the tomb with her. But, although his state of mind can swing to extremes, his dialogues with Juliet, and his soliloquy before he takes the poison, display maturity and his unflinching (坚贞不渝) commitment to Juliet.

◆ Write up a character study of Romeo. Use the information above and your own investigations. Back up your ideas with quotations.

◆ In groups of four, each of you takes one of the 'relationship cards' below and researches the play to find evidence in support of the stance it takes. Then, as a group, argue the merits of each 'reading'.

Card A Juliet is sweet and innocent, a young woman whose passion is courageous, admirable and wondrous. Her love for Romeo reflects all her virtues.

Card B Juliet is far too independent and strong-willed for her own good. As a thirteen-year-old, she shouldn't be jumping into a full-on relationship with a man she hardly knows.

Card C Romeo is the embodiment of unflinching love. He shows total commitment to Juliet — loving her so deeply and powerfully that he literally lays down his life for her.

Card D Romeo is in love with the idea of love and only ever acts impetuously. Under pressure, he resorts to childish, hysterical and selfish behaviour.

◆ After discussing Romeo and Juliet's attitude to love and to each other, all of you should write up your thoughts about the presentation of Romeo and Juliet's relationship, reflecting the ideas of the group.

CHARACTERS

Friar Lawrence

Friar Lawrence is like a father figure to Romeo, who confides in (吐露秘密) him rather than in his own father, Montague. But the Friar is a puzzling character. His language and actions are open to very different interpretations. Some productions have shown him as shrewd and level-headed (头脑冷静), concerned to heal the breach between the Montagues and Capulets. In other productions, he has been played as cunning and dishonest or as a bungling (错误百出的), nervous schemer (阴谋家).

On his first appearance he seems a wise moral commentator, as he speaks of everything having the capacity for good or evil. He advises caution ('Wisely and slow'), and wishes to use the marriage of Romeo and Juliet to bring peace to Verona. But his deeds do not match his words. He acts hastily, breaking Church law by marrying Romeo and Juliet in secret. He devises a plan to deceive Juliet's parents, from whom he conceals her marriage. He risks poisoning Juliet, and abandons her in the tomb at her moment of greatest need. His impulsive actions help cause the death of the lovers.

- ◆ In the final scene, the Prince says 'Some shall be pardoned, and some punishèd'. Imagine that Friar Lawrence is called to account for his part in the tragic outcome. Half the class prepares as prosecuting counsel (控方律师), the other half as defence counsel (辩护律师). Base your lines of enquiry and questions on the issues outlined above. In each case, try to get to the truth of each assertion.

- ◆ Put your teacher into the role of Friar Lawrence and conduct the trial. Let the class decide how much to blame he really is. Should he be pardoned or punished (and, if so, what would be your recommendation for sentencing)? Link your judgements to evidence, using quotations from the play.

The Nurse

The Nurse is Shakespeare's development of a character type in classical Greek and Roman drama: the long-winded (爱唠叨) and rude-talking servant. She is a mother figure and close confidante (女性知己) of Juliet, and she seems to have genuine affection for the girl. The Nurse acts as a

go-between for the lovers, helping Juliet deceive her parents. Her earthy, rambling (说话漫无边际), repetitive style gives her great stage presence, and directors often use her to bring humour to the play.

The Nurse sometimes appears to be the most sympathetic character in *Romeo and Juliet*. But for all her likeability, and her close relationship with Juliet, her advice that Juliet should marry Paris seems like a heartless act of betrayal, which leaves Juliet vulnerable and isolated.

- ◆ Prepare mini-presentations on the Nurse's role and character in Act 1 Scene 3, Act 2 Scene 4, Act 2 Scene 5 and Act 3 Scene 5. Which lines from the text do you think typify her character? Can you identify common language or speech patterns?

ROMEO AND JULIET
柔密欧与茱丽叶

- Imagine that the Nurse is placed on the psychiatrist's couch. One person becomes the Nurse, who is psychoanalysed by their partner or other members of the group. You could probe some of the inconsistencies in her character. Is she frank or secretive about her real feelings? A bit of a creep or arrogant? Trustworthy or sly and dishonest? A woman of principle or a pragmatist (爱管闲事的人)? A woman who knows about love or just speaks about it?

- Write up the psychiatrist's report with your honest assessment of the Nurse's personality.

Mercutio

Mercutio is perhaps the most complex character in the play. Romeo gives a good description of him: 'A gentleman … that loves to hear himself talk' (Act 2 Scene 4, line 123). He is an entertainer – clever and witty, but also earthy and coarse. He loves playing with language, particularly when he can give it sexual double meanings. In contrast to Romeo's idealisation of love, Mercutio mocks love, seeing it only in terms of sex. His flights of fancy are full of dazzling invention, but much of his imaginative creativity can also be seen as feverish (狂热) and neurotic (神经质).

Mercutio feels intense friendship for Romeo, and possesses a strong sense of male honour. He seems to be always on the edge of looking for a fight. His courage in defending the honour of his friend Romeo results in his death. Some people argue that Mercutio becomes such an engaging character that Shakespeare thought it necessary to kill him off before he completely dominated the play. There is a sense of loss at his death, but perhaps Shakespeare made Mercutio's early demise dramatically inevitable as the key to the tragedy – spurring Romeo to revenge.

- The outline above analyses Mercutio both as a character (with his own personality) and a dramatic construct (a figure used to enhance key aspects and themes of the play). In pairs, each of you chooses one approach (character or dramatic construct) and investigates Mercutio's presentation. Share your findings with each other and review their respective merits.

The parents: *Who Do You Think You Are?*

Lord Capulet appears at first to be friendly and generous. At the party he reminisces about his youth, and is determined to stop Tybalt making trouble. But he shows a different side to his character when Juliet refuses to marry Paris. He becomes short-tempered and tyrannical, exploding in uncontrollable fury when Juliet refuses to obey him. However, when she dies (both in pretence and in reality) he is overcome with grief and remorse (懊悔).

Lady Capulet seems distant from her daughter. She displays little or no maternal affection. She lacks sympathy for Juliet's feelings ('tell him so yourself'), when Juliet refuses to marry Paris. She shows little sign of taking Juliet's part or comforting her when she is the target of Capulet's rage. But like Capulet, she is heartbroken at Juliet's death.

- Imagine that you have been commissioned as a researcher to investigate the background of Juliet's family in the style of the television programme that reconstructs the heritage and lineage (宗系；血统) of celebrity figures. Choose as your subject Lord or Lady Capulet (or both). Study the pen portraits above, then begin to invent their family tree. For example, bearing in mind Capulet's wealth, what trade or profession do you think his own parents might have had? And if (as his wife implies) he has had the odd fling (短暂的风流韵事) with younger women, might there be a few illegitimate (私生的) children?

- Present your imagined family trees with accompanying commentary and a brief celebrity profile of the current Capulets. Where do they now live, for example, and what is their lifestyle like?

Perspectives and themes 视角与主题

Tensions and oppositions in *Romeo and Juliet*

Oppositions and contrasts abound in *Romeo and Juliet*. You could think of them as themes of the play. The action begins with a violent clash between the feuding families. Throughout the play, divisions and conflicts haunt the doomed lovers.

Light versus dark

The play is alive with images of light and darkness. The flash and sparkle of eyes, jewels, stars, fire, lightning, torches, exploding gunpowder, the sun and moon, are set against a darker world of night, clouds, smoke and the blackness of the tomb: 'More light and light, more dark and dark our woes!' Juliet, waiting for Romeo, aches for the sun to set 'And bring in cloudy night immediately'. Romeo sees Juliet's beauty flooding the darkness of the tomb with brilliance: 'her beauty makes / This vault a feasting presence full of light'.

- Working in groups, look back through the play to find as many images of light and darkness as you can. In each case, identify the context: who is speaking, where and when. Then comment on the kind of effect or impact the images have, particularly at that point in the play.

- Examine the first meeting between Romeo and Juliet in Act 1 Scene 5, and pick out Romeo's words connected with light. Do the same for the start of Act 2 Scene 2. What do Romeo's 'light' words suggest about his attitude towards Juliet?

- Study the photographs in this edition. From the selection, choose five that you think express the conflict of light and darkness in a particularly striking or effective way. In each case, explain the reasoning behind your choice to a partner.

- Imagine that you are directing a movie version of the play. Focus on Act 5 Scene 3. Decide what colours and lighting you would use. *Film noir* (from the French 'black film') uses light to hint at the psychological state of mind of its characters. At what point would Romeo be in the shadows? When would he be in close-up? What about the other characters? Discuss your ideas with a partner and then write up your notes.

- Discuss the interplay of light and dark in the play. Romeo and Juliet's love is defined in terms of the sun, stars, moon, fire, lightning, torches and day – but it exists in a world full of the darkness of night, tombs, churchyards and clouds. Write an essay exploring the dramatic significance of this tension.

Chance versus choice: fate and free will

The Chorus opens the play with a mention of fate: 'A pair of star-crossed lovers'. The belief that fate determines our lives echoes through the play. Romeo fears that fate has unhappy things in store for him if he goes to Capulet's feast: 'my mind misgives / Some consequence yet hanging in the stars'. Juliet fears what inevitably lies ahead as she parts from Romeo: 'Methinks I see thee now, thou art so low, / As one dead in the bottom of a tomb.' Romeo and Juliet struggle to break free of what Fate threatens in dreams and premonitions. 'Then I defy you, stars!' is Romeo's defiant challenge when he hears of Juliet's death.

- There are six 'Themes' boxes in the main part of this edition, on pages 20, 140, 164, 172, 176 and 196. Remind yourself of the focus of each one, then prepare a presentation on the impact of fate on human affairs in the play.

- Take each character in turn and consider if there is any evidence that they have a choice over their own destiny. Rate the strength of their free will on a scale of 0 to 10 and display your findings as a bar graph.

Romeo and Juliet
柔密欧与茱丽叶

Love versus hate

Here's much to do with hate, but more with love
                                    Act 1 Scene 1, line 166

The love of Romeo and Juliet is threatened by a society full of hate. Juliet fears for Romeo's safety at the hands of her kinsmen: 'If they do see thee, they will murder thee.' The hateful, hate-full honour code that governs relationships between the feuding families of Verona will destroy Romeo and Juliet, Mercutio, Tybalt and Paris. Love, in Verona's masculine society, is about domination. The macho (大男子气概的) servants of Capulet joke about sex in violent, aggressive terms. The selflessness of Romeo and Juliet, equal in love and willing to die for each other, is in strong contrast to the hate that fills Verona.

◆ Use the series of oppositions outlined in the paragraph above as the basis for an extended piece of writing. In it, explore how *Romeo and Juliet* dramatises the conflict between love and hate. You might begin your preparation by heading up a piece of paper with two columns – 'Love' and 'Hate' – and gathering evidence from the play to fill out those columns. You should look not only at the incidents, but also at the dramatic effects created. There is material to get you started on pages 6 and 50.

Public versus private

The action of the play moves from outdoor to indoor, from public to private spaces. In contrast to the violent happenings in Verona's city centre and the grand occasion of Capulet's party, there are quiet, intimate scenes in the moonlit orchard or in Juliet's bedroom in the Capulet mansion. The shift from public to private, from social spaces to personal meetings, is symbolic of other tensions:

- the loyalties of groups (Montagues and Capulets) versus the loyalties of individuals towards each other (Romeo and Juliet)
- the freedoms of personal love versus the constraints of social life
- male dominance versus the vision of equality of the sexes seen in the love between Romeo and Juliet.

◆ Working as a group of five, each takes an act of the play. Go through your allocated act and, for each scene, identify whether it is set in a public or private location. Then incorporate your findings into a flow diagram. Reconvene (重新集合) and put all five acts together. What do you notice about the pattern created? Choose from within your flow chart two scenes that appear to have a profoundly dramatic shift in location – from public to private or vice versa.

◆ Cast and act out the last few lines of your first scene and the beginning of the second. Now let other students imagine that they are switching channels on television, and this changing sequence is all they see. Get them to make a list of everything they might suppose about the characters, the situations, the circumstances of the action and the play as a whole.

◆ As a class, put your reflections together and consider how effectively Shakespeare establishes the contrast between public and private.

Youth versus age – fast versus slow

The differences between old and young, between cautious, mature wisdom and youthful impetuous emotion, are striking. Romeo's passion is evident: 'I stand on sudden haste'. The contrast with the Friar's advice is vivid as he urges 'love moderately, long love doth so' and pronounces 'Wisely and slow, they stumble that run fast'. But don't think the play is a simple contrast between youth and age. Juliet's father is given to mood swings and sudden outbursts as violent as any in the young people!

The contrast between passion and caution is evident in the characters, but there are also changes in tempo (节奏) throughout the play. In Capulet's orchard, time seems to stand still as Romeo and Juliet exchange vows of love. After leisurely beginnings, scenes explode into violent action. Events force the lovers into hasty action. Capulet's decision to bring the wedding forward hurries Juliet into drinking the Friar's potion. News of her 'death' sends Romeo speeding back to Verona – and his own death.

Perspectives and themes

- In groups, choose a scene in which the pace changes dramatically. Good ones to look at are Act 1 Scene 1 or Act 3 Scene 1 where, after slow beginnings, there is a sudden upsurge in action and incident. Study the content of your chosen scene (just the action, not the language). You'll need to know it really well, so pay attention to the details. Then imagine that you are watching a silent movie version of the play. Start to run the action of the scene as if you're focusing on the detail in slow motion and then, following the rhythms of Shakespeare's story-telling, gradually speed it up. Remember – no language, just actions! The result will probably be frenetic but it will give you a good sense of the changing rhythms of the scene that Shakespeare constructs.

- Create a sequence of photographs or freeze-frames which, act by act, highlight the contrast between youth and age. In each case, try to find a suitable extract of text that you can use as a caption. Be prepared to explain your intentions to other students as they watch your images.

- Remind yourself of the content of this scene. Go through it carefully, making notes on the ways in which Shakespeare counterpoints ideas of life and death. Gather together key quotations that you feel underline this contrast. You could then broaden your investigation to take in other scenes that have a contrast between life and death at their core.

Memento mori (死亡象征) (literally, 'remember your mortality') is a genre of powerful and graphic artistic images of Death and the vulnerability of life, which dates back to classical times. Common conventions are depictions of the 'grim reaper' (a bent-backed old man with scythe [大镰刀]), human skeletons and representations of time.

- You have been commissioned to produce a *memento mori* for a new collection to be published in a book. Create one based on an image from the play. Either caption it with the original words that inspired it, or incorporate the quotation into your artwork. Think carefully about how you would choose to represent the figure of Death.

▼ *Vanitas*, a *memento mori* by Philippe de Champaigne (1602–74).

Life versus death

Although Romeo and Juliet's youthful, life-affirming relationship is at the heart of the play, and their love is full of vitality and energy, death is never far away in the divided world of Verona. Even as they celebrate their wedding night (Act 3 Scene 5), their thoughts are punctured (刺破) with ominous forebodings of death.

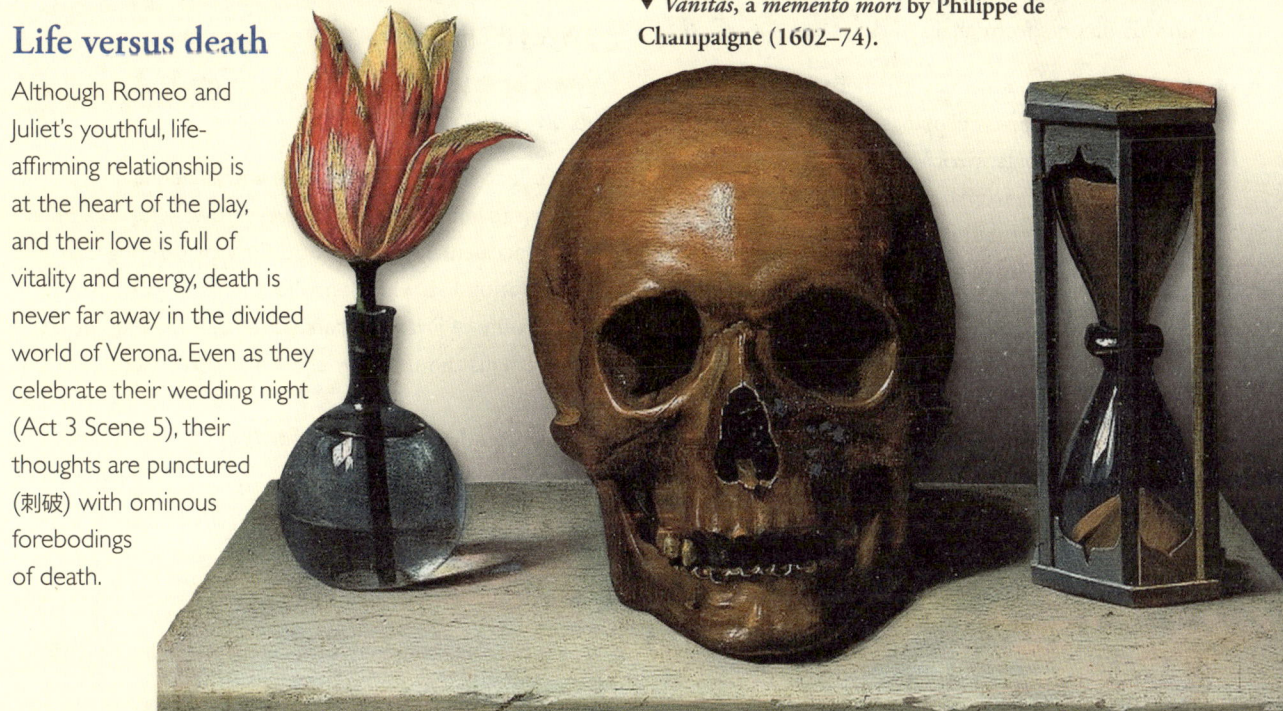

Romeo and Juliet
柔密欧与茱丽叶

Why did Romeo and Juliet die?
柔密欧和茱丽叶为什么会死?

Romeo and Juliet is a tragedy – that is, a specific type of play that ultimately ends in the death of the main characters. Often, the **tragic hero** or **heroine** (the central figure in the drama) is a victim of fate or circumstance, as well as being partly responsible for their own downfall as a result of their naivety or weaknesses in their character. It seems that there is an unstoppable force propelling them towards disaster, despite their efforts to halt it. At the end, the audience must confront the question: who or what is to blame for the tragedy? For hundreds of years, people have argued over the reason for the deaths of the young lovers. Your task here is to complete your own investigation into the possible causes.

◆ First, divide into five groups. Each group should complete research and investigation into the separate possible 'causes' listed below (1–5). Use the trigger questions in each section to firm up specific lines of enquiry. Gather evidence from the play, such as key quotations and comments from characters.

◆ Invent witness statements and other forms of testimony (证据) – letters, press clippings (剪报), diary entries, newspaper reports, sworn affidavits (宣誓书) and so on. Interview other characters who might also have something to contribute: perhaps a householder whose window overlooks Verona's public square, or a boy who had crept into Capulet's orchard to steal fruit. Use your imaginations to amass as much material as possible to support your specific line of enquiry – but don't deliberately subvert (破坏) the evidence of the text!

◆ Display all your evidence on a 'market stall'. Use the table at which you've been working, but dress it up with a banner and other visual images to show clearly the topic on which you have been focusing (for example, the 'fathers' table could be embellished (美化) with the families' coats of arms and trappings of their ancestry and lineage).

◆ In turn, all groups should send out representatives, or 'ambassadors', to each of the stalls to gather as much information as possible before feeding back to their host group. In this way, all groups will build a wide-ranging and detailed awareness of the possible causes.

1 Was it fate?

Were the deaths foretold in the stars? There are many suggestions in the play that the deaths were determined by fate.

◆ Collect references to the inevitability of the tragedy, for example 'star-crossed' (Prologue, line 6), 'the yoke of inauspicious stars' (Act 5 Scene 3, line 111). You could invent characters' horoscopes (星座) – and even call upon an astrologer (占星家) to give evidence!

2 Was it chance?

Was it just bad luck? Fortune is fickle (变幻无常), so maybe no one is responsible – it was simply a series of accidents.

◆ Collect examples of chance and accident ('misadventured piteous overthrows'), for example, the accidental meeting of the Servant, carrying Capulet's invitation list, with Benvolio and Romeo, or the non-delivery of Friar Lawrence's letter. Was Mercutio's death just an unhappy chance occurrence?

3 Was it adolescent passion?

Some critics have laid the blame on the folly (愚蠢) of Romeo and Juliet in their youthful haste and passion. But how far do you think it was the lovers' own fault? Is adolescent love at first sight a cause of the tragedy?

◆ Collect examples of haste and passion in the play to use as evidence.

4 Was it the feud?

Were the deaths caused by the enmity of the Montagues and Capulets? The two families struggle for power in Verona. Their 'ancient grudge' breaks 'to new mutiny' at the start of the play. A rigid code of honour makes the young men spring into violent, bloody action. Tybalt feels that the 'honour of my kin' has been insulted by Romeo's presence at Capulet's feast. Romeo is provoked into 'fire-eyed fury' by the death of Mercutio. He embraces the revenge code that governs relationships between the two rival factions of Verona.

◆ Collect other examples that suggest the lovers' deaths are caused by the quarrel that fractures the city.

5 Was it fathers?

Verona is a patriarchal city. Fathers have virtually absolute control over their daughters. They may give them in marriage to anyone they choose, and feel deeply insulted if their daughters dare disagree with that choice. Juliet does so, and incurs the extreme wrath of Capulet:

> go with Paris to Saint Peter's Church,
> Or I will drag thee on a hurdle thither.
>
> Act 3 Scene 5, lines 154–5

Together with patriarchy comes all the machismo (大男子主义行为) of the young men. They relish crude sexual joking, see love as brutal conquest and have no understanding of gentler, balanced relations between the sexes.

◆ Collect other examples that help you enquire into whether Verona's male-dominated society is responsible for the lovers' deaths.

Free investigation

As an alternative to the 'market stall' activity with its prescribed areas of focus, why not conduct your own free-running enquiry into the causes of the untimely and ultimately unnecessary deaths of the two lovers? You can investigate in many ways: through mock trials (模拟审判) or select committees, or by using the techniques of investigative journalism or television.

◆ Call witnesses (including those who do not speak in the play, such as 'the lively Helena' or Petruchio). Require characters to defend themselves against the charge of being guilty of causing the deaths. Don't simply try to pin blame on particular individuals. Seek other reasons for the tragic outcome of the play.

What other causes?

Although the activities above invite you to speculate imaginatively and 'invent' additional evidence to enhance your enquiries, there is also a benefit in mounting a pure 'evidence-based' analysis of the reasons behind the tragic deaths of the two young lovers. In addition to the 'causes' signalled above (points 1–5), you might also consider the following:

- Is the tragedy caused by love itself? Their love makes Romeo and Juliet feel that meeting in death is the only worthwhile ending. 'Well, Juliet, I will lie with thee tonight' (Act 5 Scene 1, line 34) is Romeo's expression of that love in death.

- Should you question the Friar's motives? He marries the lovers in secret, then devises a dangerous plan that will ensure his own part in the affair is concealed. Juliet fears that he might have given her a real poison, 'Lest in this marriage he should be dishonoured' (Act 4 Scene 3, line 26).

- Or might the cause lie in the 'rude will' of human nature? The Friar sees such self-centredness resulting in evil if it gains the upper hand over 'grace' (Act 2 Scene 3, lines 27–30).

◆ Collect your ideas in a mind map or other graphic form of display. Present them on a large sheet of paper for others to look at and interrogate (审问).

◆ Based on all your lines of enquiry and investigation, write an extended essay exploring what you think are the reasons for the lovers' deaths. Remember to use evidence and quotations from the text to support your critical judgement.

Romeo and Juliet
柔密欧与茱丽叶

The language of *Romeo and Juliet*
《柔密欧与茱丽叶》的语言

Imagery

The language of *Romeo and Juliet* is full of imagery (sometimes called 'figures' or 'figurative language'). Imagery is created by vivid words and phrases that conjure up emotionally charged mental pictures or associations in the imagination. For example, when Juliet learns that Romeo has killed Tybalt, she struggles to express her contradictory feelings. How could a beautiful person like Romeo, whom she loves so much, commit so awful a deed? How could such an attractive appearance mask such an evil action? Her outburst contains at least a dozen images, beginning with:

> *O serpent heart, hid with a flow'ring face!*
> *Did ever dragon keep so fair a cave?*

◆ Look back at Juliet's speech (Act 3 Scene 2, lines 73–85). Identify all the images she uses and, taking each in turn, comment on how it works and how it suggests the dreadful confusion Juliet is experiencing at that moment.

Some images recur throughout *Romeo and Juliet*, highlighting the themes of the play. One example is that of light and dark:

> *O she doth teach the torches to burn bright!*
> *It seems she hangs upon the cheek of night*
> *As a rich jewel in an Ethiop's ear*
>
> Act 1 Scene 5, lines 43–5

> *The brightness of her cheek would shame those stars,*
> *As daylight doth a lamp*
>
> Act 2 Scene 2, lines 19–20

> *her beauty makes*
> *This vault a feasting presence full of light*
>
> Act 5 Scene 3, lines 85–6

◆ Write several paragraphs that explore how the images quoted above use the ideas of light and darkness. Add another paragraph explaining why you think Shakespeare gives these 'light' images to Romeo at these points in the play.

Death is never far away in the conflict-torn world of Verona. The old people brood over (郁闷地沉思) it: 'death's the end of all', 'we were born to die'. Young lives are abruptly cut short. Images of death spread through the language: 'death-marked', 'untimely death', 'death-bed', 'canker death', 'Cold death', 'death-darting eye', 'cruel Death', 'detestable Death', 'present death'.

Shakespeare's imagery uses simile, metaphor and personification. All are comparisons that substitute one thing (the image) for another (the thing described).

A **simile** compares one thing to another using 'like' or 'as' – for example: 'shrieks like mandrakes torn out of the earth'; 'And in their triumph die like fire and powder'; 'My bounty is as boundless as the sea, / My love as deep'.

A **metaphor** is also a comparison, suggesting that two things that are unalike are actually the same. When Romeo says, 'O speak again, bright angel', he implies that Juliet is an angel, some glorious thing to be praised. To put it another way, a metaphor borrows one word or phrase to express another. For example, Benvolio uses all the following as metaphors for swords and sword-fighting: 'piercing steel', 'deadly point to point', 'Cold death', 'fatal points'. The Chorus in the Prologue describes the lovers as 'star-crossed' and later says that Juliet must 'steal love's sweet bait from fearful hooks'.

Personification turns all kinds of things into people, giving them human feelings or attributes. Probably the most powerful personification in the play is the image of Death as Juliet's husband-bridegroom. It recurs in different forms:

> *And death, not Romeo, take my maidenhead!*

> *Death is my son-in-law, Death is my heir,*
> *My daughter he hath wedded.*

> *Shall I believe*
> *That unsubstantial Death is amorous,*
> *And that the lean abhorrèd monster keeps*
> *Thee here in dark to be his paramour?*

The language of Romeo and Juliet

- Find the source of these examples. Then collect some others of your own choosing, and test your classmates to see if they can discover their location and context in the play.

- Look back through the 'Language' boxes, which draw attention to the overpowering presence of Death in the play (pp. 84, 134, 146 and 162). Choose some of the most striking examples of the personification of death, then present them visually as a collage (拼贴画) of quotations. Add your own analysis, exploring the connotations and impact of each example.

- Check your understanding of metaphors, similes and personification: which is which in the examples below? Identify each one and explain how it works.

    Scaring the ladies like a crow-keeper

    When well-apparelled April on the heel
    Of limping winter treads

    bloody Tybalt, yet but green in earth

    Love goes toward love as schoolboys from their books

Antithesis and oxymoron

Antithesis is the opposition of words or phrases against each other, as in 'More light and light, more dark and dark our woes!' (Act 3 Scene 5, line 36). This setting of word against word (e.g. 'light' versus 'dark') is one of Shakespeare's favourite language devices.

In *Romeo and Juliet*, conflict occurs in many forms: Montague versus Capulet, love versus hate, the marriage bed versus the grave, and all the other oppositions listed on pages 209–11. Antithesis intensifies that sense of conflict. For example, Friar Lawrence's first speech (Act 2 Scene 3, lines 1–30) contains at least fifteen antitheses as he gathers plants and thinks about the potential for good and evil in every living thing ('baleful weeds' versus 'precious-juicèd flowers', 'tomb' against 'womb', 'Virtue' against 'vice', and so on).

In another speech full of sharply contrasting antitheses, Capulet grieves for Juliet (Act 4 Scene 5, lines 84–90). He contrasts the happy preparations for the intended wedding with the mourning rites that now must mark her death. The first two lines set 'festival' against 'funeral':

All things that we ordainèd festival,
Turn from their office to black funeral

A special kind of antithesis is **oxymoron**. Here, two incongruous (不一致，不相称) or contradictory words are placed next to each other, as in 'cold fire' or 'bright smoke'. Oxymoron comes from two Greek words: *oxys* meaning 'sharp' and *moros* meaning 'dull'.

On his first appearance in the play, seeing the signs of the brawl, Romeo speaks a dozen oxymorons as he reflects on love and hate (Act 1 Scene 1, lines 167–72). His musings begin with two oxymorons, quickly setting 'brawling' against 'love', and 'loving' against 'hate':

Why then, O brawling love, O loving hate

At the end of the 'balcony' scene, Juliet uses a memorable oxymoron to describe her feelings: 'Parting is such sweet sorrow' ('sweet' versus 'sorrow').

- Work through the play, collecting as many examples of antitheses and oxymorons as you can. Write an extended essay showing how these two language devices help create the sense of conflict in *Romeo and Juliet*.

215

ROMEO AND JULIET
柔密欧与茱丽叶

Sonnets

At about the same time as Shakespeare wrote *Romeo and Juliet*, he was probably writing his **sonnets**. There are several sonnets in the play:

- the Chorus at the start and end of Act 1
- Lady Capulet's praise of Paris (Act 1 Scene 3, lines 82–95), which uses very showy and extravagant imagery (often called 'conceits') in comparing Paris to a book
- Romeo and Juliet's first meeting (Act 1 Scene 5, lines 92–105), in which the two lovers share the lines of a sonnet
- their next four lines, which are the start of another sonnet.

A Shakespearean sonnet is a fourteen-line poem. Each line usually contains ten syllables. The sonnet has three quatrains (四行连句) (each of four lines) and a couplet (对句):

- the first four lines (rhyming ABAB)
- the next four lines (rhyming CDCD)
- the next four lines (rhyming EFEF)
- a couplet (two lines) to finish (rhyming GG).

◆ Turn to the Prologue. Identify the rhymes ('dignity'/'mutiny', 'scene'/'unclean', and so on) and match them with the rhyme scheme above.

The sonnet tradition

The language of *Romeo and Juliet* shows the strong influence of the Italian poet Petrarch (1304–74). He became very popular with English poets in the time of Queen Elizabeth I. They drew on Petrarch's themes and style to write about **courtly love** (宫廷爱情).

Romeo's love for Rosaline echoes the major theme of Petrarch's poetry: a young man's unrequited love (love that was not returned) for an unattainable and dismissive woman. Romeo was infatuated with Rosaline, but she rejected all his advances.

In Act 1 Scene 1, lines 199–207 and lines 219–29, you can see other influences of the sonnet tradition: neat rhyming; elaborate conceits (for example, metaphors of war); and the wordplay of wit, puns and repetition.

◆ Conduct your own research into sonnets, the sonnet tradition and the nature of courtly love. Use your college library or the Internet to find out more about Petrarch and the tradition he inspired. The Cambridge School Shakespeare edition of *The Sonnets* will give you more help about Shakespeare's sonnet writing, but you could also look at how other poets, especially modern ones, have approached and adapted the form to write about love.

◆ After you have investigated the tradition of sonnet writing, have a go at writing your own version of a Shakespearean sonnet! (You might first like to read through the next section on verse and prose to help you with the rhythm.)

Verse and prose

Although quite a few lines in *Romeo and Juliet* end in rhymes, most of the play is actually written in **blank verse** (无韵诗; 素体诗): unrhymed verse with a 'five-beat' rhythm (iambic pentameter). Each line has five iambs (feet [前音节轻、后音节重的音步]), with one stressed (/) and one unstressed (×) syllable:

> × / × / × / × / × /
> *But soft, what light through yonder window breaks?*

The 'five-beat' rhythm (五拍节奏) (or metre [韵律]) is often obvious, but at other times, notably in the later stages of the 'balcony' scene, it is less prominent.

Prose was traditionally used by comic and low-status characters. High-status characters spoke verse. However, the Nurse (low-status) speaks a good deal of verse when she is with high-status Lady Capulet and Juliet. Also, Romeo, Mercutio and Benvolio (all high-status) use prose in Act 2 Scene 4 (probably because their talk is 'comic'). And although the conventional rule is that tragic death scenes should be in verse, Mercutio, at the point of death, speaks in prose.

The language of Romeo and Juliet

- Look again at the line quoted on page 216. Read the line in unison with a partner, pronouncing each syllable very clearly, almost as if it were a separate word. As you read, beat out the five-stress rhythm (e.g. clap hands, tap the desk).

- Now turn to the opening lines of Act 2 Scene 2. Repeat what you have just done. Can you find the rhythm? (Note that 'Juliet' would have two beats in line 3!) When you have found it, try the exercise again with verse spoken by other characters.

- Read through the rest of Act 2 Scene 2 and notice how Shakespeare gradually moves away from the rigid enforcement of the iambic pentameter rhythm. Why do you think he does this?

- Choose a verse speech and speak it to emphasise the metre (five beats). Then speak it as you feel it should be delivered on stage.

- Some scenes (such as Act 2 Scene 3 in particular) contain a good deal of rhyming. With a partner, read quickly through the scene again. First, try accentuating all the rhymes; then, on a second reading, try to make them less pronounced and obvious. Afterwards, talk together about the different effects created, and which version you think would be more powerful in a stage performance of the play.

Repetition

Repeating words or phrases was a favourite device of Shakespeare's. **Repetition** can heighten tension and add depth and dramatic impact. Apart from familiar grammatical words (such as 'and', 'the', and so on) the two most frequently repeated words are 'love' (which appears over 130 times) and 'death' (around 70 uses). Their repetition is a clear indication of two of the play's major thematic concerns.

In addition, Shakespeare packs the play (especially Acts 3 and 4) with words connected with time. Why? To intensify the gathering pace of the drama and the sweeping tide of events that overwhelms the two young lovers.

Repetition can also strengthen the presentation of character. For example, when Juliet opposes her mother in Act 3 Scene 5, lines 114–17:

> LADY CAPULET *The County Paris, at Saint Peter's Church,*
> *Shall happily make thee there a joyful bride.*
> JULIET *Now by Saint Peter's Church and Peter too,*
> *He shall not make me there a joyful bride.*

- Collect two or three extracts from the play that contain examples of language repetition (if you're stuck, it's always a good idea to look at the language of the young men, especially Mercutio and Romeo together). Think carefully about the mood Shakespeare is trying to create, then have a go at dramatising them to bring out the dramatic impact of the repetitions.

Romeo and Juliet
柔密欧与茱丽叶

Puns

A **pun** is a play on words that sound similar, but have different meanings. Shakespeare was fascinated by puns – especially in *Romeo and Juliet*. Mercutio loves to use puns, and they are often very rude and sexual. You'll find a cluster of such puns commented upon in the 'Language' boxes on pages 50, 74, 76. Remind yourself of the nature of Mercutio's coarse wordplay on those pages and compare it with the Nurse's (a box on her punning language appears on p. 114).

Even at the point of death, Mercutio can't resist punning: 'Ask for me tomorrow, and you shall find me a grave man' (Act 3 Scene 1, lines 89–90).

◆ Working in a group of five, take one of the following bullet points each and investigate further!

- Why do you think Shakespeare includes so many rather offensive, sexually charged puns in the play?
- Does every character in the play use puns?
- Discover the first pun each character uses. For example, Gregory and Sampson pun on 'colliers'/'choler'/'collar' at the very start of Act 1 Scene 1.
- What is the dramatic impact of the characters using so many puns?
- Since puns are often viewed as clever, witty and humorous examples of wordplay, why do you think Shakespeare includes so many in *Romeo and Juliet*, even at moments of great seriousness and pain?

◆ Rejoin your group and share your findings with each other.

Soliloquy

As in all Shakespeare's tragic plays, he uses the dramatic device of the **soliloquy** powerfully in *Romeo and Juliet*, particularly as the lovers' increasing isolation and vulnerability are emphasised in the second half of the play. In order to appreciate the impact of some of the language, try one of the following activities based on a soliloquy of your choice.

Bare bones soliloquy

◆ In a small group, take one line at a time and agree what you consider to be the key word. Write down that key word – just one per line. This will give you a 'bare bones' script of a handful of words.

◆ Keeping the words in their original order, present this new script in any ways that seem appropriate. Think about using choral speech, echoes, repetitions, sound effects or movement. Share your performance with the rest of the class for comment.

Two-handed soliloquy

◆ Read through your chosen soliloquy, with each person handing over the reading at each full stop, colon, semi-colon or question mark.

◆ Now consider ways of performing this speech as if it's a conversation (which it is, in a way, as it's like a piece of internal dialogue or a character debating with himself or herself). Experiment with other ways of dividing up the speech and ways of speaking to create different effects.

◆ Then think about how you might layer in movement, where you might stand (back-to-back, facing each other, one kneeling the other standing, and so on). Share your final response with others in the class.

Creating atmosphere

Shakespeare often creates atmosphere through language. Remember, for example, that his plays were originally staged in broad daylight, so words had to establish setting and atmosphere (see pp. 220–1). A good example of his technique is Act 5 Scene 3, where the language has to suggest night in a graveyard, then inside the funeral vault.

◆ Focus on this scene, or choose your own favourite scene. In a small group, talk together about its atmosphere (aggressive, fearful, joking, tragic and so on). Compile a 'language list' of phrases or lines from your chosen scene that create the atmosphere. Use your list to make up a short play with your own plot and characters. Create as powerful an atmosphere as you can by using Shakespeare's words.

The language of Romeo and Juliet

Creating character

Most of Shakespeare's characters have a distinctive way of speaking, but their style can change from situation to situation. For example, Friar Lawrence's highly stylised lines in Act 2 Scene 3 in conversation with Romeo are all in rhyming couplets, whereas in the closing scene he speaks in plain, uncomplicated language when reporting on the events in the tomb.

- Why do you think Shakespeare specifically adapts the Friar's language in this way in these two scenes?

- Choose a character, follow them through the play and compile a list of their 'typical' language in different situations. Afterwards, write a short commentary exploring what their different language styles tell you about them as people and how they interact with other characters.

The 'love' language of Juliet and Romeo

Look back to the 'Language' boxes on pages 56 and 58. They both draw attention to Juliet's ways of speaking about love as a character in love (for example, Juliet describes her developing relationship with Romeo as: 'Too like the lightning, which doth cease to be / Ere one can say "It lightens".')

- Use this and other references from those pages as a starting point for an exploration of how the two main characters describe and define their experiences of love.

- Create two posters (one for each character), in which you assemble all your references and evaluations. How similar do you find their ways of speaking about love, the kind of words, images and expressions they use? Are there any distinct differences?

Romeo and Juliet in performance
《柔密欧与茱丽叶》的演出

Performance on Shakespeare's stage

Many of Shakespeare's plays were performed at the Globe Theatre in London, one of many specially built outdoor playhouses that appeared at the end of the sixteenth century.

Performances took place mostly during the summer months and in broad daylight, so there were no special lighting effects. Shakespeare's language had to establish the time, setting and atmosphere of each scene. This is particularly noticeable in *Romeo and Juliet*, where several key episodes either take place in darkness or refer strikingly to the thematic interplay of light and darkness (see p. 209). In addition, Shakespeare often used the words of the script to suggest how the actors should move and behave. For example, Friar Lawrence's opening line to Romeo at the start of Act 3 Scene 3 is 'Romeo, come forth, come forth, thou fearful man'.

There were no elaborate sets on the bare stage of the Globe Theatre, but the actors wore attractive and expensive costumes, usually the fashionable dress of the times.

The audience was positioned on three sides of the stage. The 'groundlings' (站票观众) paid a minimal entrance fee and stood in the pit ([圆形剧场中的] 无座观众池) around the stage. Those who paid more were seated in three tiers around the outside of the theatre. It is believed that there would have been a lot of background noise during performances – especially from the groundlings, who were often restless and probably enjoyed some kind of lively interaction with the performance itself. In order to ensure that the audience fully engaged with key ideas and issues, Shakespeare uses a good deal of repetition in his language. You will notice this is a feature of the writing in every scene!

In Shakespeare's day, Juliet, the Nurse and other female parts were played by boys because women were not allowed to act on stage. On stage, only a few props were used (swords, chairs, and so on). As you look through *Romeo and Juliet*, you will notice that some basic props become very important to the action of the play. These include:

- swords and daggers
- masks and torches
- a rope to help Romeo to climb up to Juliet's window
- Juliet's ring
- the sleeping potion
- the Friar's letter to Romeo
- the Apothecary's poison.

◀ The interior of the Globe Theatre in Shakespeare's day.

Romeo and Juliet in performance

◆ Take one or more of the items listed. Produce two sets of designs for the props you have selected, one for a period Elizabethan production and one for a very modern version.

The play features several important settings or locations:

- Verona
- a room for the Capulet party
- Juliet's balcony/window of her bedroom
- Friar Lawrence's cell
- Mantua
- the funeral vault/tomb.

◆ Study the representation of the Globe Theatre on the previous page. Working in a small group, research Verona in Italy at the time the play was set. Together, produce a series of designs that show how these locations could be represented in Shakespeare's theatre.

◆ A professional theatre designer would produce a three-dimensional model of the set, with its key features reproduced in miniature. Have a go at creating such a model for yourselves, perhaps by using a shoe box as the basic structure.

◆ Compare your set designs with those of other students. How different do you think the audience's response will be to the different sets?

The Globe has now been rebuilt on London's Bankside, close to the site on which it first stood. Many of the productions there are staged as Shakespeare's Elizabethan audiences probably saw them. In 2004 and in 2009, *Romeo and Juliet* was performed in Elizabethan costume.

▲ Romeo kneeling over the 'dead' Juliet in a performance at Shakespeare's Globe in 2004.

▼ A 2009 Globe performance of Mercutio fighting with Tybalt.

ROMEO AND JULIET
柔密欧与茱丽叶

Performance after Shakespeare

It seems that *Romeo and Juliet* has always been a popular play, but, like virtually all of Shakespeare's plays, it has been rewritten and adapted over the centuries. This was mainly done to reflect the tastes and social circumstances of the times, or to boost the dramatic impact and the spectacle of the play in performance.

In the eighteenth century, David Garrick's rewritten version of *Romeo and Juliet* was very popular. He cut much of the dialogue, but added a funeral procession (see p. 169) and a final conversation between Romeo and Juliet in the tomb. The play was acted in the fashionable costumes of the day, as you can see in the picture (right). In the nineteenth century, productions of *Romeo and Juliet* became obsessed with historical accuracy. Period costumes and settings were designed with meticulous attention to detail.

- ◆ Pick out features in the picture below that show attempts to recreate twelfth-century Verona on stage.

- ▼ Henry Irving's 1882 production at the London Lyceum. Identify lines in Act 5 Scene 3 which match this picture.

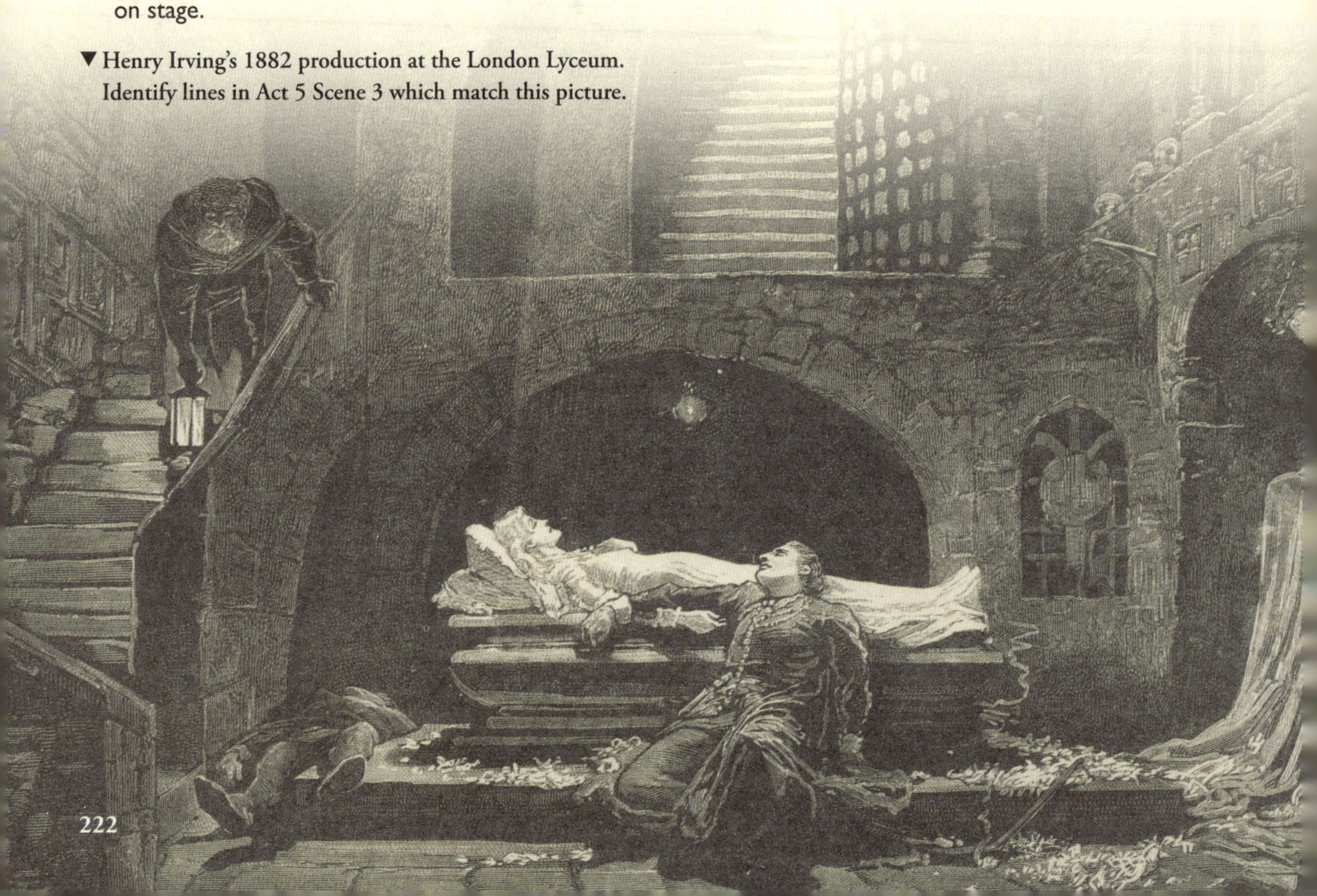

▲ Spranger Barry as Romeo and Miss Nossiter as Juliet, Covent Garden, London, 1753.

ROMEO AND JULIET IN PERFORMANCE

Modern productions – distinctive interpretations

Most directors, set designers and production teams work in harmony to create a particular 'vision' for their staging of the play. However, many comment that one of the challenges of producing *Romeo and Juliet* is its very popularity – it's a story well known to audiences and often enacted on stage. So how does each production make it fresh and interesting?

In the 'Stagecraft' boxes in the main part of this edition, you have been encouraged to consider, and try out, ideas for lifting the script off the page.

Six 'script boxes' follow, which focus on key elements of the play:

1. Dramatic openings
2. Dramatic endings
3. Location and setting
4. The Capulet ball (Act 1 Scene 5)
5. The 'balcony' scene (Act 2 Scene 2)
6. Interesting stagecraft

Inside each of the boxes you'll find information about how particular productions have approached specific aspects of the play and attempted to make them distinctive or unusual.

◆ In pairs, select one of the numbered boxes and work through the ideas described in it, discussing each one in turn. Which do you find the most interesting and why? In your discussion, consider what the director might have had in mind by approaching the play in this way.

◆ Talk together about how any of these ideas for staging have helped further your understanding of *Romeo and Juliet*. Add your evaluative comments to the Director's Journal that you began on page 22.

1 Dramatic openings

a One movie opening made strong use of contemporary CNN-style news reporting, helicopter surveillance (监视), and security tapes.

b In one production, the fight scene was staged with the graceful movements of a ballet. Swords were waved by men as if they were underwater.

c In a ferocious (凶残) opening, the face of a brawler (争吵者) in this production was smashed against concrete wall. Romeo delivered the Prologue.

d In a production set in a Sicilian village, the fight was conducted with agricultural scythes.

e One opening skipped the first forty lines and went straight into a violent and brutal fight. Benvolio was tied to a stake by Tybalt – jets of steam and sheets of fire erupted around them. The Prologue was a voiceover.

2 Dramatic endings

a The lovers' double suicide cut to a press conference. The Prince delivered the Prologue to the flashbulbs of reporters' cameras.

b The ghosts of Romeo and Juliet emerged from the tomb full of mourners, to view their own memorial.

c The back wall split open, revealing the crypt (教堂地下室), tomb and iron railings that kept Romeo out of the funeral vault.

d The play moved into the modern world – police radios and sirens (警笛) could be heard. The impassive (无动于衷) observer Balthasar spoke the ending. The final incidents were jotted down by a plainclothes (便衣) police officer.

Romeo and Juliet
柔密欧与茱丽叶

3 Location and setting

a One production was set in nineteenth-century Italy, with clothes lines strung across narrow streets.

b In another, brutal 'Clockwork Orange' (《发条橙》, 一部英国犯罪片) style production, gangs inhabited a concrete subway.

c Soft music and subtle lighting created a dream-like, surreal atmosphere.

d A complicated set of doors, arches and windows opened up to present vistas of other rooms. The atmosphere suggested an Italian Renaissance painting. The lighting was like candlelight.

e Costumes were black leather, creating a gritty, urban feel. The Prince was a Mafia Don (黑手党). Violent gangs, using vicious flick-knives, ruled the streets.

f The set suggested 1920s Shanghai when the opium trade flourished. The Montagues were tea-sipping Europeans, the Capulets Oriental (costumed with silks and fans).

g This production portrayed the maddening midday heat of a volatile (极不稳定) state. Gang warfare was rife. The Capulets were white, the Montagues black.

h Located in a Sicilian village, the terracotta-tiled piazza became a focal point for the action.

i The culture of 1940/50s Italy dominated. There was no visual distinction between the Montagues and Capulets as both were dressed in formal black.

4 The Capulet ball (Act 1 Scene 5)

a Capulet's ball was staged as a family get-together. Mercutio appeared in drag (男扮女装) costume.

b The guests were 'frozen' in an amber glow, as the two lovers were picked out in white spotlight.

c Paris was more in love with Lady Capulet than her daughter Juliet.

d Romeo spotted Juliet through the glass walls of a fish tank.

e The Charleston dance was followed by the Chinese Lion Dance, lit in deep red.

5 The 'balcony' scene (Act 2 Scene 2)

a The balcony was transposed to a swimming pool.

b On a minimalist (极简抽象派) bare stage with very few props Juliet's white bed acts as balcony (and, later, her funeral bier).

c The scene was played on the back of a large symbolic statue of a black horse.

d The position of the lovers was reversed – Juliet was in a courtyard standing below Romeo.

6 Interesting stagecraft

a Additional performers were used as a 'Chorus' to echo the lovers' lines, which reverberated (回响) around the stage. These voices spoke Romeo and Juliet's thoughts after their wedding night.

b The costumes were cream and beige, with light dappled the stage through a weeping willow tree.

c Lady Capulet was clearly having an affair with Tybalt.

d The ghosts of Mercutio and Tybalt were present on stage at the end of play.

e A rectangular stone plinth (柱基) doubled as Juliet's bed and her tomb.

f The production showed a 'play within a play'. Set in a Sicilian town, the residents stepped onto the stage to play a part.

g Romeo and Juliet were in modern dress; the other characters were in Renaissance costume. The interval was taken deep into Act 3 (rather than the customary end of Act 2).

Transforming genre

All kinds of transformations of Shakespeare's play have been made. For example, there is a ballet by the Russian composer Sergei Prokofiev, an opera by Gounod, and an American stage musical and movie, *West Side Story*, with music by Leonard Bernstein.

▲ Russia's Bolshoi Ballet performs Prokofiev's version of *Romeo and Juliet*.

◀ Romeo lies dying as Juliet prepares to stab herself in a performance of Gounod's opera version.

▼ The musical *West Side Story* (《西区故事》) updated the play and set it in 1950s New York City.

Romeo and Juliet
柔密欧与茱丽叶

Romeo and Juliet on film

The Italian film director Franco Zeffirelli chose images of youth and beauty in Renaissance paintings as an inspiration for his 1968 movie. He also made great use of the outdoor world: the sun-baked Italian setting was hot and intense. Searing (灼热) sunlight on dusty streets was set against strong torchlight for the interior scenes, which were filmed inside authentic stone buildings. The Montagues dressed in blue, the Capulets in red and orange.

The director Baz Luhrmann (see the pictures on pp. 47, 184 and below) also sharply distinguished the feuding families by their clothes. The Montagues wore casual beachwear, including colourful Hawaiian shirts. The Capulets wore expensive designer clothes, ornamental jewellery and bullet-proof vests. In addition, Luhrmann transported the play to 'Verona Beach' (a fictional North American setting) and gave it a contemporary soundtrack. The action of the play is high-octane (表现力强，令人兴奋), featuring drug trips, car chases and gunfights.

When a stage play is transferred to the medium of film, it offers the director considerable artistic freedom. In addition to a variety of camera angles (panning shots, close-ups, etc.) special effects and the addition of a soundtrack, the 'action' can be presented in a more

naturalistic way. Editing techniques and multiple 'takes' can also ensure that what you see is a 'perfect' interpretation of the director's intentions.

- Make a list of some of the qualities and effects of a good stage production that could be lost in a film version.

- Choose one scene, or part of a scene, that you think lends itself to being filmed. Write a design brief, showing clearly how this would work.

Romeo and Juliet in performance

Stage your own production of *Romeo and Juliet*

Talk together about the period and place in which you will set your play. Will it be medieval Italy? A present-day place where conflict exists between two social groups? A 'timeless' setting? When you have made your decision, choose one or more of the following activities. Your finished assignment can be a file of drawings, notes and suggestions, or an active presentation.

◆ Design the set – how can it be used for particular scenes?

◆ Design the costumes – look at past examples, but invent your own.

◆ Design the props – furnishings and hand props (e.g. swords).

◆ Design a lighting and sound programme – for one or two scenes.

◆ Design the publicity poster – make people want to see your play!

◆ Design a 'flyer' – a small handbill to advertise the production.

◆ Design the programme – layout? Content? Number of pages?

◆ Write character notes for actors' guidance.

◆ Work out a five-minute presentation to show to potential sponsors.

Visit a production of *Romeo and Juliet*

Shakespeare wrote *Romeo and Juliet* to be acted, watched and enjoyed – not to be studied for examinations! So visit a live performance. Prepare for a school or college visit using the following:

◆ Everyone chooses a character (or an incident or scene) to watch especially closely. Write down your expectations before you go. Report back to the class on how your expectations for 'your' character or scene were fulfilled or challenged.

◆ Choose your favourite line in the play. Listen carefully to how it is spoken. Does it add to your understanding?

◆ Your teacher will probably be able to provide one or two published reviews of the production. Talk together about whether you should read the reviews before or after you see the play for yourself. After the visit, discuss how far you agree or disagree with the reviews.

◆ Write your own review. Record your own perceptions of what you actually saw and heard – and your feelings about the production.

◆ Two points to remember: preparation is always valuable, but too much can dull the enjoyment of a theatre visit; every production is different. There's no such thing as a single 'right' way to 'do' Shakespeare – but you might think that there are 'wrong' ways!

Romeo and Juliet
柔密欧与茱丽叶

Practitioners' perspectives

Nancy Meckler, director of the RSC production of *Romeo and Juliet* in 2006, speaks in 'Director's Talk' about some of her ideas for the production:

The thing I found really interesting was that if everybody already knows the story is there any way the people on stage can share with the audience the fact that we all already know the story? Very early on, when I first was asked to do it, I had this idea that it would be performed by a community of people living in Italy who already know the play, and who perform it once a year. So it means that the people who are performing it already know the story, and the audience that's watching already knows the story. That would free me from the idea that we all have to pretend that you don't know what's going to happen.

We talked about a village that had warring families in it – somewhere in Italy, and in the end we settled on Sicily. The idea is that these two warring families – or clans – have come to perform *Romeo and Juliet* on the edge of town in a wasteland space.

So we thought about a rather desolate wasteland where these people gather once a year to put on a play. That's why they've built a stage and at the back [indicates the back wall] that's meant to make us think of an outdoor movie screen, because in Italy you often get outdoor cinema. When we first began it really did look like an outdoor film screen and it was going to be tattered and torn. Then as time went on and Katrina Lindsay worked on the design, she began to think that she didn't want the design to be so real, and that maybe the screen should be almost transparent, so that you could light through it and sometimes you could see images behind it. So the set started off by being a realistic place and then it became less real – if that was a cinema screen you wouldn't be able to light through it in that way. The main thing was that we wanted somehow to be on the edge of nowhere, to be in a neutral space. If these clans were killing each other and they were going to put on a play, it had to be in a very neutral space.

I had the idea very early on that the fights in *Romeo and Juliet* shouldn't be realistic, because I feel that sometimes with realistic stage fights it takes us out of it a little bit, because we think, 'Oh look, they're doing a stage fight, they must have rubber tips on the ends of the swords'. Sometimes the actors have to be really careful because it has to be so carefully choreographed (设计舞台动作), so you don't always get the sense of the violence and the aggression. So I wondered if there would be a way of staging the fights where we could look at the aggression and not at the art of stage-fighting.

What I love about *Romeo and Juliet* is that it's quite an early play of Shakespeare's and he doesn't really have a sub-plot going but he just keeps throwing in these little servant scenes in the middle. In the middle of the tragedy you get a silly servant scene, and I love that – the way he turns it round. There's one servant scene that we've left in that's often cut because people think it's too silly at too serious a moment. It's the musicians' scene and we've still got it in there. I love the idea of bringing out the whole idea of comedy and tragedy being together like that.

Of course as a play, it's so much about opposites: much of the imagery is about dark and light – how Juliet's eyes light up the night in a particular way, and when she's in the grave she lights up the grave. When Romeo sees her for the first time, he talks about her being a swan among crows, and she's like a bright light in a dark night.

There's so much imagery of dark and light, black and white, life and death. Friar Lawrence talks about the fact that the earth is a womb that brings forth life but it's also a tomb that buries life. There's so many things about opposites in the play that somehow making the comedy silly and the tragedy tragic, putting them right next to each other, feels like it's a real expression of the way he wrote it.

There's something primal about the idea that two young people with their lives ahead of them have to be sacrificed in order for a community to decide to make peace. Peace movements, even now, are so often started by people who say, 'We can't bear the fact that we keep losing our young people. It's our young people that end up dead in this war and we adults have got to find a way to stop killing our children.' Perhaps it's only when enough children die that the adults can find a way to make peace, because it is often the young and the innocent that get it, isn't it?

Romeo and Juliet in performance

Neil Bartlett, director of the RSC production in 2008, also speaks in 'Director's Talk':

One thing that's really important to Shakespeare is that it needed to take place in a Catholic country where the rules of religion are absolute, there is no space for, 'Oh I believe this and you believe that.' It's no accident in the play that you hear people swear 'by the Virgin Mary', 'by Our Lord', all the time. There's lots of priest action in Romeo and Juliet! *It's a very religious society.*

I wanted to anchor (基于，取材于) it very firmly in Italy. It's a very conservative society. This is not a world in which the Nurse can say to Juliet, 'Why don't you think about going to university?' Or, 'Here, read this book.' No one says to Romeo, 'Actually if you ever heard the word "macho" perhaps you want to think twice about the way you're behaving in your life.' It's very, very conservative (both with a small 'c' and with a capital 'C') culture. So I've set it slightly back in the past. It's somewhere … I don't know, in the 1940s.

But I stress the 'somewhere'. It's not set in Rome in 1949 and everyone's recovering from the war. The setting, as you can see [indicates stage] is very simple. That's your lot: there's a floor, there's a wall.

Also the clothing of the 1940s is very good for this play, in that the 1940s were a time when everything appeared to be very prim and proper (一本正经). Women wore tailored suits, sensible shoes and hats, and men wore suits. But actually it's sexy as hell! It's that classic Italian thing of saying, 'I'm a mature, responsible, respectable woman and these are my breasts. Are you staring at them? Please stare at them again.' That whole double-whammy (双重灾难) of women in a Catholic culture.

The women in this play are very sexy, I think. Lady Montague is a tiny part, though beautifully played in this production by Katy Krane, but the Nurse and Lady Capulet and Juliet are fantastic female parts, the three of them, and they're vibrantly sexual in their different ways. Very raunchy (淫秽, 色情) women.

◆ In the extracts on these pages, the two directors share their thoughts about some crucial issues that must be addressed in designing a production of Romeo and Juliet:

1. The audience already knows the story.
2. Where to set it (place and period).
3. How to stage the fights.
4. The balance of comedy and tragedy.
5. Highlighting the 'oppositions' in the play.
6. Why the lovers die.
7. The importance of religion.
8. How to present the women.

Read the extracts carefully, looking for the directors' views on the issues listed above, and make notes on what they say. Then prepare a short presentation for your class on what you think about their ideas – where you agree and where you disagree.

ROMEO AND JULIET
柔密欧与茱丽叶

Writing about Shakespeare 笔论莎士比亚

The play as text

Shakespeare's plays have always been studied as literary works – as words on a page that need clarification, appreciation and discussion. When you write about the plays, you will be asked to compose short pieces and also longer, more reflective pieces like controlled assessments, examination scripts and coursework – often in the form of essays on themes and/or imagery, character studies, analyses of the structure of the play and on stagecraft. Imagery, stagecraft and character are dealt with elsewhere in this edition. Here, we concentrate on themes and structure. You might find it helpful to look at the 'Write about it' boxes on the left-hand pages throughout the play.

Themes

It is often tempting to say that the theme of a play is a single idea, like 'death' in *Hamlet*, or 'the supernatural' in *Macbeth*, or 'love' in *Romeo and Juliet*. The problem with such a simple approach is that you will miss the complexity of the plays. In *Romeo and Juliet*, for example, the play is about the relationship between love, family loyalty and constraint; it is also about the relationship of youth to age and experience; and the relationship between Romeo and Juliet is also played out against a background of enmity between two families. Between each of these ideas or concepts there are tensions. The tensions are the main focus of attention for Shakespeare and the audience, and they also happen to be how drama operates – by the presentation and resolution of tension.

Look back at the 'Themes' boxes throughout the play to see if any of the activities there have given rise to information that you could use as a starting point for further writing about the themes of the specific play you are studying.

Structure

Most Shakespeare plays are in five acts, divided into scenes. These acts were not in the original scripts, but have been included in later editions to make the action more manageable, clearer and more like 'classical' structures. One way to get a sense of the structure of the whole play is to take a printed version of the play (not this one!) and cut it up into scenes and acts. Then display each scene and act, in sequence, on a wall, like this:

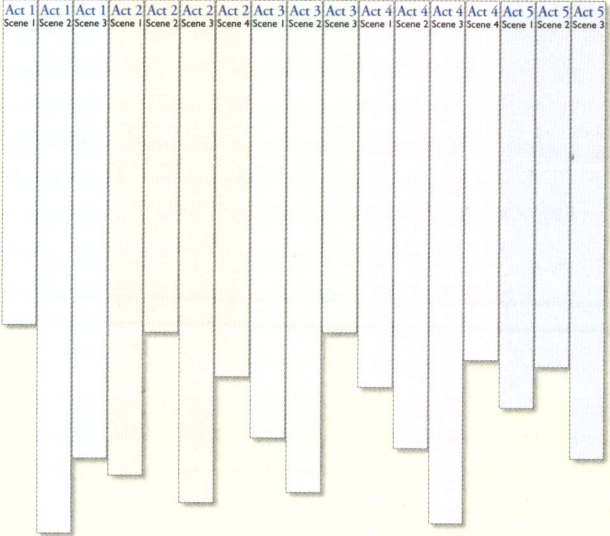

As you set out the whole play, you will be able to see the 'shape' of each act, the relative length of the scenes, and how the acts relate to each other (such as whether one of the acts is shorter, and why that might be). You can annotate the text with comments, observations and questions. You can use a highlighter pen to mark the recurrence of certain words, images or metaphors to see at a glance where and how frequently they appear. You can also follow a particular character's progress through the play.

Such an overview of the play gives you critical perspective: you will be able to see how the parts fit together, to stand back from the play and assess its shape, and to focus on particular parts within the context of the whole. Your writing will show more awareness of the overall context as a result.

The play as script

There are different, but related, categories when we think of the play as a script for performance. These include *stagecraft* (discussed elsewhere in this edition and throughout the left-hand pages), *lighting*, *focus* (who are we looking at? Where is the attention of the audience?), *music* and *sound*, *props* and *costumes*, *casting*, *make-up*, *pace* and *rhythm*, and other *spatial relationships* (e.g. how actors move across the stage in relation to each other). If you are writing about stagecraft or performance, use the notes you have made as a result of the 'Stagecraft' boxes throughout this edition of the play, as well as any material you can gather about the play in performance.

What are the key points of dispute?

Shakespeare is brilliant at capturing a number of key points of dispute in each of his plays. These are the dramatic moments where he concentrates the focus of the audience on difficult (sometimes universal) problems that the characters are facing or embodying.

First, identify these key points in the play you are studying. You can do this as a class by brainstorming what you think are the key points in small groups, then debating the long-list as a whole class, and then coming up with a short-list of what the class thinks are the most significant. (This is a good opportunity for speaking and listening work.) They are likely to be places in the play where the action or reflection is at its most intense, and which capture the complexity of themes, character, structure and performance.

Second, drill down at one of the points of contention and tension. In other words, investigate the complexity of the problem that Shakespeare is exploring. What is at stake? Why is it important? Is it a problem that can be resolved, or is it an insoluble one?

Key skills in writing about Shakespeare

Here are some suggestions to help you organise your notes and develop advanced writing skills when working on Shakespeare:

- Compose the title of your writing carefully to maximise your opportunities to be creative and critical about the play; or explore the key words in your title carefully. Decide which aspect of the play – or which combination of aspects – you are focusing on.
- Create a mind map of your ideas, making connections between them.
- If appropriate, arrange your ideas into a hierarchy that shows how some themes or features of the play are 'higher' than others and can incorporate other ideas.
- Then sequence your ideas so that you have a plan for writing an essay, review, story – whichever genre you are using. You might like to think about whether to put your strongest points first, in the middle, or later.
- Collect key quotations (it might help to compile this list with a partner), which you can use as evidence to support your argument.
- Compose your first draft, embedding quotations in your text as you go along.
- Revise your draft in the light of your own critical reflections and/or those of others.

The following pages focus on writing about *Romeo and Juliet* in particular.

Romeo and Juliet
柔密欧与茱丽叶

Writing about *Romeo and Juliet*
笔论《柔密欧与茱丽叶》

The purpose of this section is to help you to write about *Romeo and Juliet* in an informed, coherent and convincing fashion. Before you begin to commit to writing down your ideas, remember to keep two key considerations in mind:

1 *Romeo and Juliet* is a play, so you should always appreciate its form and genre. In the 'fight scene' (Act 3 Scene 1), for example, there is a huge amount of 'stagecraft' built in to the writing (entrances, exits, 'stage business', action and so on). It's all about what the audience sees, hears and experiences.

- Look at the script on page 95 of this edition. Try writing about how the language might be brought to life on stage. Speculate about different ways of playing this short episode.

2 *Romeo and Juliet* is not about 'real' people and 'real' situations, so don't treat it as such. When Shakespeare pays close attention to the timings in the play, it's as much about making a dramatic point (the two lovers are caught up in an unstoppable and fast-moving tide of events), as trying to make it all credible and naturalistic. The play is a dramatic construct and often characters, for example, are vehicles for ideas about themes and structure. Remember the Prince? Shakespeare presents him very sketchily as a figure (and he's been played on stage in a variety of ways) but he has a crucial role in the drama.

How many different kinds of writing might you tackle? You could write about:

- an extract (a key speech, such as Juliet's before her wedding night, or a longer passage of dialogue, such as the lovers' dialogue in the 'balcony' scene)
- a key scene (such as the Capulet ball in which Romeo and Juliet meet)
- a character (the Friar), or group of characters (the women in the play)
- a core theme (the conflict of love and hate)
- an element of the text re-creatively (that is, rewriting it in another genre, or from another perspective, or in the persona of one of the characters).

- Individually, consider each of these 'types' of writing in turn. See if you can come up with three additional focuses or frameworks for questions besides the ones that are suggested in brackets. Then pass your ideas to a partner for consideration. Together, settle on two questions for each category that you think would generate interesting written responses. Keep these in mind as you work through the next section.

Writing about an extract or a key scene: the whole of Act 4 Scene 3

1 Locate the extract in the play, and contextualise it. What has just happened? (The Friar's plan) What is about to come? (Juliet will deceive her mother and Nurse and drink the potion.)
2 Concentrate on exploring the specific mood or atmosphere of the extract. (Juliet's deception gives way to her dark fears and imaginings, explored in her soliloquy.)
3 How might the lines be spoken – tone, emphasis, pace, pauses, and so on? What are key words and images (of fear and death)?
4 Think about Shakespeare's stagecraft – how he assembles and groups characters (the three women at the start of the scene), the interplay between them, the use of entrances/exits and the blocking (舞台调度) on stage. The 'silent' character of the Nurse.
5 Link the details of the extract to key themes or issues rooted in the text as a whole (dramatic irony, Juliet's isolation, the pervasiveness of death).
6 Show how the extract links to the dramatic construction of the play (the escalation of the tragedy).

- Working in groups of six, take one numbered section each of the above essay framework. Plan your answer by researching your specific area of focus. Then divide up a large sheet of sugar paper into six sections. Take turns to fill in the notes you have compiled. Use this large sheet as a resource to help you produce an essay plan of no more than one side that you could include in a revision booklet to be used for examination preparation.

Writing about a character

Planning an essay on the character of Mercutio

Summarise what Mercutio does in each act: his interactions with other characters; his decisive actions.

Explore how Mercutio relates to other characters and note down the different ways he treats them. How do they speak to him and about him?

Focus on the type of language that Mercutio uses – the imagery he employs, the tone he strikes, his typical way of speaking. Identify quotations which will back up your points. Link Mercutio's role to key themes and aspects of the drama.

Finally, think about the possible reasons why Shakespeare killed him off in Act 3.

Writing creatively

Many assessments offer you the opportunity to write about *Romeo and Juliet* creatively, as well as critically. Act by act, throughout this edition, you have been encouraged to try a number of creative-writing activities. The great thing about such activities is that you can be as imaginative and original as you like within the framework of such responses: *Romeo and Juliet* is a complex, rich and intriguing text that offers lots of opportunities for creative approaches.

Summing up

Keep in mind the focus on *Romeo and Juliet* as a dramatic text. What features of the play as a theatrical performance enhance the impact of key issues? Remember that there is no single, right interpretation – both from you as a critic, but also from a director. How might an audience respond – in Shakespeare's time, and now? How do you respond? What are your own personal responses to the question and how can you justify them?

Possible questions

Below you'll find questions on character, theme, extracts and creative tasks. Have a go at one of each, or invent your own!

1 The Nurse is the most sympathetic character in *Romeo and Juliet*. Discuss.
2 *Romeo and Juliet* is a tragedy of fate. Discuss.
3 Discuss the presentation of male pride and honour in the play.
4 Explore the dramatic construction of Act 3 Scene 1.
5 Explore the contrasts between love and hate.
6 In role as one of the characters, write about a key incident in the play from your point of view.
7 'A mixture of inconsistencies and contradictions'. Consider the presentation of Friar Lawrence.
8 In what ways can you consider Act 3 to be a pivotal (核心的) act of the play?
9 Romeo simply does not match up to the concept of a tragic hero.
10 Write an additional speech for a character, or script a section of dialogue between a character who appears in the play and one who doesn't.

ROMEO AND JULIET
柔密欧与茱丽叶

William Shakespeare 莎翁年表
1564–1616

1564	Born Stratford-upon-Avon, eldest son of John and Mary Shakespeare.
1582	Marries Anne Hathaway of Shottery, near Stratford.
1583	Daughter Susanna born.
1585	Twins, son and daughter Hamnet and Judith, born.
1592	First mention of Shakespeare in London. Robert Greene, another playwright, described Shakespeare as 'an upstart crow beautified with our feathers'. Greene seems to have been jealous of Shakespeare. He mocked Shakespeare's name, calling him 'the only Shake-scene in a country' (presumably because Shakespeare was writing successful plays).
1595	Becomes a shareholder in The Lord Chamberlain's Men, an acting company that became extremely popular.
1596	Son, Hamnet, dies, aged eleven. Father, John, granted arms (acknowledged as a gentleman).
1597	Buys New Place, the grandest house in Stratford.
1598	Acts in Ben Jonson's *Every Man in His Humour*.
1599	Globe Theatre opens on Bankside. Performances in the open air.
1601	Father, John, dies.
1603	James I grants Shakespeare's company a royal patent: The Lord Chamberlain's Men become The King's Men and play about twelve performances each year at court.
1607	Daughter Susanna marries Dr John Hall.
1608	Mother, Mary, dies.
1609	The King's Men begin performing indoors at Blackfriars Theatre.
1610	Probably returns from London to live in Stratford.
1616	Daughter Judith marries Thomas Quiney. Dies. Buried in Holy Trinity Church, Stratford-upon-Avon.

The plays and poems

(no one knows exactly when he wrote each play)

1589–95	*The Two Gentlemen of Verona, The Taming of the Shrew, First, Second* and *Third Parts* of *King Henry VI, Titus Andronicus, King Richard III, The Comedy of Errors, Love's Labour's Lost, A Midsummer Night's Dream,* **Romeo and Juliet,** *King Richard II* (and the long poems *Venus and Adonis* and *The Rape of Lucrece*).
1596–99	*King John, The Merchant of Venice, First* and *Second Parts* of *King Henry IV, The Merry Wives of Windsor, Much Ado About Nothing, King Henry V, Julius Caesar* (and probably the Sonnets).
1600–05	*As You Like It, Hamlet, Twelfth Night, Troilus and Cressida, Measure for Measure, Othello, All's Well That Ends Well, Timon of Athens, King Lear.*
1606–11	*Macbeth, Antony and Cleopatra, Pericles, Coriolanus, The Winter's Tale, Cymbeline, The Tempest.*
1613	*King Henry VIII, The Two Noble Kinsmen* (both probably with John Fletcher).
1623	Shakespeare's plays published as a collection (now called the First Folio).

Acknowledgements 鸣谢

Cambridge University Press would like to acknowledge the contributions made to this work by Rex Gibson.

Extracts from 'Director's Talk' on pp. 228–9 are reproduced courtesy of the Royal Shakespeare Company.

Extracts from Michael Billington's review of *Romeo and Juliet* at The Courtyard, Stratford-upon-Avon on pp. 204 and 205 copyright © Guardian News & Media Ltd 2010.

Picture Credits

p. iii: Olivier Theatre 2000, © Geraint Lewis; p. v: Royal Shakespeare Theatre/Barbican 1997, © Donald Cooper/Photostage; p. vi: top RSC/Barbican Theatre 2000, © Donald Cooper/Photostage; p. vi bottom: Mokhwa Repertory Company (Korea)/Barbican Theatre 2006, © Donald Cooper/Photostage; p. vii top: Shakespeare's Globe 2004, © Geraint Lewis; p. vii bottom: RSC/Royal Shakespeare Theatre 2006, © Geraint Lewis; p. viii top RSC/Swan Theatre 1989, © Donald Cooper/Photostage; p. viii bottom: RSC/Royal Shakespeare Theatre 2004, © Donald Cooper/Photostage; p. ix top: Ludlow Festival 2009, © Donald Cooper/Photostage; p. ix bottom: Open Air Theatre/Regent's Park 2008, © Donald Cooper/Photostage; p. x: Haymarket Theatre/Basingstoke 2001, © Donald Cooper/Photostage; p. xi top: Haymarket Theatre/Basingstoke 2001, © Donald Cooper/Photostage; p. xi bottom: RSC/Royal Shakespeare Theatre 1995, © Donald Cooper/Photostage; p. xii top: Ludlow Festival 2009, © Donald Cooper/Photostage; p. xii bottom: *Romeo and Juliet* directed by Franco Zeffirelli 1969, © Paramount/The Kobal Collection; p. 2: RSC/Royal Shakespeare Theatre 1991, © Donald Cooper/Photostage; p. 6: Mokhwa Repertory Company (Korea)/Barbican Theatre 2006, © Donald Cooper/Photostage; p. 8 RSC/Royal Shakespeare Theatre 2004, © Donald Cooper/Photostage; p. 10 RSC/Royal Shakespeare Theatre 2004, © Donald Cooper/Photostage; p. 12: Shakespeare's Globe 2009, © Geraint Lewis; p. 20: RSC/Royal Shakespeare Theatre 1995, © Donald Cooper/Photostage; p. 24: Chichester Festival Theatre 2002, © Donald Cooper/Photostage; p. 26: Bristol Old Vic 2010, © Donald Cooper/Photostage; p. 30: David Gelles as Romeo and Kevin O'Donnell as Mercutio in a 2011 Shakespeare & Company performance, photo by Kevin Sprague; p. 32 left: Kevin O'Donnell as Mercutio in a 2011 Shakespeare & Company performance, photo by Kevin Sprague; p. 32 right: Sid Solomon in The Acting Company's production of *Romeo and Juliet*, produced in association with the Guthrie Theatre 2011/photo by Paul Kolnik; p. 38: RSC/Courtyard Theatre 2010, © Donald Cooper/Photostage; p. 40: Iraqi Theatre Company/RSC/Swan Theatre 2012, © Donald Cooper/Photostage; p. 47 top: *William Shakespeare's Romeo + Juliet* directed by Baz Luhrmann, © 20th Century Fox/The Kobal Collection; p. 47 bottom: RSC/Royal Shakespeare Theatre 2004, © Donald Cooper/Photostage; p. 54 left: Shakespeare's Globe 2009, © Donald Cooper/Photostage; p. 54 right: RSC/Royal Shakespeare Theatre 2006, © Donald Cooper/Photostage; p. 58: RSC/Courtyard Theatre 2010, © Donald Cooper/Photostage; p. 62: Olivier Theatre 2000, © Geraint Lewis; p. 64: Mokhwa Repertory Company (Korea)/Barbican Theatre 2006, © Donald Cooper/Photostage; p. 72: 'The Death of Cleopatra', © North Wind Picture Archives/Alamy; p. 74: Theatre of Memory/Middle Temple Hall 2008, © Donald Cooper/Photostage; p. 82: RSC 2008, © Donald Cooper/Photostage; p. 89 top: Mokhwa Repertory Company (Korea)/Barbican Theatre 2006, © Donald Cooper/Photostage; p. 89 bottom: Chichester Festival Theatre 2002, © Donald Cooper/Photostage; p. 94: Haymarket Theatre/Basingstoke 2001, © Donald Cooper/Photostage; p. 100: Royal Ballet Sinfonia/Birmingham Hippodrome 2006, © Linda Rich/ArenaPAL; p. 102: RSC/Royal Shakespeare Theatre 1995, © Donald Cooper/Photostage; p. 106: RSC/Royal Shakespeare Theatre 2000, © Donald Cooper/Photostage; p. 110: RSC/Royal Shakespeare Theatre 2000, © Donald Cooper/Photostage; p. 118: Shakespeare's Globe 2004, © Elliott Franks/ArenaPAL; p. 124: RSC/Royal Shakespeare Theatre 2000, © Donald Cooper/Photostage; p. 128: 'The wheel of fortune', © The Art Gallery Collection/Alamy; p. 130: Iraqi Theatre Company/RSC/Swan Theatre 2012, © Donald Cooper/Photostage;

p. 139 top: RSC/Royal Shakespeare Theatre 1995, © Donald Cooper/Photostage; p. 139 bottom: RSC/Royal Shakespeare Theatre 1995, © Donald Cooper/Photostage; p. 142: RSC/Royal Shakespeare Theatre 1995, © Donald Cooper/Photostage; p. 144: RSC/Royal Shakespeare Theatre 2000, © Donald Cooper/Photostage; p. 150: Open Air Theatre/Regent's Park 2002, © Elliott Franks/ArenaPAL; p. 152 RSC/Royal Shakespeare Theatre 2000, © Donald Cooper/Photostage; p. 169: Playbill from 1756 Theatre Royal Drury Lane, © The Harvard Theatre Collection, Houghton Library; p. 174: RSC/Royal Shakespeare Theatre 1995, © Donald Cooper/Photostage; p. 184: *William Shakespeare's Romeo + Juliet* directed by Baz Luhrmann, © 20th Century Fox/The Kobal Collection; p. 186: Opera North, Leeds 2008, © Donald Cooper/Photostage; p. 190: RSC/Royal Shakespeare Theatre 1995, © Donald Cooper/Photostage; p. 198: RSC/Royal Shakespeare Theatre 2000, © Donald Cooper/Photostage; p. 201 top: Shakespeare's Globe 2004, © Geraint Lewis; p. 201 bottom: Greenwich Theatre 1998, © Donald Cooper/Photostage; p. 204 top: Shakespeare's Globe 2009, © Donald Cooper/Photostage; p. 204 bottom: RSC/Courtyard Theatre 2010, © Donald Cooper/Photostage; p. 205: Chichester Festival Theatre 2002, © Donald Cooper/Photostage; p. 206: Ludlow Festival 2009, © Donald Cooper/Photostage; p. 207: RSC/Royal Shakespeare Theatre 2004, © Donald Cooper/Photostage; p. 211: 'Vanitas' by Philippe de Champaigne; p. 215 Olivier Theatre 2000, © Donald Cooper/Photostage; p. 219: Itim Theatre Company, Tel Aviv/Barbican Centre 1994, © Donald Cooper/Photostage; p. 220: Shakespeare's Globe, © The Granger Collection/Topfoto; p. 221 top: Shakespeare's Globe 2004, © Donald Cooper/Photostage; p. 221 bottom: Shakespeare's Globe 2009, © Donald Cooper/Photostage; p. 222 top: Spranger Barry as Romeo and Miss Nossiter as Juliet, Covent Garden, London, 1763, © The Harvard Theatre Collection, Houghton Library; p. 222 bottom: Henry Irving's production of *Romeo and Juliet* at the London Lyceum, 1882, © The Harvard Theatre Collection, Houghton Library;
p. 225 top: Bolshoi Ballet/Royal Albert Hall 1993, © Donald Cooper/Photostage; p. 225 middle: The Royal Opera 2000, © Donald Cooper/Photostage; p. 225 bottom: *West Side Story* directed by Robert Wise and Jerome Robbins 1961, © Mirisch-7 Arts/United Artists/The Kobal Collection; p. 226 top: *Romeo and Juliet* directed by Franco Zeffirelli 1969, © Paramount/The Kobal Collection; p. 226 bottom: *William Shakespeare's Romeo + Juliet* directed by Baz Luhrmann, © 20th Century Fox/The Kobal Collection; p. 227: RSC/Royal Shakespeare Theatre 2000, © Donald Cooper/Photostage.

Produced for Cambridge University Press by White-Thomson Publishing
+44 (0)843 208 7460
www.wtpub.co.uk

Managing editor: Sonya Newland
Designer: Clare Nicholas
Concept design: Jackie Hill